# BASIC PROBLEMS OF OBC & DALIT MUSLIMS

# BASIC PROBLEMS
# OF
# OBC & DALIT MUSLIMS

*Edited by*
ASHFAQ HUSAIN ANSARI

SERIALS PUBLICATIONS
NEW DELHI

First Published - 2007

ISBN : 81-8387-088-0



***Published by***

**SERIALS PUBLICATIONS**
4830/24, Prahlad Street, Ansari Road
Darya Ganj, New Delhi-110002 (India)
Phone : 23245225. Fax : 91-11-23272135
E-mail: serials@satyam.net.in

## CONTENTS

## PART - II



## PART - III

**(Reproduction of the thin Volume-Earlier Published)**

# EDITOR'S NOTE – FIRST & FOREMOST

*Ashfaq Husain Ansari*

On 14th of April 2004 a function was organised by the 'National Action Forum for Social Justice' at Andhra Bhawan, New Delhi. A thin booklet edited by me containing less than hundred pages was released by Justice Rajender Sachar who few months later took the charge of Prime Minister's High level Committee, now known as Sachar Committee. The thin booklet was titled "Basic Prablems of Backward Muslims" Its foreword was written by Mr. P.S. Krishnan, I.A.S. (Retired) former secretary Government of India Ministry of Welfare now known as Ministry of Social Justice and Empowerment. He later joined as member-secretary of the NationalCommission of Backward Classes and there he was for two consecutive terms. Besides other important assingments he was also assigned the task of chairman of Working Group for Empowerment of Backward Classes in X Five Year Plan of which I was also made one of the members. During the meeting of this working group we discussed some of the basic problems of backward Muslims also. In some of these discussion my former colleague in the U.P. Backward Calsses Commission, Dr. H.S. Verma who was also one of the members of this working group, participated On the advice of these two learned colleagues I collected few articles. In the meantime I also wrote some articles on the subject. They forced me to get this thin volume printed because no meaningful literature on the problems of backward Muslims was available. After going through the articles by the eminent social scientists which I had collected and the articles I wrote, Mr. Krishnan offered to write a foreword.

The thin volume "Basic Problems of Backword Muslims" was released at Andhra Bhavan by Justice Rajendra Sachar on 14th April, 2004 on the occasion of the birth anniversary of Baba Sahab Dr. Bheem Rao Ambedkar. Mr. P.S. Krishnan whose organisation 'National Action Forum For Social Justice' organised the function, presided. Among the distinguished persons present on the occasion were the then chairman of National Commission of Backward calsses, Justice Ram Surat Singh, Cahirman of the Scheduled Caste Commission Dr Suraj Bhan, Mr Oscar Fernandes, at that time general secretary of All India Congress committee, Mr. D. Raja Secretary of the Communist Party of India and eminent socialogist Prof Imtiaz Ahmad, besides others.

In March 2005 an enlarged Hindi edition of the book "Pichre Musalmano ke Bunyadi Masayal" was also releasd at Gorakhpur. This enlarged Hindi edition, besides the translation of most of the articles of the thin Volume, includes the articles of Madhu Limay Maulana Asrarul Huq Qasmi, Abdul Rahman Abid, Ali Anwer, Zafar Agha, Prof. Anwar Pasha and Mohammad Ibrahim Qureshi among others. It also contains rejoinders to Syed Shahabuddin and Prof.Iqbal Ahmad Ansari.

"Pichre Musalmano ke Bunyadi Masayal" was released at Zila Panchayat Hall Gorakhpur on 05-03-05 by Minister of State for Home Affairs, Government of India Mr. Sri Prakash Jaiswal in the august presence of Justice Ram Surat Singh, the then chairman of National Commission of Backward Classes, who presided. Mr Mohammad Ibrahim Quraishi the then chairman of Madhya Pardesh Minorities Commission Mr. P.S. Krishnan former member-secretary National Commission of Backward Calsses, Mr. Udit Raj Chairman of Indian Justice Party and also of Lord Budha Club and Mr. Ali Anwer now a Rajya Sabha member.

It may not be out of place to mention that Urdu book on the History of Momin Conference "Momin Conference ki Dastavezi Tareekh" edited by me was earlier released at Vithal Bhai Patel House on 30th Septemer, 2000 at the National Conference on Social Jutice held at V.P. House ground Rafi Marg, New Delhi in the distinguished presence of Sri Subhash

Yadav, the then Deputy Chief Minister of Madhya Pradesh, Sri Krishnappa the then Minister of Karnataka Government, Sri Ram Raj (now Udit Raj) Shri K. Veeramani, Dr. Yoganand Shastri then Development minister Delhi government released the book, Shri Chandrajeet Yadav presided.

Thereafter I wrote a letter to Smt.Sonia Gandhi, president of the Congress Party and chairperson of U.P.A.on 24 June 2005 which I reproduce here.

> *"I understand that persons associated with Congress High Command are learned persons and they very well know that bulk of the Muslim community is included in the list of Other backward Classes. The nine judges Mandal Judgement (Indra Sawhany v/s Govt. of India) very clearly expressed that besides Hindu OBCs, Muslims, Christians and Sikhs are getting the benefits of 27% OBC reservation. Justice Venkatchallia, Chairman of the Constitution Review Commission (NCRWC) has very clearly stated in paragraph 10-11-2 of the report:*
>
> *"At present the political representation of minority communities in legislatures, especially Muslims, has fallen well below their proportion of population. The proportion of BCs among them is next to nil. This can lead to a sense of alienation. It is recommended for political parties to build up leadership potential in the minority communities including BCs, SCs and STs among them for participation in political life."*

*It further stated more clearly:*

> *"Backward calsses belonging to religious minorities who have been identified and icluded in the list of backword calsses and who in fact constitute the bulk of the population of religious minorities should be taken up with special care along with their Hindu counterparts in the developmental efforts for the backward calsses."*

*The above referred paragraphs from the NCRWC clearly confirm that OBC sections of Muslims "are included in the list of backward classes and who in fact constitute the bulk of population of religious minorities." These "bulk" differ from state to state but generally they are between 75 to 85 per cent of the minority population and minority generally means Muslims. Mandal Commission report also confirms this percentage of Muslim BCs which includes Dalit Muslims also. There are no two opinions that bulk of Muslim population consists of*

*Muslim backwards who are identified and included in the list of backward calsses. The nine judges constitution bench judgment also confirms this.*

*Inspite of the facts mentioned above the Congress High Command formed the opinion under the influence of its elite Muslim leadership that Muslims are not getting the reservation benefits and hence Congress in its Election Manifesto 2004 has declared that when it comes to power it will provide reservation to Muslims in admission to educaional institutons and jobs in civil services without going into the fact that Muslims who are socially and eductionally backward are already included in the list of Backward classes in state and central list and those Muslims who are included in the list of backward classes constitute the bulk of Muslim community and the percentage of these bulks differ form state to state which roughly comes to 75 to 85 per cent of Muslim population.*

*Social stratificaion among Muslims is a known and accepted fact. It is confirmed by sociologists and anthropologists world wide and also by Encyclopedia Americana and Britanica. Now the Ashraf Muslim leadership also confirms this social stratification of Ashraf, Ajlaf-Arzal groups of Muslims. Ashraf Muslim cannot be included in the OBC list because they are treated socially and educatuonally forward. Para 552 of the Mandal Judgement has formulated the criteria for inclusion in the OBC list which is as under.*

> *"552- The backward class of citizens referred to in Article 16(4) is the socially backward class of citizens whose educational and economic backwardness is on account of their social backwardness. A caste itself may constitute a class. However in order to constitute a backward class the caste concerned must be socially backward and its educational and economic backwardness must be on account of its social backwardness.*
>
> *The economic criteria by itself connot identify a class as backward unless the economic backwardness of the calss is on account f its social backwardness,"*
>
> *NineJudges Constitution bench Judgment of Indra Sawhney v/s Union India (Mandal case).*

*The population ratio of these forward Muslims (Ashraf) is 15 to 25 per cent of the total Muslim population. All the hue and cry for Muslim Reservation is for this 15 to 25 per cent Muslim population. The bulk of Muslim population that is 75 to 85 per cent of the Ajlaf-Arzal backward Muslims is included in the list of backward classes in the state and central list and is getting the benefits of OBC in job and admissions. It may not be out of place to mention that OBCs are not getting reservation in central educational institutions and also in minority educational institutions.*

*Without going into details at this satge I would like to mention that all the excrcise by the Congress led UPA Government is for the 15 to 25 per cent of the Muslim population. It has nothing to do with the bulk of Muslim population who constitute 75 to 85 per cent of the Muslim population. These bulk 75 to 85 per cent of the Muslim population are not getting their due share, be it admission to eductuonal institution job reservaion of central and state services, political representation in state legislatures and parliament and in the decision making bodies of political particse be it Congress, the Samajwadi Party, the BSP, the RJD, the NCP and the left parties.*

*The representation of these bulks (Muslim OBCs) in the Lok Sabha from Ist to 14th is also very-very poor--out of around 7500 members of Lok Sabha from Ist to 14th Lok Sabha only 400 Muslims in all could get elected and out of 400 Muslim Lok Sabha members only 60 Muslims belonging to OBC category could get elected. The position of representaton of the OBC Muslims in Rajya Sabha and Upper Houses of State legislatures is very poor.*

*The actual picture of under representation of OBC Muslims who are included in the list of OBC is narrated above in short. The details can be provide if required Ashraf Muslims are posing as if Muslim are out of the reservation list but the picture is just the reverse-15 per cent of the Ashraf Muslims are getting 85 per cent representation in every sphere and 85 per cent of the OBC Muslims are getting only 15 per cent reservation, be it in admission or jobs or political representation in political parties.*

*I fail to undrstand why this gross neglect on the part of this section of the Muslim Community in the Congress Party is still there under your leadership. The bulk of the Muslim community, who are no doubt included in the OBC list at the centre and state deserves representation in the organisation of the government and the Congress Party. Even the National Commission of Minorities and National Commission of Backward Classes both have no representation of backward Muslims.*

*I want to place these facts before you, the chairperson of UPA and president of the Congress Party with the hope that justice will be done to the OBC Muslims which includes Dalit Muslims also.*

*You will not mind if I frankly say that OBC Muslims are not only under represented in the decision making bodies of Congress Party at every stage from DCCs to PCCs and AICC. For a long time the working Committee is without any representation of OBC Muslims. The committees and commissions formed by the UPA government have not a single person among its members from OBC Muslims. Governors and other constitutioal positions also have no Muslims of this category."*

Besides most of the articles of the thin volume "Basic Problems of Backward Muslims" the present volume includes articles by eminent socialogists and political activists, Late Madhu Limaya Swami Agnivesh, Praful Bidwai, Asghar Ali Engineer, Prof. D.L. Sheth, Prof. Nadeem Hasnain, Mr. Dileep Karanth, Prof. Anwar Pasha, Prof. K.Z. Amani, Mr. D. Raja, Dr. Udit Raj, Prof. H.N. Ansari, besides rejoinders to Syed Shahabuddin, Prof. Iqbal Ahmad Ansari and Prof. Tahir Mahmood. Shamsul Islam, Ashok Yadav Sharad Yadav Prof Yogindra Sinkand, Saiyid Hamid and Prof Iqbal A. Ansari do not fully accept the social stratification among the Muslims but by and large they subscribe to the views of the editor with their own definition. An interview of Mr. Ali Anwer, President of the All India Muslim Pasmanda Mahaz amd Member Rajya Sabha from Bihar is also included. Relevant extracts from an affidavit filed by Government of India with the Supreme Court in the case of a P.I.L. on the subject are also reproduced as a LAST WORD of this volume. Most of the contributions in this volume are taken from English Hindi and Urdu newspapers and magazines. My job was to reproduce these articles dealing on the subject of 'Predicament of OBC&Dalit Muslims' into one volume, of couse, with due courtesy of the authors and the newspapers and magazines. The copy right will remain with the contributors.

Before concluding this First and Foremost chapter I would like to thank my neighbour and esteemed colleague who always respects me as elder brother, Mr. Mohammad Ahsan Ansari, retired Deputy Development Commissioner and now a leading social and education activist, without whose active and almost day to day co-operation it would not have been possible for me to bring out this volume. Most of the translations from Urdu and Hindi into English were done by him. I must also thank Dr. Ahmad Husain, Mr. Feroz Ahmad Advocate, Supereme Court, Mr. Anwar Ahmad and Er. Shams Anwar for their patronage and support to the cause of OBC Muslims.

I hope the readers will appreciate that a collection of articles by eminent sociologists, political leaders and social activists under one binding will serve the purpose of creating awareness among the leaders of all political parties and social groups.

One of my Delhi based friends, senior journalist and editor of "Alpjan" quarterly a chronicle of Minorities Mr. Anees Chishtee who has offered to look after and co-ordinate with the publishers on our behalf has greatly relieved me from this important job. Without expressing my sincerest thanks to Mr. Anees Chishtee, this first and Foremost Editor's Note can not be concluded.

# PART - I

# 1

## RECOGNITION AND ENTITLEMENT:
### *Muslim Castes Eligible for Inclusion in the Category 'Scheduled Castes'*

*Imtiaz Ahmad*

I am asked to make a presentation on Scheduled Caste converts to Islam. This raises a substantial difficulty. 'Scheduled Castes' is a legal and administrative term denoting castes among Hindus, Sikhs and Neo-Buddhists which possess three principal attributes: engagement in traditionally defiling occupations, exclusion from the main residential areas within localities and untouchability practiced against them by other castes on account of a presumed superiority of ritual status. There are other diacritical distinctions and restrictions that reinforce their distinctly low status. Similar castes among Muslims and Christians are not included in the category 'Scheduled Castes' though there have been demands from time to time that this should be done.

If I follow the direction to make a presentation on Scheduled Caste converts to Islam, I would perforce have to limit myself only to those Scheduled Caste converts to Islam who embraced that faith after the 'Scheduled Castes' became a legal and administrative entity. Cases of members of the Scheduled Castes converting to Islam are known (Meenakshipuram conversions are a case in point), but such cases have been few and far between.[1] Once such conversion occurs, the proselytes are denied the recognition and entitlement of the 'Scheduled Castes'. No useful purpose is likely to be served by concentrating on this limited section both because the number of such cases is small and the more substantial question is that of those Muslims castes which share the characteristics of the castes currently included in the category 'Scheduled Castes' but are denied recognition and entitlement as 'Scheduled Castes'. I am therefore going to redefine the scope of my presentation to include Muslim castes that are denied recognition and entitlement as 'Scheduled Castes' and not limit this discussion to Scheduled Caste converts to Islam which constitutes a very limited section of Muslims.

Several issues require discussion for an understanding of the situation of those Muslim castes which share the attributes of the Scheduled Castes, but are denied recognition and entitlement as Scheduled Castes. I shall discuss these issues before going on to reflecting on their situation in contemporary India.

## CONVERSION TO ISLAM

Broadly speaking, there are to views about conversion to Islam and attitudes on this issue have been greatly coloured by the rise of nationalism and the political discourse as it evolved during and after British rule. One view, which enjoys widespread uncritical acceptance because of the communalist interpretation of history during the nineteenth century, is that conversion to Islam was forced by Muslim rulers who were fired by zeal to spread Islam. It is this view that has contributed towards interpretations of the sack of Somnath by Mohammad Ghazni and other temples by other rulers as acts aimed at conversion and was harnessed in mobilising Hindu sentiments during the Ayodhya Movement where Babar was portrayed as a Muslim zealot. The other view is that conversion to Islam took place through the efforts of the Sufi saints who sanctified and legitimised folk religious and cultural practices making it possible for intermediate and low castes, whose culture was greatly imbued with folk religious and cultural elements, to be drawn into the Islamic fold.

There is no need for our present purposes to go into this controversial question, but one point ought to be made in passing. It is that the heaviest concentrations of the Muslim popu1ations are to be found in areas where Muslim political power was never effectively established or was established much later. On the other hand, these areas had been the strongholds of Buddhist domination before the revival of orthodox Hinduism. The theory that conversions to Islam were limited to the lower castes among the Hindus cannot thus explain the heavy concentration of Muslims in those areas.[2] What appears more plausible is that large segments of the Buddhist population in those areas embraced Islam as the Buddhist faith receded into the background. Under constant threat of religious persecution at the hands of resurgent Hinduism, Islam may have provided an escape to this erstwhile Buddhist population. Sufi missionary activities may have played a part in this process as the institutional framework of the Sufis was highly communitarian and, after the decline and abolition of the Buddhist Sangha, the Sufi shrines and hospices may have further served as a source of attraction to the Buddhist group to convert to Islam.

This had a decisive influence in shaping the caste demography of the Muslim population. Muslim high castes comprised by foreign irnmigrants who had accompanied the invading armies or who emigrated during subsequent peaceable times account for a small proportion of the Muslim population. The artisna1, menial and peasant castes constitute the largest segment accounting for roughly between 82-64 per cent of the Muslim population depending upon the region and its early cultural history. Lowliest Muslim castes comparable to 'untouchable' castes among Hindus constitute a small fraction of the total Muslim population. Furthermore, they are not uniformly distributed throughout the length and breadth of the country. There are no known cases of such Muslim castes in South India, except perhaps in Andhra Pradesh,[3] but members of several such Muslim castes are known to exist in Uttar Pradesh, Bihar, Maharashtra, Gujarat and Kashmir Valley. This peculiar Muslim caste demography is accounted for by a number of factors: presence of dominant Muslim castes, presence or absence of 'untouchable' Hindu castes to perform scavenging and other demeaning functions and prosperity levels of Muslims of the area, etc.

## CASTE AMONG MUSLIMS

Caste had been the organizing principle of Hindu social organization,[4] though its rigidity and contours changed greatly through the different historical periods. Perhaps, as has been asserted often, caste was not quite as rigid and fixed during the Vedic times as it became during the period following the articulation of the *Manusmriti*. Nonetheless, caste early became the defining basis of status, economic resources and political power. It was almost natural that converts to Islam who had earlier operated within the caste system brought their pre-conversion conceptions of the social system, and retained their earlier caste identities. It is also almost natural that conversion to Islam, a sudden turning to a new light, would have automatically introduced some changes in their social organization as a result of interaction with the principles of the Islamic faith.[5]

Early Muslim rules as well as intellectuals, including the ulema, did not see anything wrong with the persistence of such pre-conversion orientations. Actually, they rationalized and legitimated them as the natural order of things. Zia Barni elaborated a theory that the 'merits' and 'demerits' of all people have been 'apportioned at the beginning of time and allotted to their souls'. People's actions are not of their volition, but rather an expression and result of 'Divine Commandments'.[6] Muhammad Habib and Afsar Umar Salim Khan, translators of Barni's work, painfully admits, 'Barni's God, as is clear from his work, has two aspects–first, he is the tribal deity of the Musalmans; secondly, as between the Musalmans themselves, he is the tribal deity of well-born Muslims.[7] Subsequently, the ulema employed the Islamic juridical concept of kafa'a to provide legitimacy to the existing social divisions in society.

Empirical studies which initially took the form of decennial census adduced considerable evidence that castes (or caste-like groupings, which is a much later categorization) existed among Muslims and could be identified through a hierarchy of status orders that had several significant attributes: source of descent so that those claiming to be the descendants of the Prophet or one of his Companions enjoyed precedence over local converts, and association with an occupation leading to each caste confining marriages to its members. Using evidence from decennial censuses, Ghaus Ansari[8] argued that Muslims in India were divided into three broad categories whom he called the *ashraf* (noble born), *ajlaf* (mean and lowly) and *arzal* (excluded). Each of these categoriẹs was further divided into a number of groups for which, following the practice of the deceonia1 censuses, he chose to designate as castes. Since Ansari was relying on the evidence supplied by the enumerations conducted as part of the decennial censuses, he could not examine the process of mutual interaction among these sub-communities whom he designated as caste. He generally suggested that the three broad categories he had identified constituted a hierarchy in which the sub-communitles called castes were ranked in an order of social precedence. How this hierarchy was constituted and what was the basis on which the rank order was settled were questions that Ansari could not discuss on account of the limitations of the data he used. This deficiency was met by Ahmad who brought in evidence from castes in close mutual interaction and also noted the differences that existed between the Hindu and Muslim caste systems.[9]

Muslims are as a rule while they admit that caste or caste-1ike groupings exist among them, display a high degree of ambivalence on the subject of caste among Muslims. This ambivalence has many expressions and has resulted in two distinct tendencies among Muslims. Many Muslims, who admit that caste differences obtain among them, often come up with the plea that rather than caste some other term should be used to Muslim castes. Ethnic groups, *biradaris* or caste-like groupings have been considered and used as substitutes. Others deny the existence of caste among Muslims altogether, arguing that Islam is an egalitarian religion and does not recognize distinctions of caste and status honour. These Muslims refuse to recognize that Islam and Muslims are not necessary one and the same and that there might be a gap between Islamic beliefs and ideology and actual social behaviour.

Both tendencies arise from Muslim anxieties about their position in India. Those Muslims who argue that rather than caste some other word should be used to designate social divisions among them are guided by the anxiety that if caste was used it would betray affinity with the Hindus. The Muslim community was very substantially formed through conversion from the indigenous groups and the fear that it might relapse back into Hinduism has prompted it all through history to clearly distinguish itself from Hindus through evolving diacritical distinctions that they feel are more Islamic and set Muslims apart from Hindus. Accordingly, while they are willing to admit that caste-like formations exist among Muslims, they would much rather like some other word to be used to designate Muslim castes.

On the other hand, those Muslims who are prone to denying the existence of caste among Muslims altogether do so out of an anxiety for projecting the community as a monolith in the context of its standing as a minority in India. Benur traced this dimension in the context of the rise of the nationalist movement in India. He writes: 'The Hindu nationalists, using religion and culture as the bases of nationalism, tried to push only the Hindus as the 'national' community, and the Muslim as the 'illegitimate' residents of India. The Muslim elites also tried to project the Muslims as religious monolith and advanced the theory of distinct 'Islamic' identity of the Muslims. But because the Muslims were divided by the caste hierarchy, it was inconvenient for them to project the Hindus as monolith Hence, they put forward the theory of 'unity in diversity' and argued that the Hindu culture was the 'unifying force' behind the so-called diversity of the Hindus. The Hindu elites, i.e. the Brahmanical upper classes pushed the Brahmanical value system and philosophy as the 'essence' of so-called Indian culture. The Muslim elite adopted a similar view about the Muslims, reducing everything to Islam. .... So, it was contended that the Indian Muslims are without any caste system and they are one homogeneous community'.[10]

This tendency[11] has permeated down to sociologists who display a remarkably uncanny ambivalence towards caste among Muslims. At the behavioural level, they are willing to concede that there are elements of caste in Indo-Muslim society. However, as soon as the discussion shifts from behaviour to ideology they recoil form their position, seeking to add caveats or hedge around the issue by admitting unabashedly that when they apply the term in the context of a Muslim group they are using it in a loose sense. Two recent writings by Husnain[12] and Nazir[13] exemplify this tendency. Husnain locates his discussion in the context of the question whether the concept of caste can be applied to the system of social stratification of a community professing a faith other than Hinduism. His conclusion is bald and simple: 'It is true that the egalitarian social order of Islam stands in sharp contrast with the ideology of caste yet the 'Indian Islam' and 'Hindu Caste System' have been able to achieve a substantial compatibility'.[14] He then goes on to offer a host of explanations for why this should be the case. He writes: Hutton sounds convincing when he says that when Muslims and Christians came to India, the caste was in the air and the followers of even these egalitarian ideologies could not escape the infection of caste. Moreover, the overwhelming majority of Indian Muslim population comes form the lower Hindu castes who have been coming into the fold of Islam to escape from social persecution and the oppressive socio-economic disabilities. They were also attracted and lured by the social egalitarianism of Islam but the search for equality proved a mirage. In many cases there were improvements in their socio-economic condition yet the goal of social equality remained illusive. Moreover, in most of the cases the people embracing Islam gave up their religious faith but not the caste that was brought forward even to a new socio-religious milieu. Thus, it would be apt to say that while Islam may not be having castes or caste-like groupings, the Indian Muslims do have'.[15]

No sooner that he has made this sociological formulation, Husnain becomes uncomfortable. As if fearing that he might have committed an almost sacrilegious act by declaring that there is caste among Indian Muslims, he wishes to recoil from it. Cryptically, he adds: 'But in the present paper an attempt is being made to stay clear of the issue whether the model of social stratification among the Indian Muslims is the replica of the Hindu caste system or not. The author, in this paper, shall be using the term caste and caste system among the Indian Muslims in a conveniently loose manner. It is undisputed that there are groups of people among the Muslims who are organised more or less like the Hindu castes but this is also true that many of them are less rigid because Islam, theoretically at least, permits marriage between different classes of believers.[16] Not only that. He looks for crutches that would enable him to perform this summersault. He finds one in the following statement of Nazir, which he quotes approvingly:' ....It is necessary to make a distinction between a caste system and caste labels: the former refers to a local system of hierarchically ordered corporate groupings involving division of labour, occupational specialization, unequal dependence, and recruitment by birth only; the latter refers to a set of non-local, no corporate named groups which provide a ranking hierarchy, and which do not involve occupational specialization, unequal dependence, and recruitment by birth only.[17] 'Perhaps,' concludes Husnain, 'the 'caste system' and 'caste like grouping' among the Indian Muslims with all its fluidity may be better analysed and better understood through this observation'.[18]

This assumes that Hindus live under 'the caste system'. Muslims only use castes labels. Several theoretical and empirical questions are raised by this assumption. First, how is this assumption made? Is it made on the basis of a piece of empirical research? Or, is it made on entirely *a priori* grounds. As far as I am aware, there has to date been no empirical research which can be said to have established beyond the shadow of a doubt that Muslims do not live under a caste system and only use caste labels. Indeed, if such empirical research existed, the dilemma these authors (and others) face over how to characterize Muslim social stratification in India would not exist It exists because available empirical research has demonstrated that Muslim social stratification in India and beyond is marked by features of the caste system. It is, therefore, dear that the assumption is made on *a priori* grounds. As believing Muslims committed to upholding the widely proclaimed Islamic egalitarianism as axiomatic, they cannot face up to the behavioural reality that Muslims live under a caste system. They not only assume the distinction between 'the caste system' and 'caste labels' but go on to suggest that it constitutes a viable framework for analysing and understanding Muslim social stratification in India. It is used as a smokescreen to avoid facing the harsh behavioural reality of caste among Muslims in India.

Second, is there an empirical basis to the assertion that Muslim social organisation in India is 'a set of non-local, nor-corporate named groups which provide a ranking hierarchy, and which do not involve occupational specialization, unequal dependence and recruitment by birth only'?[19] Nazir does not make explicit the level at which he is talking. Is he talking about the categorization of Muslims into the broad categories of *ashraf, ajlaf* and *arzal*. If that is his point of reference, then his characterisation of Muslim social organisation as a set of non-local, non-corporate groups can be said to have some validity. However, it would invalidate the distinction between 'the caste system' and 'caste labels' since similar broad division exists in the form of *varna* categories in 'the caste system'. Ansari used the three broad categories of *ashraf, ajlaf* and *arzal* in the collective sense but dearly recognised that they were divided into smaller named groups that were distinguished from one another by occupation, endogamy and sociability. Thus, if Nazir's reference is to the groups at this level then his description of Muslim groups is wholly erroneous. Let us look closely at the empirical evidence in order to determine whether the distinction he posits between 'the caste system' and 'caste labels', and by implication between Hindu and Muslim modes of social organisation, is confirmed by available studies.

Sociological research on Muslims in India as opposed to lay and impressionistic writings continues to be thin. Evidence brought together by Ahmad (1973) and subsequent research demonstrates that Muslim groups which are the point of reference here, for which words *biradari* and *zat* are commonly used, are local and corporate entities. Even *birudaris* or *zats* such as Saiyyid, Sheikh and Ansaris, which are dispersed widely and found in different parts of a district, state or the county, are identified by their affiliation to a particular territory and restrict their marriages to members within that territory. Of course, how that territory is distinguished varies widely. For Sayyids, Shiekhs and Pathans, which resent being characterised as *biradaris* and prefer to be described as *zats,* the association to territory is expressed through appending the name of the territory to its name. Thus, one hears of Sayyids of Satrikh, Sheikhs of Allahabad, Kidwais of Baragaon or Kasauli and Pathans of Malihabad. In the case of *biradaris* that have an internal organisation of government and social control (called *biradari* or *zat panchayat)* this territorial association is defined by the jurisdiction of the *biradari panchayat.* The Ansaris in Rasulpur, where I carried out fieldwork, were divided into concentric circles of three and thirteen villages. They confined their marriages to thirteen villages though Ansaris existed in neighbouring areas as well.

This is not all Considerable evidence exists to show that the *biradaris* or *zats* are associated with particular occupations, are inter-dependent (tied into patron-dient relationships of the *jajmani* type), and are endogamous. This does not mean that all members of a *biradari* or *zat* necessarily practice the occupation with which their group is traditionally associated. There has been much variation throughout history among *biradaris* and *zats,* as indeed there has been within castes, in the extent to which their members remain tied to the practice of their traditional occupation. *Biradaris* and *zats* higher up in the social hierarchy did not usually have a traditional occupation and there was no close association between *biradari* or *zat* and traditional occupation. On the other hand, *biradaris* and *zats* further down the social ladder had traditional occupations and their association with occupation was strong. This was not significantly different from the picture of groups in what Nazir would characterise as 'the caste system'. Risley's following observation makes this explicit 'In theory each caste has a distinctive occupation, but it does not follow that this traditional occupation is practised by its members. .... The traditional occupation of the Brahmans is the priesthood, but in practice they follow all manner of pursuits. Many are clerks or cooks, while some are solders, lawyers, shop-keepers and even day-labourers, but they remain Brahmans all the same. The Chamars of Bihar are workers in skin, but in Orissa they are toddy--drawers. In Orissa and the south of Gaya the Dhobi is often a hewer of splitter of wood. In Bihar and Bengal the Dom is a scavenger or basket maker, but in the Orissa state he is a drummer or basket maker and has nothing to do with the removal of night soil in Chittagong and Assam he is a fisherman, in Cashmere a cultivator and in Kumaon a stone mason.[20]

The argument that Muslim groups, *biradaris* and *zats,* are not based on recruitment by birth only is equally fallacious. Like the groups in what Nazir would call 'the caste system', Muslim *biradaris* and *zats* are based on recruitment by birth only. There is no process by which one can become a Saiyid, Shiekh or Julaha except that of birth. It is for this reason that when someone marries into another *biradari* or *zat,* he is not integrated into another *biradari* or *zat* but retains 1m 01' her original *biradari* or *zat* association. There exists a possibility in the case of *biradaris* and *zats* to attempt social mobility and end up becoming a Sayid, Shiekh or Pathan in course of time through inventing a rationale and a genealogy. Where such social mobility occurs, the basis of recruitment to the *biradari* or *zat* does not change. The *biradari* or *zat* just ends up becoming another *biradari* or *zat,* and comes to be known by another name, to which recruitment continues to be based on the principle of birth. This is again not significantly different from the situation in 'the caste system' where castes have the possibility of changing their antecedents and name through the process of social mobility. Thus, the point that both *biradaris* and *zats* are 'less rigid because Islam, theoretically at least, permits marriage between different classes of believers'[21] is not empirically established. It is asserted without a substantial basis in any empirical research.

This raises fundamental questions. Why Husnain and Nazir as well as a host of other researchers who have worked on the sensitive question of the existence of caste among Muslims are so strongly persuaded to posit that there are significant differences between 'the caste system' and the system of *biradaris* and *zats?* Is it that these differences actually exist but empirical research has so far failed to unearth them? Or, is it that they are persuaded into asserting these differences contrary to empirical evidence out of extraneous considerations? Is it that they are prone to emphasizing these differences because as believing Muslims they are familiar with tire Islamic discourse that asserts that Islam preaches social equality and are afraid to take a contrary position? Or, is it that asserting these differences is a defense mechanism whereby they can simultaneously adhere to their disciplinary obligation as social scientists as well as their religious obligation to uphold what is commonly considered the Islamic flew on social stratification? My own view has been that the tendency to emphasise differences between 'the caste system' and the system of *biradaris* and *zats* arises from some such considerations, but I would refrain from making any such point here. I would like, instead to explore whether their starting point that Islam is an egalitarian religion and preaches social equality theologically and sociologically valid. This is central to understanding their standpoint.

## ISLAM AND SOCIAL EQUALITY

There is need to ask three different questions of the Islamic text if we are to understand Islam's position with respect to social stratification and social equality. First, whether Islam is opposed to social stratification as such or is merely opposed to social inequality. Second, what is truly the Islamic attitude towards social inequality that existed in the society in which Islam evolved and took roots? Finally, whether the social equality that it proclaims, and to which reference is always made when it is suggested that Islam is an egalitarian religion, is a description of an existing state of affairs in society or is merely an ideal that is given to mankind as a direction in which it should strive. It is necessary to ask these questions in order to understand the nature of the emphasis on egalitarianism and social equality in Islam. Basic to these questions is the sociological dictum that no society beyond the most primitive can be truly egalitarian. This was the point at the heart of Veblen's *Theory of the Leisured Class* (1932) wherein he argued that as societies generated economic surplus there almost always developed some form of social stratification. Pitrim A. Sorokin articulated this point as a general statement.

On even the most casual reading of the Islamic scriptural text one is struck that quite irrespective of the emphasis it places on equality of human beings Islam's orientation is remarkably hierarchical. Its hierarchical orientation comes in a wide variety of fields. First, the relationship of the believers with non-believers is conceived in hierarchical terms with the believer the *dhimmi* and the *kafir* constituting a clear hierarchy. Second, the relationship of Allah to the believer is conceived in hierarchical terms. It is a relationship of subordination and subservience so much so that the individual believer must prostrate before Allah in daily prayers and must at the same time see himself as utterly powerless in relation to Him. Any number of passages exist in the Islamic scriptural text endorsing the relatively lowly standing of the believers, whether as individuals or as a collective entity, in relation to Allah. Third, the relationship of the wife to her husband is clearly conceived in hierarchical terms even if the text does not distinguish between them in terms of the religious duties enjoined upon them. This is sometimes cited by Muslim feminists and Muslim modernists to argue that Islam guarantees equality of gender and does not place a Muslim woman in any inferior position to a man. However, in reality a woman is subordinate to a man and the relationship between them is seen as constituting a hierarchy wherein the woman stands in relation to a man in the same position as the individual stands in relation to the community and the community stands in relation to Allah. Fatima Mernissi characterises this orientation of Islam in relation to women by the concept of *nusuz,* which implies an unequal relationship. Finally, the relationship between the master and slave is conceived in clearly hierarchical terms even if the master is called upon to deal with the slave with kindness and merit is assigned to those who would free their slaves. Thus, it is clear that the framework of Islamic thinking is deeply imbued with the notion of hierarchy and social stratification.

It is true that the Arab society in which Islam evolved did not possess great differences of wealth, but economic differentiation between ordinary Bedouins and the trading classes did exist One can easily imagine that they would have differed with respect to their wealth, material possessions and lifestyles and Islam could not have brushed them under the carpet. It would have been required to deal with them, as they would have been reflected in their behaviour and mutual attitudes. As far as the Islamic scriptural text is concerned, it clearly recognises such distinctions in society and prescribes appropriate forms of behaviour for each. It asks those deprived in social and economic terms to be content and to live according to their means. It is repeatedly said in the text that Allah is All-seeing and would reward the poor for their poverty on the day of judgement. At the same time, the wealthy and rich, while they are allowed to live in their riches and to spend according to their economic standing, are warned not to be too proud of their material possessions. Moreover, they are asked to show kindness to those who are deprived and poor and to part with a portion of their wealth and income for the poor. Even the poor are conceived in hierarchical terms: first come the near ones followed by orphans and then the destitute and the deprived. If some kind of social stratification had not existed in society, Islamic scriptural text would neither have referred to those differences, nor indicated appropriate forms of behaviour for them. It would also not have sought to device an economic framework for the redistribution of wealth in a manner that the poor are able to meet both ends meet. It is, thus, clear that the emphasis that Islamic scriptural text places on social equality does not describe an existing state of affairs.

If the worldview of the Islamic scriptural text is hierarchical and it admits social and economic differences in society, then how should we interpret its emphasis upon social equality? One way to interpret this can be to ignore that Islamic orientation is hierarchical and that it recognises social and economic differences in the society in which it originated and to argue that it stands for egalitarianism as an absolute value. I would argue that those who maintain that Islam contemplates no social stratification are interpreting Islam in precisely this way. Even when they encounter social differentiation and stratification, they glibly ignore it and flag the proclaimed egalitarianism of Islam as a social reality. The other way of interpretation can be to recognise a fundamental difference. This is the difference between the society as it exists and as it ought to exist and to maintain that the Islamic proclamation in favour of social equality is more in the nature of an ideal for the future than a description of an existing state of affairs.

This distinction should not be entirely unfamiliar to us in India. As is well known, Indian society has been the most unequal society, social inequality being institutionalised in the caste system. India's constitution went on to declare India to be a casteless and classless society. In so doing, the constitution was not proclaiming that social inequalities of the past had entirely disappeared and the society was egalitarian from the time it was promulgated. The only sensible way would be to recognise that, while social inequalities persist, the ideal that the Constitution provides is that of egalitarianism. This is also true of Islam. It proclaims social equality to be an ideal, but recognises social inequalities existing in society. By this token, there is no contradiction between Islamic support for an egalitarian society as a future goal and presence of caste or class differences as a social reality.

## DALIT MUSLIMS

The expression 'Dalit Muslims' has been finding increasing mention in the discourse of traditionally backward Muslim communities in recent years. However, there does not yet exist any clear understanding of what this expression actually means or which castes or groups it is supposed to denote. On the one hand, it has been used to denote a whole range of Muslim castes which are currently included in the category of the Other Backward Classes. On the other hand, it has been used to denote those Muslim castes or groups which converted from the 'untouchable' Hindu castes or are so severely stigmatised and are subjected to such extreme forms of social exclusion that would render them comparable to the Scheduled Castes.

The Mandal Commission compounded and reinforced this confusion. As is already well-known, the Commission's task was to identify Other Backward Castes and to determine whether they should be eligible for reservation along the lines of the Scheduled Castes and Scheduled Tribes. There was no difficulty in this with respect to Hindu castes because administrative policy clearly recognised a distinction between Scheduled Castes and Other Backward Castes. Because the presidential order of 1950 clearly and arbitrarily laid down that 'No person who professes a religion different from the Hindu religion shall be deemed to be a member of a Scheduled Caste', the Mandal Commission lumped the severely stigmatised and extremely excluded among the Muslims with Muslim Other Backward Castes for purposes of affirmative action. Therefore, when the urge for equality and social justice seized the imagination of the lowest social groups in other religious traditions and the word Dalit came to be seen as a short-cut carrier of that aspiration, the expression 'Dalit Muslims' came to be used for a wide variety of groups other than those severely stigmatised and excluded and on that ground comparable to Hindu 'ex-untouchable' castes for whom the term 'Scheduled Castes' was reserved.[22]

One can arrive at an assessment of the extent of confusion that prevails at present with respect to the expression 'Dalit Muslims' by reading between the lines in the statements of those claiming to speak on their behalf as well as by considering the castes that they have been tempted to include under that category. N. Jamal Ansari writes: ... it is an established fact that Indian Muslim community is divided into castes and has a large deprived section. ... Before discussing constitutional provisions in respect of Dalits and exclusion of all 'Dalit Muslims' from those provisions, I think we must define 'Dalit Muslims'. Dalit means downtrodden, oppressed, suppressed and backward. Also, Dalit stands for untouchable and depressed classes. The term 'Dalit' applies to members of those menial castes that have been graded lowly which they have inherited by accident of birth'.[23] Likewise, Ali Anwar uses the words *'pasmanda'* (meaning downtrodden and backward) and Dalit interchangeably and includes under 'Dalit Muslims' castes like Bhatiyara, Tikyafarosh, Itafarosh, Halalkhor, Khakrob, Mogalzada and Chirimar only some of which can be said to be severely stigmatized and excluded.[24] Clearly, in all such statements and lists, as their reading suggests, the expression 'Dalit Muslims' has been used as a generic term to denote all Muslim castes that are educationally and socially backward.[25]

## CONCLUSION

There are roughly about 17 Muslim castes distributed in different parts of India who would qualify to be eligible for inclusion in the category 'Scheduled Castes'. On what basis are they distinguishable from the Muslim Other Backward Castes? Ansari did suggest in this early work that the relationships between the *ashraf* and *ajlaf* on the one hand and the *arzal* on the other were shaped by considerations of social distance taking on the characteristics of untouchability. He mentioned that the members of the category called *arzal* were excluded both physically and socially. From a physical point of view, they tended to inhabit excluded localities and did not mix with the members of the other two categories. When it came to social intercourse, their relationship was characterized by strict maintenance of social distance and deference so that the members of the *arzal* castes had minimal and limited interaction with the members of the other castes. Once again, Ansari was constrained into not saying anything more that this by the nature of the evidence that came out of the enumerations of the decennial censuses and some stray observations the census authorities offered in their reports from time to time.

More focused research on social stratification among Muslims in the early seventies and subsequently relied upon empirical methods, painstakingly collecting information on actual, day-to-day interactions among Muslim castes. This research succeeded in providing a more grounded picture of the situation of the castes that Ansari had called *arzal*. It demonstrated that in terms of day-to-day social interactions the *arzal* existed on the margins of society. Even so, the range of dimensions of interaction that this research explored was restricted to areas of commensality, endogamy and sociality.[26] It showed that the *arzal* engaged in the lowly occupation of scavenging, confined their marriages within the group and were excluded into separate residential quarters in the villages as well as the towns in which members of the other categories did not live. This research also noted the existence among the *arzal* castes of a system of internal government and social control with a hereditary official who regulated the life of group members and punished any transgressions of group norms besides settling domestic or intra-group disputes. Since much of this early research was focused on local communities, villages and towns, and covered groups falling into what Ansari had designated as *arzal* and *ajlaf,* the range of information on the *arzal* castes does not go beyond this limited range. For example, it is silent on the exclusion of the *arzal* castes in the ritual and religious spheres28 as well as on whether the religious specialists who cater to the *ashraf* and *ajlaf* castes also minister to them.

Considering the severely stigmatised and extremely excluded so-called *arzal* castes, two questions need to be disposed off. One is whether these castes should be recognised and entitled to benefits currently given to the 'Scheduled Castes'? One argument often advanced is that Muslims do not have castes and therefore the benefit of reservation to 'Scheduled Castes' cannot be extended to them. This is a fallacious argument to say the least. Public policies are not based on ideologies, which is an extremely contested arena with no ground for believing that the State's understanding of the Islamic ideology is necessarily correct. Public policies are based on objective realities and seek to address social problems as they exist at the ground level. If extremely excluded and severely stigmatised castes exist among Muslims, there is no ground that the strategy of ameliorating such groups should not be applied to them. There exists a strong case for extending the benefits of the 'Scheduled Castes' to severely stigmatised and extremely excluded Muslim castes, and any attempt to shy away from this obvious action would expose the State to the allegation that it is indirectly seeking to prevent the depletion of the 'Hindu community' by ensuring that the Schedule Castes stay within the Hindu fold and if they hanker for those benefits they should change over to Hinduism and one of the other religions of Indian origin whose deprived sections are included in the category 'Scheduled Castes'. The State's secular credentials will remain in doubt so long as this argument is adhered to.

The second question is whether these Muslim castes should be recognised as 'Scheduled Castes' only when there is demonstrable evidence that they converted from one of the Scheduled Castes. This was also the test applied in the determination of Sosai's claim to be granted concessions being extended to the 'Scheduled Castes'. Among other things, his claim was rejected, as he could not demonstrate beyond the shadow of a doubt that he or his ancestors had necessarily descended from one of the 'Scheduled Castes'. It is necessary to remember that in most of these cases we are dealing with castes whose caste histories are wholly unrecorded. Moreover, where is the basis for presuming that all such castes in other religious traditions are necessarily descendants of the 'Scheduled Castes'? It is possible that they may have come into existence autonomously as a result of subsequent colonisation under Muslim domination. Muslim elites may have forced some groups, irrespective of whether they earlier belonged to the 'Scheduled Castes' or not, to perform certain functions for them and their current stigmatization may not be the result of their conversion to Islam but may owe itself to their subsequent domination. Under the circumstances, requiring the severely stigmatised and extremely excluded castes, whether among Muslims or Christians, to pass the test of originating out of the 'Scheduled Castes' would amount to failing them on *a priori* grounds. This would militate against the spirit and intentions of the Constitution.[28] The scale of justice has to be balanced to ensure that similarly placed social groups are treated equally and evenly without religion (an anathema in a secular state) being brought into play to deny some of them equal treatment under the law.

Paper presented at the workshop on 'Conferment of Scheduled Caste Status to 'Untouchables'/Dalits converted to Christianity/Islam: Issues and Challenges' held at Tata Institute of Social Sciences, Mumbai on August 18-19, 2006.

## NOTES

1. Contrary to popular perceptions and State eagerness to enact legislations seeking to regulate conversions on the premise that large-scale conversions to Islam are indeed taking place Muslim proselytization efforts virtually ceased after Independence. Some Muslim groups continue to hold on to the concept of *dawat* (invitation to Islam), but are conscious that the political climate is too hot and problematic to attempt proselytization on a large scale. Unless castes come forward for reasons of their own (as happened in Meenakshipuram), conversions to Islam are now mostly individual and sporadic. For a discussion of the dynamics of the Meenakshipuram conversions, see Imtiaz Ahmad 'Threats and Responses: Conversions in Tamilnadu', *Economic and Political Weekly*, vol. 17, no. 43, 1982, pp. 1737-39 and 'The Tamilnadu Conversions, Conversion Threats and the Anti-Reservation Campaign: Some Hypotheses', *New Quest* 34, 1982, pp. 219-26.
2. For a more detailed discussion on this point, see Imtiaz Ahmad, 'Exclusion and Assimilation in Indian Islam', in Attar Singh (ed.) *Socio-Cultural Impact of Islam in North India*, Chandigarh, Punjab University, 1976.
3. One explanation for the presence of Muslim scavengers in Hyderabad appears to be the presence of sizeable Muslim elite which needed scavengers in order to maintain family toilets. Outside of Hyderabad, particularly in outlying districts where an elite class did not exist Muslim scavenging castes are not to be found. Because Uttar Pradesh and ihar had a sizeable elite class the largest number of Muslim lowest castes is found in these areas. Again, while they are found in and around Kolkata, they are almost non-existent in rural West Bengal.
4. See K.M. Pannikar, *Hindu Society at Cross-Roads,* London, Allen and Unwin, 1961.
5. There is an interesting debate on caste among Muslims according to which Muslim system of social stratification is claimed to have evolved independently and is seen as having no relationship with the Hindi caste system. Charles Lindholm has argued that many of the features found in Muslim society are similar to those found

among Muslims in other parts of South Asia and on that basis has argued that the Muslim social stratification found in India is an extension of the system found elsewhere (see Charles Lindholm, 'Paradigms of Society. A Critique of Theories of Caste among Indian Muslims' *European Journal of Sociology*, 1965, pp. 131-140). Many Muslims are themselves inclined to take a similar line of argument. This argument would have been tenable if Islamic scriptural sources had provided a blue-print of an Islamic social stratification system. This not being the case, the argument fails to sustain itself. It is plausible that Islam did modify certain social practices including that of caste. Whatever practices were not sanctified by Islam but existed in India were attenuated. Whatever practices existing in India were in conformity with the Islamic ethos bècame more rigid. Thus, purdah practices, which already existed even in India, were rendered more rigid and strict and caste principles were relaxed or made less restrictive.

6. For a more detailed treatment of Barni's as well as other contemporary scholars' views on social divisions in society, see Yoginder Sikand.
7. Quoted in Sikand.
8. Gaus Ansari, *Muslim Castes in Uttar Pradesh*, Lucknow, Ethnographic and Folk Culture Society, 1959.
9. Imtiaz Ahmad, 'Introduction', in Imtiaz Ahmad (ed.), *Caste and Social Stratification among Muslims*, Delhi, Manohar Book Service, 1973.
10. Fakruddin Benur, 'The Dynamics of Caste Problems of the Indian Muslims', Paper presented at a seminar on Dalit Muslims organized by Deshkal Society, New Delhi, 2004.
11. This tendency is, incidentally, not limited to Muslim elites, but is also reflected by leaders who claim to represent the cause of lower Muslim castes. For example, Ali Anwar, president of the Pasmanda Muslim Mahaz, Bihar, notes, 'In Islam in principle caste and conceptions of high and low or touchable and untouchable do not exist. I want to state this rights in the beginning because whenever this question is discussed some people immediately start citing the Quran and the Hadith. I want to state that the discussion is not about Islam but on adherence to it' (Paper presented at a seminar on Dalit Muslims organized by Deshkal Society, New Delhi, 2004).
12. Husnain.

13. Nazir.
14. Husnain, p. 2.
15. Husnain, pp. 207-08.
16. Husnain, p. 207
17. Nazir, p. 2898.
18. Husnain, p. 208.
19. Nazir, p. 2898.
20. Hutton, *Census of India*, 1902, pp. 350-51.
21. Hasnain, p. 208.
22. On what grounds the presidential order of 1950 decided, in opposite to the explicit wording of the Constitution, remains an enigma and has not been adequately researched upon. It is clear that the distinction arose out of the strong Hindu undertones of nationalism as it took shape in India. Since the idea of nationalism simultaneously propagates the notion of a national community which in this case was seen as the 'Hindu community', there was fear that if the extremely stigmatized and excluded castes in other religious traditions were allowed eligibility as Scheduled Castes there would remain no check on conversion of lower groups to them (already the idea that the lower groups had converted to Islam because of their lowly position in Hindu society was widespread). The idea that the term 'Scheduled Castes' should be restricted to Hindu 'ex-untouchables' was introduced to prevent conversion of lower Hindu groups to other religions and thereby to prevent any subsequent depletion of the 'Hindu community'. What role did the presence at that time of Dr. Rajendra Prasad at the helm of affairs played in this process is also worth investigation in the context of his subsequent strong opposition to the passing of the Hindu Code Bill.
23. 'Oppression of Dalit Muslims through Constitution of India', Paper presented at a seminar on Dalit Muslims organized Deshkal Society, New Delhi, 2004.
24. There are some who question the tendency to denote backward and downtrodden Muslim castes as Dalit Muslim. Benur writes, 'A question can be asked at this juncture. How it is appropriate to call these bahujan Muslims or backward Muslim masses as Dalit Muslims? By calling these Muslims as Dalit Muslims, what we aim to achieve? Creation of awareness among the Muslim masses? Removal of marginalisation? Generating sympathy wave? Calling

these Muslims as Dalit Muslims are we radicalising caste politics? (Fakruddin Benur, 'The Dynamics of Caste Problems ofthe Indian Muslims', Paper presented at a seminar on Dalit Muslims organized by Dehskal Society, New Delhi, 2004.

25. Perhaps the reason for this is their desire to consolidate a wider constituency. Shabbir Ansari, leader of the Mahrashtra Backward Castes Federtation, and Ibrahim Qureshi, convener, National Coordination Council, Muslim OBC of India, Bhopal, have maintained a distinction between Muslim Other Backward Castes and Dalit Muslims. Qureshi lists 8-10 Muslim castes who are eligible for inclusion in the Schedule Caste category (see his paper presented at the Muslim OBC Conference organized by the PM's High Level Committee, New Delhi, 5-6 September, 2005. Eajaz Ali has been very clear and his movement focuses exclusively on severely stigmatized Muslim castes.

26. From my observations of growing up in a Muslim family I am able to recall a number of instances of both open and silent discrimination practiced against these castes. We had a Lalbegi woman come to clean the toilets in our house. She was on the best of terms with my mother would sit for hours together gossiping with her. Whenever my mother would offer her *pan*, she would fold her hand in her *dupatta* and riase it. My mother used to drop the *pan* in her hand, making sure that her hand did not touch the Lalbegi woman's hand. On occasions of marriage the family would come and sit in a corner and wait until all guests had eaten and left. It would then be given food in vessels they brought with them. They did not eat the food there, but instead took it with them to be eaten at home. On sacrificial eid the family was not given any portion of the meet. It was given the intestines, which were kept aside for them. It is possible that some of these forms of discrimination have changed, but there is no evidence to show that they have disappeared. The Commission on Religions and .....Minorities should sponsor studies to evaluate the discrimination and its changing forms in a few areas to find out the current state of these castes.

27. Some evidence exists to show that there is discrimination against these Muslims in the religious spheres. I found during fieldwork in eastern Uttar Pradesh that members of these castes did not go the mosque for prayers and if they went they had to stand in the back rows. It has been mentioned by many observers that such groups often have their own mosques. N. Jamal Ansari notes that

'in certain areas of Uttar Pradesh and Bihar there are separate mosques and burial grounds' for these castes (Paper presented at the seminar on Dalit Muslims organized by Deshkal Society, New Delhi, 2004). Establishment of own mosque would call for a level of prosperity for the groups as a whole. Whether they have attained such levels of prosperity is something on which very little information exists.

28. In Parasram V. Shivchand case it was held that in order to determine whether a particular caste is a Scheduled Caste one has to look at the notification issued by the President on that behalf. This questionable view calls for a review.

# 2

## MUSLIM RESERVATION?

### *"Backward Section of Christians, Muslims, and Sikhs Must Get Reservation But Not Their Elites."*

***Madhu Limaye***

Caste is a peculiar aspect of Indian Society. ('Indian' in the older sense of the term) How this Caste system spread out in the areas from Hindukush to Manipur and from Kashmir to Kanya Kumari, (which Arabs called Al-Hind), still remains a secret. But it so looks that this system did not remain within the confines of any one religion, sect or language. Not only Hindus but Christians, Sikhs and Muslims also were affected. Most of personal names, family names and titles changed alongwith religious conversions. But if we go into depth, we would find castes to exist in all religious communities.

Initially when the British Govt. started 10 yearly census, the caste of every individual used to be recorded. Later on, with the advent of communal politics, petty, progressive-ism came to surface and census of castes stopped. Data of Caste-wise population could not be collected from 1941 onwards. There is mention of Scheduled Castes and Scheduled Tribes in the constitution. List of these classes, as are approved in constitution, have been prepared. With each census, statistics of Scheduled Castes and Tribes are got collected. But Scheduled Caste and Tribes do not consist of identical groups. Hundreds of sub-castes and tribes are included into these. We do not have information either in respect of these castes and tribes, their educational level, income or housing status.

Some communalists did not approve of the caste enumeration, as they thought that this would disturb the unity of their communities. Hence they tried to suppress the reality of caste-wise division. Several of the Marxists and progressivists said that the caste system would vanish with stopping the 10 yearly caste census. From the experience till date it becomes amply clear that castes have not vanished, instead the caste feeling has increased. By suppressing the real facts and statistics, the scientific policy framing has adversely been affected. Consequently a wave started for giving reservation on this or that ground and states went on increasing the percentage of reservation beyond limits.

Collecting scientific and reliable data of castes and professional groups is the only way for framing realistic policies for abolition of castes. Hoping that such a deep seated disease would end within a decade was altogether laughable.

**UGLY REALITY**

Unfortunately, our political leaders are presently grappled with an insanity. Our Constitution has after full consideration , left out the communal reservation and kept such article as 15, 16 and 340 etc. In Centre and States like Orissa and W. Bengal where there is supremacy of the higher-ups, for the first time the principle of reservation to OBCs, though with laxity is being put to practice. Now Welfare Minister Sita Ram Kesri who had to be constantly goadedd for being active in the field of social justice, following some main Congress Leaders has suddenly started pleading for giving reservation to the religious minorities. Kesri's sympathies had all along been with backward sections and definitely his secretaries can make him understand, in the Bhojpuri Language, as to what has been spoken by several of his learned officers (including Kesri's Gita Mandal Report) about castes in Sikhs, Christians and Muslims. If he asks his secretaries alone to give translation of scientific advertisements of Khatri, Saini, Sikhs, then he can be able to know this aspect of the ugly truth. If he goes to West Bengal and meets Christians,

Benerjis and Chaterjis or Protestant Brahmin Christians of Maharashtra, Goa's catholic Brahmins and Keral's famous Syrian Christian families and ask, them as to on which basis they somlemnise their marriage, then he would stop talking of all people. But I feel that he is not talking all these out of ignorance. He has discussed with me on these matters and has concurred with me that reservation ought to be given to backwards of Christians, Muslims and Sikhs. But the facility of reservation must not be given to "Brahmin-Thakurs" of these communities at all.

In the same way as the tendency of pre-Muslim Indian sects had been of tolerance towards all religions in accordance with the teachings of Upanishad, that there are several routes to establish similarity with the etarnal truth- Ishwar or Allah- similarly Islam's ideal and tendency has been towards equity. But none of these two could fully succeed in achieving this ideal.

Ziauddin Barni has been a famous Muslim historian of medieval india. His support for hier archial structure and contempt for lower castes is a well-known fact. (The political Theory of Dilli Sultanate, editor- M Habib & Smt. Khan). Similarly Sir Syed Ahmed Khan, who had shown the path of modern education and modernity to Indian Muslims used to see the lower caste people with contempt and got scared by a mere imagination of their rule over higher caste people (Writing and speaches of Sir Syed Ahmed Khan, pp. 207-208).

Several men of letters have underlined the feelings of high & low in Indian Muslims, so far so, that the names of some backward castes in Muslims still exist there as they were earlier like-Dhobi, Teli, Darzi, Dhimar, Nai, Kumhar, Gujar, Lohar etc. in earlier census reports the names of Pinjari, Qasai and several other castes also find mention. In this regard, some learned studies have also been made like- 'Muslim Castes in Uttar Pradesh' and 'Castes among Non- Hindus' athored by Ghaus Ansari.

Some times back, it had been written by Rown Gonsalves that Goa's church is the only church of all catholic world whose common priests are Catholic Brahmins. In this state, Caste is the basis of strong groups-in Hindus as well as Catholics (Hindustan Times, 4 Dec. 1944).

In this very context Mahatma Gandhi had written in 1941, to a Bengali well-wisher, "Undoubtedly the evil of untouchability exists in Christians as well as Muslims, it is the gift of Hindus, chronic communicable disease of untouchablility . Hindus can help other communities by abolishing the disease of untouchability. But the residual work would have to be done by these communities themselves." (Collected Work of Mahatma Gandhi Part 70, p-139, but then India was not free). Now we are free and hence the Indian State ought to give relief to the lower castes of all communities alongwith those of Muslims and Christians.

It has been said in Mandal Report, " undoubtedly the social and educational backwardness in non Hindu communities is almost similar as in Hindus. Although caste system is the speciality of Hindu society, yet this evil is found in different measures in all non-Hindu Communities also. There are two main reasons for it- firstly, caste system is the main element for building a mentality and it leaves a deep effect on a person's social awareness and cultural values. Consequently the sense of socially high and low very much remained in former Hindus, even after religious conversions." (Mandal Report, Part I p-55).

The day to day statements of Kesri finding place in print irriated me to such an extent that I asked him in writing as to whether he was law unto himself and whether he followed the principle of collective responsiblity of the Cabinet of Ministers or not?

If Kesri is real friend of the ignored sections of the backwards and minorities then by dividing the other backward classes into 'backwards' and 'most backwards' he should keep the backward sections of Muslims and Christians, included into the Mandal and other reports and most of whose condition is really pathetic, alongwith the most backward classes of the Hindu (as has been done in the Mungeri Lal Commission's schedule-I) And then out of the total 27%, 15 or 14 reservation should be ensured for these most backward sections. He should be aware of the fact that Supreme Court has held such classification to be in-appropriate. But Kesri would not care for any justification. He has turned intoxicated for vote bank politics and not for social justice.

***Courtesy : 'Maya Magazine'***

# 3

# MUSLIMS IN INDIA: CASTE AFFINITY AND SOCIAL BOUNDARIES OF BACKWARDNESS

*Nadeem Hasnain*

Muslims in India constitute the largest religious minority and a sigificant segment of Indian society. They constitute about 12 percent of the total population and in terms of numbers about 12 crore. Thus, they form the second largest Muslim population in the world next only to Indonesia.

The distribution of Muslim population in India today is the result of a process extending over almost a millennium. They have been living for ages as an inseparable part of the rural and urban social milieus and bound together by the age-old ties in economy, customs and traditions. Significantly, Muslims in India are neither a cultural community nor a compact ethnic population. They live through layers of identities in a complex society. At some palces, they may be seen through a provincial-linguistic/ethnic category as in Ladaakh (Jammu and Kashmir), a tribal-*biradari*/kinship group as in Lakshadweep and through such tribal groups as Gaddi and Bakrewal in Jammu and Kashmir, through a sectarian perspective such as *Sunni, Shia, Ismaili,* etc., or through various Islamic schools such as Deobandi and Barelvi.

The socio-cultural/ethnic heterogeneity of Indian Muslims as described above has at least one thing in common and that is social stratfication, by and large, on the lines of Hindu society with whom they have been living and interacting for more than a thousand years.

## ISLAM, MUSLIMS, CASTE AND SOCIAL STRATIFICATION

The question-whether the concept of caste can be applied to the system of social stratifcation of a community professing a faith other than Hinduism-has often been posed. It is true that the egalitarian social order of Islam stands in sharp contrast with the ideology of caste, yet the 'Indian Islam' and 'Hindu caste system' have been able to achieve a substantial compatibility. Hutton (1951) sounds convicing when he says that when Muslims and Christians came to India, the caste was in the air and the followers of even these egalitarian ideologies could not escape the infection of caste. Moreover, an overwhelming majority of Indian Muslim population come from the lower Hindu castes who have been coming into the fold of Islam to escape from social persecution and the oppressive soci-economic disabilities. They were also attracted and lured by the social egalitarianism of Islam but the search for equality proved a mirage. In many eases, there were improvements in their socio-economic conditions, yet the goal of social equality remained elusive. Moreover, in most of the cases, the people embracing Islam gave up their religious faith but not the caste that was brought forward even to a new socio-religious milieu. Thus, it would be apt to say that while Islam may not be having castes or caste-like groupings, the Indian Muslims do have.Thus, the interface between ideology and social structure in the context of caste may be full of academic issues requiring discussion.

But, the present chapter stays clear of the issue whether the model of social stratification among the Indian Muslims is the replica of the Hindu caste system or not and, consequently, the terms such as caste and caste system among the Indian Muslims would be used in a conveniently loose manner. It is undisputedly true that there are groups of people among the Muslims who are organized more or less like the Hindu castes but this is also true that they are less rigid because Islam, theoretically at least, permits marriage between different classes of believers. Nazir (1993:2898) takes a fresh look on this whole issue:

> *"It is necesary to make a distinction between a caste system and caste labels: the former refers to a local system of hierarchically ordered corporate groupings involving social division of labour, occupational specialization, unequal dependence, and recruitment by birth only; the latter refers to a set of non-local, non-corporate named group which provide a ranking hierarchy, and which do not involve occupational specialization, unequal dependence, and recruitment by birth only."*

Perhaps, the 'caste system' and 'caste-like groupings' among the Indian Muslims with all their fluidity may be better analyzed and understood through this observation. Even within this framework, as Harjinder Singh (1977) remarks. "there might be regional variations in the nature of Muslim stratification in India."

Ghaus Ansari (1960), in his pioneering study on caste amd social, stratification among the north Indian Muslims. places Muslim castes into three categories: (i) *Ashraf*, (ii) *Ajlaf*, and (iii) *Arzal*.

*Ashraf* includes the Muslim nobility that claim to be the descendants of early Muslim immigrants, either Sayyad, Shaikh, Mughal or Pathan, as well as descendatns of higher Hindu castes such as Muslim Rajputs. Clean occupational castes, such as Julaha (weavers), Darzi (tailors), Qassab (butchers), Hajjam (barbers), Kunjra (green grocer), Mirasi (bards, singers and musicians), Manihar (bangle makers), Dhuniya (cotton carders), Gaddi (graziers, milkmen), etc. were included in the category of *Ajlaf* (mean). The third category of *Arzal* (literally very mean) includes the unclean or ritually polluting castes such as Bhangi of Mehtar (sweepers and scavengers).

With the establishment and acceptance of caste/caste-like social hierarchy among the Muslims with its own norms and patterns of behaviour, space for upward mobility also emerged among the Muslim castes. The process of sanskritization among the Hindu castes has also subsumed the Muslim castes. When Ahirs (the Hindu milkmen caste) trace their origin to the Chandravanshi Yadava and Krishna, the Muslim Julahas (weavers) add 'Ansari' with their name referring to the Ansars (highly revered companions of Muhammad). Likewise, Qassabs/Chikwas (Musim butchers) add 'Qureshi' with their names referring to the tribe Quraish Muhammad came from. Certain other middle-level Muslim castes add 'Khan' with their names extending their claims to a Pathan or Afghan ancestry. So, in the process, Julahas (weavers) became Momin Ansar, Hajjams (barbers) became Salmani, Kunjras (vegetable vendors) became Raeen, Darzis (tailors) became Idrisi, Bhistis (drawers of water) became Abbasi, Lohars (ironsmith) and Badhai (carpenters) became Saifi, and so on. As a result of welfare and development programmes, several such occupationally specialized castes attained prosperity and with heightened political conseiousness, organized themselves into caste-based orgaizations or *jammats/biradaris*. This, in turn, promoted social solidarity among them. Thus, on the lines of the Hindu castes, the Muslim castes too have adopted the lifestyle and behaviour pattern of their higher castes such as Sayyed and Shaikh in the process of sanskritization.

## MUSLIM BACKWARD CASTES, COMPENSATORY DISCRIMINATION AND RELATED ISSUES

Three backward segments of population, were identified and targeted for special treatment with the advent of independence and subsequently promulgation of the Constitution of India. These were scheduled castes (SCs), scheduled tribes (STs) and other backward classes (OBCs). Various compensatory discrimination policies are directed at these categories, related to job, education, welfare and development. If we try to situate Muslim population in these categories, we find that SCs cannot be Muslims as this category is restricted to Hndus, Sikhs and Buddhists. The STs can be Muslims but Muslim tribes are few such as a microscopic popultion of small tribal groups of Lakshadweep, Gaddis and Bakrewals of Jammu and Kashmir. This obviously means that only the third category of OBCs seems open to them. For a long time, the Muslims, despite their socio-economic backwardeness, could not take advantage of this mainly because it remained a vauge catagory and criteria for inclusion in this category were not specified in the Constitution. Although some states had implemented reservation for OBCs on the basis of recommandation of the state-level backward classes commissions, the reservation issue for OBCs attained cnetrality only in 1990 when V.P. Singh government decided to implement the Mandal Commission's recommendation for goverment jobs at the national level. The Mandal Commission had declered 82 Muslim groups as backward.

Dwelling upon the status of OBCs among the non-Hindu communities (mainly Muslims), the Mandal Commission (1980) observed.

> *"There is no doubt that social and educational backwardness among the non-Hindu communities is more or less of the same order as among the Hindu communties. Though caste system is peculiar to Hindu society yet, in actual practice, it also pervades the non-Hindu communities in India in varying degrees. There are two main reasons for this phenomenon: first, caste system is a great conditioner of the mind and leaves an indelible mark on a person's social consciousness and cultural mores. Consequently, even after conversion, the ex-Hindus carried with them their deeply ingrained ideas of social hierarchy and stratification. This resulted in the Hindu converts inadvertently acting as Trojan horses of caste system among highly egalitarian religions such as Islam, Christianity, Sikhism, etc. Secondly, non Hindu minorities living in predominantly Hindu India could not escape from its dominant social and cultural in fluences. Thus, both from within and without, caste amongst non-Hindu communities received continuous sustenance and stimulus."*

After giving a good deal of thought to these difficulties, the Mandal Commission evolved the following rough and ready criteria for identifying non-Hindu OBCs:

(i) All untouchables converted to any non-Hindu religion.

(ii) Such ocupational communities, which are known by the name of their traditional heriditary occupation and whose Hindu counterparts have been included in the list of Hindu OBCs (e.g. Dhobi, Teli, Nai, Kumhar, Lohar, Darzi, Badhai etc).

Though we do not have any separate census enumeration for Muslim OBCs, those engaged in advocacy for them claim their population to be of the order of 80-85 percent of the total Muslim population of India. In sociolgical terms, in the *Ashraf-Ajlaf-Arzal* categorization, all the Muslim castes/ groups coming within *Ajlaf-Arzal* social categories qualify for the status of OBCs.

## MUSLIM OBCs: EMPOWERMENT AND COMMUNAL QUOTA

Though a majority of Muslims are already covered under the existing provisions of reservation for the OBCs, there has always been a grouse among them that they would not be able to compete with the educationally and economically advanced Hindu OBCs like Yadav, Kurmi, Koeri, etc, who are able to swallow thier share of the common cake just as what they have done in relation to the Hindu 'most backward classes/castes' (MBCs). On the other hand, there has been a general hostility among the relatively more advanced Hindu OBCs to the idea of a separate sub-quota for either the Muslim OBCs or the Hindu MBCs. Significantly, for sometime now, a section of Muslim leadership has been demanding a separate quota in reservation for Muslims as a whole despite the fact that the Muslim OBCs, constituting an overwhelming majority of the entire Muslim population of India, are alredy covered under the existing provision for the OBCs. The liberal-secular Muslim opinion is opposed to this demand on two grounds: it will provide a ready issue and handle to the aggressive *Hihdutva* forces to promote hostility towards the Muslims and it is unjust because some groups within each religious community are traditionally 'forward' and socially, educationally and ecocomically advanced as compared to the rest of their population as well as in the absolute sense of the term. The Sayyed, Sheikh, and other *Ashraf* castes of north India, the Thangal, Arakkal, Koya and Keyi of Kerala Muslims, the Khatri and Jat among the Sikhs, the Syrian among the Kerala Christians and so on are the advanced higher castes. Thus, the argument that an entire relgious community is socially and educationally backward negates the sociological reality and goes against the principle of social justice.

The response of the leadership of Muslim OBCs is also very meaningful and significant. They are stongly apprehensive that if Muslims as a whole, as a religious community, are extended reservation, the relatively better off caste groups shall be cornering and gobbling up most of the opportunties for educational and economic advancement. This povides a frertile ground for intra-community competitiveness leading to bickering and social conflicts. Morever, this also goes against the very objective and rationale of empowerment of relatively weaker and backward segment of Indian society. Thus, the demand for a communal quota finds hardly any takers among the Muslim OBCs and this has also contributed to the mobilization of Muslim OBCs against the upper strata of Muslims.

The efforts for the empowerment of Muslim OBCs, along with Hindu, Christian and Sikh OBCs, have exploded the myth (perpetuated largely by the Muslim elite) that the entire Muslim commmunity is a monolith devoid of any economic, social and cultural complexities. The report of the Mandal Commission has also contributed to the politicization of the internal social classification of the Indian Muslims. One of the significant fallouts of this phenomenon is the decreasing political power of the higher caste Muslim leadership who enjoyed a virtual monopoly over Muslim leadership. As the trend indicates, the Muslim OBCs shall produce their own leadership not only at the grassroots level but also at the provincial and national levels encompassing all the institutions of Indian society. However, the present scenario of growing ascendancy of militant *Hindutva* forces and its fallout such as the recent Gujarat carnage and state-sponsored terrorism against the Muslim minority seems to be the last hope of the Muslim elite. Obviously, an overriding sense of insecurity leads to ghettoization at both physical and mental levels and the entire population tends to close down their ranks and the traditional elite usually grabs the leadership. Incidentally, the separatist-comunalist-fundamentalist leadership among the

Indian Muslims has always come from the feudal and elite segment playing the politics of identity.

In his article, published in a booklet brought out by the Centre of Backward Muslims of India (2000). Sheth rightly points out:

> *"The proponents of reservation for all Muslims should in the interest of intellectual honesty and political candour make their demand as a "religious minority" but not as a backward class. Even this would mean a major amendment to the Constitution: one that would violate the secular spirit of the Constitution. India's Constitution recognises the cultural rights of minorities as fundamental rights and forbids discrimination on ground of religious affiliation, but it is foundationally opposed to any idea of "communalquota"*

The new demand of Muslim reservation is simply a strategy to introduce through the backdoor the principle of comunal quotas into the Constitution.

Even if the allegation of some of the Muslim leaders about some discrimination and bias against Muslims in the recruitment in some areas of government jobs is true, the remedy seems to be more detrimental to their intrests than the problem.

## POLITICAL MOBILIZATION OF MUSLIM OBCs

In the socio-political mobilization of todays Muslim OBCs, Muslim weavers' movement seems to be the first attempt by any such Muslim group. Although the origin of this movement is shrouded in controversy and difference of opinion, Ansari (2000), in a richly documented work on Momin Ansars and their movement, writes that some leaders founded, informally, in 1912 in Calcutta, a forum that was largely welfare-oriented organization. The first convention of Momin Conference was formally held in calcutta in 1928 and from this year onward the Momin Confernce gained an all-India stature and became the representative organization of 3-4 crore Momins of undivided India.

Since handloom industry was first to be hit in the Indian cottage industry sector by the East India Company, weavers were threatened by impoverishment. So, social humiliation and struggle for existence seems to be the prime motivating forces behind this pioneering movement. It mobilized not only Momins but also other Muslim artisan castes. It used to hold an all-India convention every year in major cities of India and for the first time, perhaps, Muslim weavers along with some other artisan castes started looking to the future with hope and motivation for empowerment.

Commenting on the changing profile of Momin Conference, Anwar (2001) points out that up to 1937 its activities were confined to promoting social consciousness and welfare among the Momins. The turning point came in 1938 when it started assuming political overtones when the Muslim League came out with the demand for a separate homeland for the Muslims, the backward Muslims adopted an aggressively nationalist posture and opposed the demand for Pakistan. Right from its very inception the Momin Confernce was convinced about the caste/class character of the Muslim League and its leaders and it had no doubt that the League and its demand were promoting the feudal and elitest vested interests and the lower strata of Muslims were only being harnessed as cannon fodder. The feudal lords, capitlists, *nawabs* and *jagirdare* felt threatened by the mass upsurge of Indian masses and they knew that the Congress Party had not much in its socio-ecomic and political agenda for these vested interests. Its corollary in the post-independent Indian polity may be seen in the form of promotion of Ayodhya issue to blunt the impact of implementation of Mandal Commission's recommendations. It was an intelligent diversionary tactic. Together with Jamat-e-Ulema-e-Hind, the Momin Comference exposed the claim of the Muslim League of representing the entire Muslim population and promoted the nationalist secular agenda of the Congress party with partition of the country the Momin Conference aligned with the Congress Party along with the Jamat-e-Ulema-e-Hind backed by the *Ulema* of Deoband who conributed significantly to the freedom struggle opposing Muslim League for its dvisive agenda. With the passage of time, the Momin Conference lost its strength and became almost defunct. Besides the Momin Conference, the Raeen Conference representing the caste of vagetable vendors and the Mansoori Conference representing the oilseed pressers, also played their role in the socio-political mobilization of Muslim OBCs between 1930s and 1950s.

The period between 1950s and 1980s witnessed hardly any notable movement of Muslim OBCs. Commenting on the post-independence backward classes movement, especially among the Muslims, noted political commentator Bidwai (1996) says:

> *"The Muslim OBC initiatives go back to the 1980s in activism in Maharashtra inspired by Lohia and Karpoori Thakur. However, as a movement the intitiative has gathered strength only in the last few years, partly under the intellectual impetus provided by the Muslim Marathi Sahitya Parishad, first organized in 1990 and held four times so far. The Maharashtra organizers borrowed heavily from the Bahujan Samaj social reform legacy of Shahu Maharaj and Jyotiba Phule and the modernist viesw of Ambedkar. The All India Muslim OBC Sangathan held its first convention on August 29, 1996. The convention was a success. Although uneven, the delegates' composition revealed the commonality of interests and concerns between Qureshis (butchers and meat sellers) and Julahas (weavers), Nais (barbers) and Raeens (vegetable growers or Malis), and Dhobis (washermen) and Telis (oil pressers). The convention's demands include, predictably, extension of Mandal Commission recommentations to all Muslim OBCs, more scholarships, etc., and less predictably, land reforms, funding for small entrepreneurs, and restoration of consessions to scheduled caste (i.e., non-OBC) Muslims which were withdrawn in 1984."*

There also seems to be a conscious effort to relate to *dalit* Muslims and Hindu OBCs and create bonds of solidarity across religious divides. The trans-religious subaltern solidarity could be the nemesis of the religion-based identity politics pursued by the communal and fundamentalist organizations of Muslims such as *Jamat-e-Islami*.

In this series of political mobilization of Muslim OBCs, the latest is the establshment of *Pasmanda Muslim Mahaaz* (Backward Muslim Front) in a convention on 25 October, 1998 at Patna. Though its activities, till date, seem to be confined to Bihar, it has set in motion the efforts by the politically conscious Muslim OBCs in other states.

## MUSLIM OBCs AS ETHNOGRAPHIC CATEGORIES: A BRIEF OVERVIEW

It is now historically established that most of the Muslims in India did not come from Arabia or othr regions from where the message of Islam came. Muslim traders represented the earliest phase of Islam in India and nomadic Sufi saints who were instrumental in attracting the oppressed and exploited lowest strata of Hindu society into the fold of Islam. Making a very interesting and significant observation on the transformation of a lower Hindu caste into a lower Muslim caste, Eijaz Ali (1997) reveals:

> *"Most of the religious conversion among the Hindus occurred in Harijan castes and not from such backward castes as Yadav, Kurmi or Koeri. The converted castes/*biradaris *changed their names from Julaha to Momin, Khatik to Kunjra, Pasi to Dhuniya, Chamar to Qasai and so on. But the names of occupations and structure of Julaha are found in both (Hindu and Muslim) communities, Kunjra are still known as Khatik in some regions and Qasab or Qasai (butchers) have come from the Chamar caste.*
>
> *The fact of the matter is that it is the Chamars who had agreat expertise in skinning and buturing was forbidden and then they started butchering live animals except pig.*
>
> *They were alredy expert in other related nuances. Even today, at severul places, the settlements of Chamars and Qasais are adjacent to each other (translated from Hindi)."*

When we look at the occupationally specialized backward castes of both Hindus and Muslims, we can identify three categories. Ghaus Ansari (1960) and others have also substantiated this:

(i) Castes that are now entirely Muslim.

(ii) Castes that have larger Muslim than Hindu sections.

(iii) Castes that have larger Hindu than Muslim sections.

In the first category come those occupational castes that are now entirely Muslim; thier corresponding Hindus castes either do not exist, or if they exist, they have altogether different names. Some such castes are Atishbaz (firework makers), Chand (jesters), Bhishti (water carriers), Gaddi (graziers), Mirasi (musicians and singers), Qasab (butchers), Momin Julaha (Muslim weavers), etc.

In the second category, which have larger Muslim than Hindu share, include castes such as Darzi (tailors), Dhuniya (cotton carders) Kunjra or Kabariya (green grocers), Manihar (bangle/bracelet makers), Saiqalgar (metal sharpeners) and Rangrez (dyers and cloth printers).

The third category may contain those castes that have a larger Hindu than Muslim share. In this category of clean occupational castes come Kumhar (potters), Nai or Hajjam (barbers), Teli (oil pressers), Dhobi (washermen), etc. The Muslim Bhangi/Mehtar/Lal Begia (sweepers and scavengers) constitute, perhaps, the only untouchable section of the Muslim population.

A significant aspect of the occupational castes among the Muslims is the disappearance of certain caste groups due to social or techno-economic change. The Rangrez (dyers and cloth printers), Bhatiyara (inn keepers) and Saiqalgar (metal sharpeners have almost disappeared as social units.

The 'Peoples of India Project' carried out by the Anthropological Survey of India gives brief but rich and reliable ethnographic accounts of all the castes and communities of India including the Muslim OBCs.

A notable fact about the Muslim OBCs, especially the relatively larger caste groups, is that though some members may have moved out from their traditional occupations, still most follow their forefathers. This occupational mobility has been detrimental, yet it has another dimension that is equally important. Like their counterparts in the population, they have been hardworking from the beginning. Many enterprising members of different caste groups made the best of professions and attained prosperity. The Ansaris and Qureshis of Uttar Pradesh and Rajasthan are the obvious examples. Some other groups among them who upgraded their technology and adoted marketing strategies and showed competitive entrepreneurial skills, prospered such as the artisans/entrepreneurs of Meerut, Moradabed, Aligarh and Ferozabad from western Uttar Pradesh and Bhadohi and Varanasi in eastern Uttar Pradesh. Yet, at the same time, we find a vast multitude of masses living in impoverished conditions in rural as well urban areas of the country. These technological communities of India and their Hindu counterparts deserve a better deal from the society and state.

## NOTE

1. In order to fill the large information gap on a very large number of communities in India, the Anthropological Survey of India (ASI) launched a research project named *Peoples of India Project (1985-92)*. Out of 6,748 communities initially listed by the ASI, this project was able to identify, locate and study 4,693 communities in all the states and union territories of India. Out of a large number of volumes resulting from the project, the three volumes edited by K.S.Singh (1998) provide brief but latest and rich anthropological profile of all of the communities.

## REFERENCES

Ali, M.Eijaz (1997), "Bhartiya Musalmanon ki utpati aur aarakshan" (Origin of Indian Muslims and Reservation), *Hum Dalit*, February.

Ansari, A.H. (2000), *Momin Conference ki Dastavezi Tarikh* (Documentary History of Momin Conference: in Urdu) Delhi, Momin Media.

Ansari, Ghous (1960), Muslim Castes in Uttar Pradesh, Lucknow, Enthrographic and folk Culture Society.

Anwar, Ali (2001), *Masawaat ki jang: Bihar ke Pasmanda Musalmun* (Struggle for Equality: Backward Muslims of Bihar) New Delhi, Vaani Prakashn.

Bidwai, Parful (1996), "Age of Empowerment: Muslim OBCs Discover Mandal", *Times of India*, 11 October.

Hutton J.R. (1951), *Caste in India*, Bombay, Oxford University Press.

India, Government of (1980), The Second Backward Classes Commission (Chairperson: B.P. Mandal), Report, 7 Volumes in Two Parts, New Delhi, Manager Publication.

Nazir, Pervaiz (1993), "Social structure, ideology and language: Caste among Muslims", *Economic and Political Weekly*, December 25.

Sheth, D.L. (2000), "Muslim reservation: Firqavaarana quotey ki gunjaish nahin" (Muslim reservation: No scope for communal quota in A.H.Ansari (ed.) *Pasmaanda Musalmanon ke Masael*

(Problems of Backward Muslims), Gorakhpur, Centre of Backward Muslims of India.

Singh, Harjinder (ed). (1977) *Caste among non-Hindus in India,* New Delhi, National Publishing House.

Singh, K.S. (ed). (1998), *India's Communities, 3vols.,* New Delhi, Oxford University Press.

*Courtesy: " The OBCs and the Ruling Classes in India*

# 4

# FORWARD MARCH OF BACKWARDS: ALL BELIEVERS IN SOCIAL JUSTICE MUST TAKE A STAND ON RESERVATION

***Parful Bidwai***

The Controversy Sparked Off By Human Resources Development Minister Arjun Singh's April 5 remark that the Union cabinet will extend 27 per cent reservations for students from the Other Backward Classes (OBCs) in all the Central universities and the Indian Institutes of Technology and Management and similar institutions has developed into a polotical storm. The storm hasn't subsided despite the government's decision to temporarily shelve the move following the Election Commission's demand for an explanation as to why this "announcement" shouldn't be treated as a violation of the Model Code of Conduct for elections. Another contentious angle has been added to the controversy because the National Knowledge Commission was not consulted before the decision was taken.

Yet, opponents of the reservation proposal have begun to mobilise themselves in a concerted way-especially through e-mail list serves and Internet blogs to generate opinion against the move. Some of them reject the very idea of affirmative action, while some others question the relevance of quotas in educational institutions for the OBCs. Some of the attacks are not only intemperate, but downright hysterical-a sign of the strong sentiments and vehemence the issue has provoked.

It's vitally inportant that the issue be soberly debated in depth and in all its various dimensions. To do this, we must separate its central core from contingent considerations or passing circumstances.

Take the debate over Arjun Singh's ramark, made almost casually at a public function, and whether it constitutes a breach of the election Model Code. This is a bit of a red herring. Ever since the government moved to have the constitution amended to facilitate reservations in educational institutions after the Supreme Court judgement in three cases pertaining to private professional colleges, it has been clear that it would sooner or later introduce quotas.

Arjun Singh said as much last December. Similarly, the Knowledge Commission was bypassed. But then, nobody is clear about its role, merit and real functions, which overlap with those of many Ministries. Nor is it apparent that it has any particular expertise on the issue of affirmative action. Besides, there are sharp differences within the Commission on reservation.

So it's best to leave these contingent issues aside and go straight to the heart of the matter. Are the critics of OBC reservations right in saying that quotas in Central educational institutions are uncalled for and that most OBCs don't deserve them? Will the quotas detract from "merit" and thus eventually undermine the quality of institutions like the IITs which have built an enviable global reputation for thmselves?

Is it true that the global experience with affirmative action shows that it cannot redress entrenched disadvantages or inequalities and create better opportunities for the socially underprivileged? The very first premise in any argument for affirmative action has to be the pervasiveness and deep roots of the Indian system of hierarchical social organisation, centred on caste. Inequalities bulilt into the deepest structures of this society. Systemic discrimination has ensured that the vast majority of the people are excluded from public life for centuries.

The Dalits are the worst victims of this. The caste system considers them "impure" or "polluted" and hence puts them outside the pale. The bulk of the low and lower middle castes, which comprise the OBCs also face vicious forms of discrimination and exclusion, albeit somewhat less violent than do Dalits. This constitutes a systematic denial of social opportunity to a majority of our people, which destroys the possibility of their realising their human potential.

One of India's gravest tragedies is that such inhuman discrimination is sanctioned or legitimised by the Dharmashastras, in particular, the Manusmriti, which declares that Dalits and Shudras (including most OBC castes) must serve the twice born upper castes or savarnas with the utmost obedience and loyalty. Failure to do will attract the most severe of penalties- including amputation of limbs, pouring of molten lead into the ears, and outright beheading. Many vile inhuman and degrading casteist practices persist in India to this day. Contemporary social scince has established after extensive studies that systemic past discrimination can produce great inequality of opportunity, indeed widen it, even when there's no present discrimination. Differences in initial points based on social privilege or disadvantage will generate hugely different outcomes.

Similarly, individual career achievements are determined not by talent or merit alone. They are greatly influenced by the indvidual's membership (or lack of it) of a dominant, well-placed educated group and his/her access to "the right" social contacts information (about careers and other matters) familiarity with the language of power, and easy availabilty of role-models and mentors from a privileged community. Such deep inequalities of opportunity cannot be reduced, leave alone eliminate, without levelling the tilted playing field throuhg affirmative action.

The purpose of affirmative action is not to promote individual betterment, but to acknowledge historic injustices against a group and compensate them through means such as quotas in schools and colleges, and preference in recruitment. The bulk of India's OBCs deserve affirmative action. As for Dalit, the case is so overwhelmingly strong that it doesn't need restating. The Mandal Principle is a sound plank on which to base affirmative action. Reservations or quotas are only one type of affirmative action.

There are others too-including voluntary declarations by government or employers that they would give preference to disadvantaged groups in recruitment and grant special promotions to, say judges or officers from the oppressed minorities, etc. Those who oppose affirmative action radically, in principle, on the ground that it's anti-merit, are comprehensively wrong in assuming that our society and government run on the basis of merit, as distinct from social status, clan loyalties, wealth, sifarish, political influence, overt bribery, etc. Even the best of our competition examinations don't accurately assess merit. Take the case of the IITs, where admissions are dominated by candidates from privileged families who can afford to send them to the coaching centres of Kota in Rajasthan for long months at the expense of lakhs of rupees.

The IIT entrance examination only partly tests the aptitude or intelligence of a candidate. Success at it also involves mastering the "art" of anticipating problems answering objective questions, managing time, and other techniques in which the Kota system coaches you. The argument that some of our professional intitutions are already stretched and short of faculty has some merit. But this is a practical issue and can be addressed through special recruitment drives, higher salaries and other managerial-organisational devices. It's not an argument against OBC reservations in principle.

There are some who argue that OBCs don't deserve preferential treatment because they are among the worst oppressors of Dalits and will aqueeze them out of colleges and eventually jobs. This is frankly, a pernicious proposition. It's true that the social positions and interests of Dalits and OBCs don't always coincide. In fact, they sometimes clash-as when the OBC is a petty landowner, who seasonally employs landless dalits.

It's also true that dominant groups take advantage of such differences to exploit both sections of the people. However, the fact is, Dalits and OBCs have a lot more in common between themselves than they have with the savarnas, their collective oppressors and tormentors. This only underscores the need for solidarity form below to build a common plebeian front against casteism. Reserving 27 per cent of Central university seats for OBCs will not squeeze or compress the Dalits' 15 per cent quota-which is contested by nobody. Opponents of OBC reservations in institutions of higher education are trying to drum up a campaign at least a muscular show of oppositon, in order to create a Mandal-II situation.

In 1990, the anti-Mandal agitaton took off at least partly because VP Singh's move was seen as an attempt to puncture the BJP's mandir platfrom. The BJP backed the violent anti-Mandal protests, and the Congress too clandestinely supported them. The present resevations-for-OBCs proposal is not a defensive or reactive countermove. Not a single party today opposes the Mandal Principle or affimative action for OBCs. The political edge of 16 years ago is missing. Besides, there's a higher degree of acceptance among many savarnas of the inevitability (if not the desirability) of efforts to bring Dalits and OBCs into the mainstrem and create social opportunity for them. The "Forward March of the Backwards" is a reality. Thus, the present anti Mandal sentiment is unlikely to move in a massive way from cyberspace to the streets. It'd be interesting to see how the Congress reacts to the anti-reservations protest.

The OBCs are the one constituency whose support has eluded the party. If it hesitates and vacillates on the reservations issue, OBCs will continue to spurn the Congress as a political option. If, however, the Congress sticks firmly to its pro-quota stand, it can hope to win some OBC support and score against opponents like the regional parties, the Samajwadi Party and Bahujan Samaj Party. The issue isn't politics alone. At its core is social justice. All believers in social justice must take a stand on reservations.

***Courtesy : "Nation and the World"***

# 5

# OBC QUOTA: STIRRING WIDER ISSUES

*Swami Agnivesh & Valson Thampa*

THE ESCALATING stir by medical students against the implementation of the 93rd Amendment, which is now Article 15 (5) of the Constitution, is as symptomatic as it is significant. No one, neither the academics nor the politicians, had any problem when the constitutional amendment enabling the state to make laws to empower the socially and economically sdisadvantaged sections, besides the Scheduled Castes and the Scheduled Tribes, was being made. But now that the stage of its implementation has come, the volcano of grievance has begun to erupt.

Of course, we are familiar with the cxcuse. Medicos, and those who justify and fuel their sense of grievance, argue that they did not know that this was in the offing! And the Knowledge Commission, with the iconic Sam Pitroda at its apex, may provide it a facade of legitimacy, But what this implies is inded too signifcant to be glossed over. Doctors enjoy a significant place in society. "Next to God, doctor" is a popular saying in this country.

Doctors should be the custodians of the health not only of individuals but also of society. It is for this reason that medical ethics are more stringent than professional and business ethics in other sectors of service. But to serve society, one has to know it. To know is to engage; and to engage is to love. Very often ignorance results not from the dearth of information but from the lack of love. We are ignorant because we are indefferent amd we are indifferent largely because we are self-absorbed. Self absorption implies an outlook that limits one's relationsip to the larger context-the country in this instance- wholly to what one may get out of it. This implies blindness to what one can do for the country.

The natural outcome of this outlook is hypersensitivity to 'rights' and total insensitivity to 'duties'. For the medical fraternity, or any educated person, to confess they did not 'know' that the 93rd Admendment could have had this sort of implication is simply to expose themselves to ridicule. So the alibi of ignorance is unacceptable.

If it is not ignorance, what is it then? This brings us to the endemic problem in India:our appallingly poor track record in implementation. We have a plethora of progressive and pro-active laws. our Constitution is one of the finest achievements of legislative wisdom anywhere in the world. We are almost there, but we will not make it we dribble the ball with splendid adroitness up to the D and, then, dither. Our national score sheet would have made far better reading but for this.

Yet, it is not as though nothing has been implemented. The implementation index of a scheme or a policy remains sensitive to the social segment that is meant to benefit from it. Measures that benefit the privileged classes are less vulnerable to executive neglect or red tape. Correspondingly, it is far more difficult to implement policies that are likely to affect the advantages of the priveleged segments of the society.

## HONEST GOVERNANCE

The mark of honest governance is the executive will to bridge the gulf between the letter and the spirit-between legislative mandate ad executive action-of the Constitution. In the present case, the present government, especially Arjun Singh, the Human Resources Development Minister, needs to be commended for its clarity of vision and earnestness of purpose. We do the nation a gross injustice in seeking to subvert the implementation of the Constitution on the apprehension either that merit is likely to be compromised in the process or that a party is likely to bebefit electorally in its wake. To obstruct the initiatives of a government is to legitimise bad governance as well as to widen the gulf between law and policy.

The generic issue here is not whether or not the 93rd Amendment should be implemented. It is, on the contrary, whether we can tolerate the rule of law or not. Our commitment to the rule of law is not proved when we look for it when upholding the rule of law is to our advantage. It is proved more authentically when we stand by it even when it is in conflict with our personal or class interests. The insistence of the medicos that Article 15 (5) of the Constitution should not be implemented is, in principle, akin to the stance of the Sangh Parivar that matter pertaining to faith are above the law. What is equally disturbing is the indication intellectual and acadmic elite of this country are losing their faith in a fair debate. The quota issue could have been openly and objectively debated.

But that option was foreclosed and the way of coercion was adopted percipitously. This is worrisome because this is not a one off intance. We have been watching sadly the erosion of a culture of robust debate in our parliamntary democracy. Rather than debate, issues are clinched by holding Parliament to ransom. A more alarming symptpm of our contrived collective faith in violence, and the corresponding loss of faith in debate and dialogue, cannot be thought of. This is the road we should not, and cannot afford, to take.

The anxiety that the proposed reservation for the Other Backward Classes (OBCs) will subvert mertit seems plausible but is , in fact, purblind. Much depends on what we mean by merit. In this country of vast socio-cconomic disparities and inequities, it is unjust and misleading to define merit in an academic fashion. Shall we not say that merit in the context of health care, should also include compassion and the spirit of service? Should there not be a way by which 'merit' is translated into actual relief for the millions of our people in rural and tribal areas?

The time has come for us to consider making rural and tribal placements, at least for a period of three years, compulsory for all prospective doctors. A doctor who is indifferent to social justice is an aberraton. Also, there is no reason why the state should subsidise the medical education of the rich, mostly to enable them to find greener pastures abroad or in lucrative private practice in the metropolises. The cost of medical education must be indexed to the paying capacity of students.

Shocking events, one after the other, in recent times alert us to the ethical degradation that the medical profession is going through. The fact that medical students can, without any qualms, resort to sharpening the edges of their demands with the suffering of the people, by boycotting work, needs to be seen a symptom of this larger malady.

The root of ethical behaviour is the ability to see one's interests in harmony with the larger interests. Upsetting this ethical balance, this human equilibrium, in the interest of protecting one's own sectarian or class interests is a trend that needs to be seen clearly for what it portends for the society as a whole.

It strikes at the root of creating a wholesome social order without which neither merit nor progress makes any sense.

*Courtesy : The Hindu*

# 6

# OPEN DOORS OF EDUCATION TO ALL: Article 30 Did Not Give the Minorities Freedom to Block SC, ST and OBCs

*D. Raja*

The Other Backward Classes (OBC) Parliamentary Forum and Bharatiya Janata Party (BJP) have generated needless confusion over an important piece of legislation-The Constitution (One Hundred and Fourth Amendment ) Bill, 2005. The Bill seeks to amend Article 15 of the constitution by inserting clause (5).

The Mandal judgment in the case of Indra Sawhney Vs Union of India delivered in November, 1992, necessitated the 77th constitutional amendment in 1995. The 81st, 82nd and the 85th constitutional Amendments passed between the years 2000 and 2002 nullified the effects of Supreme Court Judgments that went against the various aspects of reservations. But tht P.A. Inamdar judgment stands out in affecting the basic tenets of the Constitution. It deprives access to education of socially and educationally backward classes, the scheduled castes and the scheduled tribes.

The Inamdar judgment firstly recognized education as a profession to be read as a fundamental right under the Article 19 (1) (g). It then proceeds to prohibit the state form imposing any reasonable restrictions on carrying out such profesion by completely abrogating state authority on such educational institutions.

It is more than clear that the intention of the polity, the Parliament and the government is to nullify the negative effect of the August, 2005, P.A. Inamdar & Ors Vs State of Maharashtra & Ors judgment of the Supreme Court. The reaction of Parliament to the judgment was immediate and well intentioned. When the 1951 judgment in the case of Champakam Dorairajan Vs Stare of Madras set aside the very basis of reservation the first amendment to the Constitution was moved to nullify it. the 'Statement of Reasons' that was mentioned in the first amendment that inserted Article 15 (4) are an important read even today.

"It is laid down in Article 46 as a directive principle of State policy that the State should promote with special care the educational and economic interests of the weaker sections of the people and protect them from social injustice. In order that any special provision that the State may make for the educational, economic or social advancement of any backward class of citizens may not be challenged on the ground of being discriminatory it is proposed that Article 15 (3) should be suitably amplified."

It is interesting that the OBC forum has the OBC parliamentarians asserting across party lines for the rights of backward classes. In fact the Indian Institutes of technology (IITs) , Indian Institute of Management (IIMs) and other institutions controlled by the Union Government do not provide reservation for OBCs. The absence of such instructions in Union Government might have compelled the OBC forum to speak out.

The OBC forum should realize that when B.R. Ambedkar moved the first amendment as the law minister in 1951, he had the foresight to provide for a wider definition of such classes. Article 15 (4) mentions advancement of any socially and educationally backward classes of citizens which meant the other backward classes in the Central list or the backward classes of the states. The OBC forum should support the government and keep up the pressure, so that full potential of the amendment is achieved through law and executive instructions.

The BJP and its NDA constituents are on an entirely different pitch. As it seems this is another attempt by the BJP to delay and stall the bill. That virtually gives sweeping powers to the state to regulate the educational institutions, including those which were products of globalization and privatization.

The BJP wants to inform the nation yet again about its dislike for the minorities. It allies in the NDA should realise that Sikhs also fall under the definition of minorities. The BJPs plea to add SCs, STs and OBCs to the reservation list of minority institutions may please some sections. But in effect, as is evident, the BJP would like the Bill to be stalled.

The Government should have ascertained as to whether such exemption to minority institutions will block the entry of the deprived and disadvantaged sections into these institutions. In fact, the first amendment to the Constitutional 1951 did not spare Article 29 (2), which is a part of the Constitution that portects the rights of the minorities but the proposed amendment tries to save Article 30.

The right of minorities to establish and administer educational institutions of their choice, under Article 30, provided them the freedom to select any kind of institution from regular colleges to medical and engineering colleges. That did not give them the freedom to block the entry of SC, ST and OBCs. In Kerala, most of the educational institution are controlled by the minority communities and such exemption would virtually debar the disadvantaged. It is necessary that minority institutions, whether aided or unaided, should not be exempted from the reservation policy.

Government should implement equality of access in aided or unaided, minority or non-minority institutions. It is time we do first things first : Open the doors of education to all.

***The writer is National Secretary,***
***Communist Party of India***
***(Courtesy : Times of India)***

# 7

# RESERVATION IN DANGER?

## *An Approach Paper on Justice Rangnath Mishra National Commission For Religious & Linguistic Minorities*

*Ashok Yadav*

Government of India's Social Justice & Empowerment Ministry declared vide its letter dated 29.10.2004 that the government had resolved to constitute a commission which would recommend measures including reservation in government jobs for religious and linguistic minorities. The commission is Rangnath Mishra National Commission for Religious and Linguistic Minorities (NCRLM).

Majority population of Muslim communities is opposing this commission for whose welfare the commission is said to have been constituted. The majority population of the Muslim community who are dalits and OBCs are vehemently opposing the constitution of this commission and have declared in no uncertain terms that the setting up of the commission is unconstitutional. Needless to say that the dalit and OBCs constitute nearly 80% of the total Muslim population.

What is of particular concern to non-minority backward classes is the inclusion of linguistic minority term in the commission and the proposal to bring linguistic minority in the fold of reservation on economic criteria. The million dollar questions is : who are the linguistic minority? Bangla speaking people in Bhiar, Hindi speaking people in West Bengal,

Kannada speaking people in Taminadu, Tamil speaking people in Karnataka are a few examples of linguistic minorities. Delhi is a place where people from every part of the country reside and therefore in Delhi people except Hindi speaking will be counted as linguistic minorities. Since as per terms of reference of the commission linguistic minorities have to be brought in reservation on economic criteria, the upper caste among the linguistic minority will get reservation. The Tamil Brahmins who do not get reservation in their homeland i.e. Tamilnadu in central list will now get reservation in the rest of India. Bengali Brahmins and Kayastha who cannot think of getting reservation in West Bengal will get the reservation if they happen to reside in places other than West Bengal. By the same logic the upper caste of Hindi belt will get reservation in central government services if they happen to be residing in, say, West Bengal, Orissa and South India states etc. *What a master strategy to extend benefit of Reservation to the upper castes?*

The British regime had not made distinction on the religion basis while granting reservation to the depressed classes (dalits in today's parlance.) But the government in independent India withdrew reservation form dalits of all faiths other than Hinduism. This was done by an executive order in 1950. Later on reservation scheme was restored to Sikhs and neo-Buddhist dalits. But Muslims and Christian dalits are still without reservation. Instead of granting reservation to Muslim and Christian dalits and thus establishing uniformity in the matter of reservation, the government of India has established NCRLM which aims at providing reservation not only to upper caste Muslims, Christians and Sikhs but also to upper caste Hindus.

Right from Mandal's partial implementation in 1990, the ruling class elites have all along been attempting for reservation on economic basis. Narasimha Rao government set up Economic Backward Class Commission, which the Supreme Court struck down. In February 2004 the NDA government set up Commission for Economically Backward Classes (CEBC),which is still going on in the UPA government. Thus there are running today two such commissions for exploring ways and means of providing reservation on economic basis (i) NCRLM and (ii) CEBC.

After Mandal, the OBCs got a unique opportunity to move up the ladder. But the opportunities were killed in the womb itself when government of India adopted the policies of non-recruitment on vacant posts, surrendering of vacant posts, contractorisation of labour in the government sectors etc. just after Narasimha government came in power. All these were done in the name of the so-called New Economic Policy. The same policy was continued by the NDA government in a dangerously aggressive manner. Though economic reasons cannot be discounted, the timing of introduction of the so called NEP is such that naturally leads us to believe that one of the motives for bringing in the so called NEP was to counter Mandal. Communalism and the right reactionary economic policies which were deceptively named New Economic Policy by the ruling elites were two pronged strategies to counter Mandal. It can never be mere coincidence that 1990 saw Mandal and 1991 saw the launch of neo liberal economic policies.

Muslim population accounts from 12% of the total population of India i.e. out of 100 crore population of India 12 crore people are Muslims. Of the total Muslim population nearly 20% i.e. about 2.5 crore people are upper caste Muslims. But their share in total MPs from first to fourteenth Lok Sabha is 4.5% i.e. somewhat less than double its share in the population. *On the other hand backward and dalit Muslim account for nearly 10% of the total population of India but their share in the total MPs from first to fourteenth Lok Sabha is less than one percent.* Muslims share in the total government jobs is about 2-3 per cent and overwhelming majority of those Muslims are uper caste Muslims. It can be well surmised that the upper caste Muslims are getting share in government jobs more or less equal to their share in the population.

Reservation on economic ground to religious and linguistic minorities will shake the very foundation of reservation and, therefore, NCRLM is a threat not only to OBCs alone but to dalit and adivasis also. We declare hereby our absolute antipathy against setting up of Rangnath Mishara NCRLM and its terms of reference and as well as CEBC set up by BJP led NDA regime. We demand in unequivocal terms for scrapping of the two commissions. We hereby give call to individuals social organizations and political parties committed to protecting interest of dalits, advasi and other backward classes to join us in our pursuit of scrapping of the two commissions.

But we will not be content with mere scrapping of the two commissions. We also demand total implementation of Mandal Commission recommendations. Thus our three demands are the following on which we see unflinching active support of all right thinking people.

1. Rangnath Mishra National Commission for Religious and Linguistic Minorities as well as Commission for Economically Backward Classes must immediately be scrapped.
2. For implementation of the remaining recommendations of Mandal Commission, the central Government must immediately bring out orders.
3. The central government must immediately put an end to the policies of commercialization, privatization and non-formalization of education, surrendering of and non-recruitment on vacant posts.

*Courtesy : 'Voice of OBC'*

# 8

# WHY EXCLUDE MINORITY INSTITUTIONS?

***Udit Raj***

The word *'Reservation'* is mostly misconstrued, misunderstood, vague and even mythical. The bill to enable reservation in private unaided Medical and Engineering Colleges has been deferred because BJP wants that the minority institutions are also to be brought under its ambit. This controversy arose because Supreme Court held on 12th August, 2005 that unaided minority and non-minority institutions had absolute right to admit students of their cho ice in medicine, engineering and other professional courses without government interference.

If BJP came into power, it was because of Mandal Anguish and heart-bun that erupted among the dominante cases, got channelised through Ram Mandir Construction Movement led by L.K. Advani. It can be safely concluded that the main intention was to oppose reservation for Backwards than to build temple at Ayodhya. Had it not been so, the long regime of BJP at the centre would have done something in that direction. The anomalies created by the Supreme Court judgement, have given an opportunity to BJP to try to get mileage while asking for reservation in the minority institutions. Though BJP may claim to have pious intentions in asking for reservation for Dalits and Backwards but K. Sudershan the RSS supremo, recently negated it when he said that reservations should go. The intention is to pit minorities against Dalits and Backwards and vice versa, and to see that the bill meets the same fate as that of the Women

Reservation Bill. However, there is some force in the stand of BJP asking for reservation in minorities institutions.

Now the leaders of minorities have to move cautiously. Most of these institutions are held by Christians, followed by Muslims, Jains and Sikhs. Muslims and Christians are demanding for their reservation in govt. jobs. And at the same time Dalits and Backwards are asking for reservations in minority institutions. Article 30 of the Indian Constitution protects the minority institutions, but that is in regard to cultural and religious interests. If law is laid to allow participation by Dalits, that will not abrogate their constitutional rights. The advantage minorities will have, will pave for a historical opportunity to bring Dalits and Backwards closer to them, which will eventually strengthen the bonds of secularism and communal harmony. Minorities do not have much to lose but in fact will gain more. They will bet a strong footing to ask for reservation in both govt. and private sectors. Majority of Muslims are from Dalit stock and hence should not have any reservation about reservation. Rather the Muslim and Christian leadership should come forward to offer and thwart the gimmick of BJP. The head of the Syro Malabar Church has appealed to Church Schools to give preference to educating poor people. "Our school should not be seen as a means for job opportunities or amassing profits." In this regard, Cardinal Verkey Vthayathil of Ernaculam Angamaly wrote in his pastoral letter issued after the recent Church synod. This letter stresses the Church role in bringing social justice in education.

Private institutions owned by majority will then be on weaker footing in opposing the move. The misuse of constitutional provisions, i.e. in regard to minorities, will also be put to an end. Dr. Krishna Swamy of Puthia Tamilagam told me that Six Medical Colleges in Tamilnadu are under the category of minority but run by the majority, like Balaji Medical College run by Jagatrakshan, an ex-MP, Venkateswar Engineering College by M.A. Chidambaram, Shanti Bhama Medical College by A.C. Shanmugam, and S.R. Medical College. Thus minorities do not have much to lose but only to gain more. The opposition from Christian is not going to there but some

Muslims might be irked. Major institutions are not with Muslims but are with Christians, e.g. five of nine private medical schools in Kerala belong to Christians. They also manage half of the fourteen self financing engineering colleges.

The common misconception is, that providing opportunities to poor and backwards lowers down the standards, but it is not so when we examine the number one institution in the world i.e. 'Havard.' The Havard University is Mecca for knowledge in the world, with its medical school being the ultimate, but it has a separate ethnic department which keeps on identifying Women, Blacks and talent from ethnic groups. Out of 8,402 medical educationalists, there are 1,150 Blacks and ethnic minorities which comes to 13.68%, 2,747 women whose percentage is more than 32%. Has this diversity lowered any of the standards or has this made it top of the world? In June, 2003, the Supreme Court of America decided a matter in favour of Black student. He sought admission in law College of Michigan University with lower marks than white students. When challenged later on, the Supreme Court upheld his admission.

Reservation is not going to solve fundamental problems but it will definitely promote social harmony. Thousands of years of discrimination can not be repaired in a few decades. Hence the argument that how long this will go on and on, should not be the concern of merit mongers. The nation is built not by a few but by all, the excellence and efficiency work in congenial atmosphere. Where there is social tension, excellence and talent will not be allowed to manifest as we witness in Bihar and some backward regions. Similarly, talent of a country is drained out because of non-congenial atmosphere. Moreover, fetching good marks in the school with the help of good equipments, facilities, and teachers should not only constitute the definition of merit.

CPM, CPI and other political parties are in favour of including minorities institutions in the ambit of reservation. However, Congress is determined to introduce the bill without amending it. i.e. excluding minorities institutions. There is a truth that Congress Party appeases more to minorities than really giving something. If the bill meets the fate of Women's

Reservation, Congress appeases both minorities as well as majorities and if bill is amended because of pressure from allies, it will take the plea that it tried hard but what to do if the govt. was to run. The Congress leaders should not forget that their calculation will backfire because today Dalits are not the same as in 60s or 70s. It is in the interest of Congress as well as the nation to bring minority institutions under the ambit of reservation.

*Courtesy : Voice of Buddha*

# 9

# CASTE AMONG INDIAN MUSLIMS

*Dilip Karanth*

The caste system, however, exists even among Indian Muslims. But many a scholar traces it to Hindu influence:

> *The Muslim caste system is a result of Hindu influence; the Indian Muslims have acquired the system........from the Hindus through constant and continuous culture contact; the system of caste groupings itself resulted in the concept of social distance between the two communities, the Hindus and the Muslims.*[1]

In this paper we will try to collect some background information which will hopefully help in sparking a debate regarding caste. That a debate is necessary is clear from a recent book by Marc Gaborieau. *Ni Brahmanes Ni Ancetres*, in which the author presents his detailed findings, after several years of filed work in Nepal, studying the Curaute, a caste of banglemakers. The book is sure to revolutionize our understanding of caste. We will present several quotes from Gaborieau's classic in this article.

Writing about the dominant trend in British ethnography. Gaboricau claims that the British took a simplistic view of castes and presented Hinduism, taken as a whole, as inherently hierarchical in structure, as opposed to Islam, taken as a whole, taken to be inherently egalitarian.[2] Any elements of hierarchy in Islamic society is taken to be a relic from Hinduism, just as Ansari has done in the quote above. This idea has become very strongly rooted in the literature on caste. This idea has been championed particularly by Muslim scholars in the 19th century, as they defended their faith against criticism by Western scholars. The basic thrust of these arguments was that:

> *Far from bringing about forcible conversions as accused of by the British, the Muslim conquerors carried out peaceful conversions, notably by means of the Sufis The chief reason for its success would have been the particular attractiveness of Islam, as an egalitarian faith, for the lower castes especially the untouchables. The cities and qasba established by the new conquerors would have been spaces of liberty; they would have permitted the most disfavored people to rise in the social hierarchy, by opening new economic outlets.*

Gaborieau points out that the best example of this theory isthe book by Arnold. *The Preaching of Islam,* for which the author collaborated with two influential Indian Muslim thinkers, Sayyid Ahmad Khan (d, 1898) and Shibli Nu'mani (d, 1914). The book, which was written in Aligarh and was first published in 1896, says among other things: "A Hindu will naturally be attracted by a religion which receives everybody with discrimination" (Arnold, 1965, 291-291); and; "It is this absence of class prejudice which constitutes the real force of Islam in India and which allows it to win so many converts from Hinduism" (pp, 118-119).

In Arnold's book we clearly see the formulations of a theme that had been or would be elaborated by many other scholars, such W.W. Hunter and James Rice. In the context of conversions to Islam in Bengal, Rice wrote that the Islamic armies "were welcomed by the out-cast *Chandals and Kaibarrta.*"[3] In the face of numerous such claims, it could be expected that modern Muslim society in Bengal would present an egalitarian picture. However, it turns out that such is not at all the case. No less a man than Dr. B.R. Ambedkar took cognizance of the existence of castes even in Muslim Bengal. Quoting the Superintendent of the Census for 1901 for the province of Bengal, Ambedkar noted:

> *"The conventional division of the Mahomedans into four tribes" Sheikh, Saiad, Moghal and Pathan "has very little application to this Province (Bengal). The Mahomedans themselves recognize two*

> *main social divisions, (1)* Ashraf *or Sharaf and (2) Ajlaf* Ashraf *means 'noble' and includes all undoubted descendants of foreigners and conerts from high caste Hindus. All other Mahomedans including the occupational groups and all converts of lower ranks are known by the contemptuous terms, 'Ajlaf', 'wretches' or 'mean people': they are also called Kamina or Itar, 'base' or Rasil, a corruption of Rizal, 'worthless'. In some places a third class, called Arzal or 'lowest of all,' is added. With them no other Mahomedan would associate, and they are forbidden to enter the mosque or to use the public burial ground.*
>
> *"Within these groups there are castes with social precedence of exactly the same nature as one finds among the Hindus.[4]"*

Bengal would become the seat of intense political activism and lobbying in the years after Ambedkar wrote these words. Caste would become a much talked of political commodity, politicians would campaign for the loyalties of the masses, the province would go on to be partitioned, and yet even as late as 1973, caste would be an abiding feature of Bengali Muslim life, M.K.A. Siddiqui, who contributed an essay[5] to an important book on the caste phenomenon among Indian Muslims,[6] points out that there are several caste groups among the Muslims in Calcutta. Siddiqui discusses several different ways in which inequality manifests itself–restrictions on commensality, hypergamy, pollution by contact, etc. He divides the castes into three categories. The castes in any one category can accept food from the others in the category, but not from castes in lower categories.

> *The Dafalis who work as priests for the Lal Begis, or the Qalanders who sometimes live in their neighbourhood, refuse to accept food or water from Lal Begis.[7]*

The groups are descent groups, "with or without occupational specialization". For example, the Lal Begis (who roughly correspond to the Bhangi caste in Hindu society) are generally regarded as unclean on account of their humble occupation– "They often experience difficulty in getting their dead buried in the common Muslim burial ground."

Hypergamy is widely practiced in the highest category, meaning that women from lower castes can be married into the higher castes (Sayyad and Sheikh), but not vice versa. The children of these mixed marriages are called "Sayyadzada" and "Sheikhzada" respectively. They do not attain the full status of their fathers, and are expected to make alliances with people of their status.

Siddiqui regards the emphasis on birth as not being sanctioned by scripture, which he says, wiped out distinctions of colour and race. However, as Islam spread to distant lands, social stratification resulted as a result of historical developments and adjustments made to local traditions. Kinship with the Prophet became a new criterion of nobility. Siddiqui discusses a few other aspects of the caste structure, and, significantly notes that "the founders of the [Sufi] mystic orders belong exclusively to categories that claim foreign origin. Most of them are Sayyads."

The situation in Bengal was similar to that in central regions of India, as shown by studies by Zarina Bhatty[8] and by Imtiaz Ahmad Bhatty studies the case of a village Kasauli in the state of Uttar Pradesh, and found the village society to be deeply caste-riven. At the top of the hierarchy was a lineage of Sayyads, and a subcaste of the Sheikhs, namely the Kidwais. These were the only *Ashraf* castes in the village. Elsewhere in India, the *Ashraf* castes include Sayyads, Sheikhs, Mughals and Pathans. These are communities claiming descent from population groups hailing from outside India. Bhatty points out that all four noble castes permit interdining, but commensality with the lower castes, consisting of groups descended from Indian coverts, is not allowed. Also Sayyads and Sheikhs intermarry, but marriages between Sayyads and Sheikhs on the one hand, and Mughals and Pathans on the other, are not socially acceptable. In the village of Kasauli, there are eighteen other castes, consisting of groups defined by occupation. Closely linked to occupation is a notion of pollution, depending on the materials handled by persons following the occupation. A kind of hierarchy is defined, with castes who come into proximity with the *Ashraf* regarded as higher.

Nats, who skin dead animals and make drums, find a place close to the bottom of the scale while Julahas and Darzis are at the top end. Dhobis, who must wash soiled clothes, are closer to the Nats than to the Julahas.[9]

Bhatty discusses the interesting case of a divide in the musician community. The *Mirasis* who perform for the higher *Ashraf* castes, are regarded as superior to the Nats, who perform the same social functions, but for the public at large. The *Mirasis* have adopted the dress of the *Ashraf*, and have learned to speak Urdu, while the Nats converse in the local dialect. Thus the *Mirasis* have improved their social standing by the imitation of and association with the upper castes, who set the norms for the whole society.

In his article on the Siddique Sheikhs of Uttar Pradesh, Imtiaz Ahmad informs us of the various considrations taken into account when determining hierarchy within the status group called the Sheikhs. There are at least four of them:

1. Affiliation with an Arab tribe.
2. Descent from a person of Arab origin who is known to have close ties with the prophet.
3. Relationship to a place in Arabia or Persia.
4. Decent from someone who is said to have entered India along with the early Muslim armies.

According to Ahmed, the Sheikh subgroups emphasize their foreign origin and links to some Islamic personage of repute. The groups who claim to be descended from the Prophet's own tribe, Quraish are regarded as the highest. Then follow the descendants of first Caliph, Abu Bakr Siddique, Next in rank are those who count the next two Caliphs, Usman and Umar among their ancestors. They are followed by descendants of the close friends and associates of the Prophet Descendants of other Persians or Arabs who may have come with the Muslim armies are ranked last.

As for the Siddique Sheikhs studied closely by Imtiyaz/ Ahmed they are not descendents of Abu Bakar.

Their Kayastha Hindu antecedents are quite well established, and their striving for recognition as *Ashraf* is a phenomenon quite well known all over India. Ahmed points out that the circumstances of the Siddique Sheikhs' conversion is not known, but after conversion to Islam, *they were allowed to retain their traditional occupation as land recordkeepers*, a fact which is also attested to by the fact that the members of the caste also served as patwaris well after the annexation of the area by the British. (emphasis added)

Ahmed makes some other very intersting observations about the Siddique Sheikhs.

*Convert groups to Islam are generally characterized as New Muslims and they are looked down upon by the social groups which are known to be descendants of foreign sources or who have succeeded in eliminating the stigma of recent conversion. This gave rise to certain differentiations in the adjustment of the Sheikh Siddiques after their conversion to Islam in the different villages. In villages that were largely or predominantly Hindu, the Sheikh Siddiques were excluded from the framework of interaction with the Hindu castes but they continued to enjoy a somewhat superior status as a Muslim group. But in villages where there were numerous other Muslim groups of superior status, the Sheikh Siddiques were not merely excluded from the social hierarchy of Hindu castes, but were also relegated to a somewhat lower position even within the hierarchy of Muslim castes.*

The continued prestige of the Siddique Sheikhs in their native villages even after conversion can probably be explained by the fact that they were already a community which enjoyed prestige among the Hindus. After all, they *were allowed to retain their prestigious occupation as land recordkeepers*. But in Muslim dominated villages, the Siddique Sheikhs commanded little prestige among the Muslims, since they were not *Ashraf*. This is an example of conversion from Hinduism which has obviously not been motivated by a desire to escape the disabilities of the Hindu caste system.

Ahmed's observations regarding the inferior status of "New Muslims" seems to be applicable widely in India. We find confirmation of this generalization in places as far removed from Uttar Pradesh as the Moplah-dominated regions of Kerala. The hierarchies in Moplah society have been studied by Victor D'Souza.[10] He reports that there are five distinct sections among the Moplahs: Thanghals, Arabis, Malbaris, Pusalars and Ossans. The Thangals who are at the top of the pyramid, are a small group of people who trace their descent to the Prophet, through his daughter Fatima. The terms Thangal is a respectful term of address, usually applied to Brahmins in Kerala. The Arabis are a group of people mostly concentrated in Quilandy (a town north of Calicut), who are descendants of Arab men and local women, but who have preserved the memory of their descent. The association of the Arabis with Arabia entitles them to a respect in Moplah society second only to that of the Thangals. The Malabaris also claim descent from Arabs, but they are those who followed a matriarchal system-the so-called "mother-right" culture. As for the Pusalars and the Ossans, D'Souza writes:

> *The so-called Pusalars are converts from among the Hindu fishermen, called Mukkuvans. Their conversion took place relatively late. Because of their latter conversion and their low occupation of fishing they are allotted a low status in the Moplah society. The Pusalars are spread all along the coastline of Kerala and they still continue their traditional occupation of fishing.*
>
> *The Ossans are a group of barbers among the Moplahs and by virtue of their very low occupation they are ranked the lowest. Their womenfolk act as hired singers on social occasions like weddings.*

The hierarchies in Moplah society also show a tendency to accord the highest place of honour to the Sayyads, and lowest place to new converts and despised groups, such as barbers. The motive for conversion could hardly have been the keen desire to escape the disabilities of the Hindu caste system. Why would converts voluntarily accept similar disabilities in the new society they were going to join ? The realities of Indian Muslim society flatly contradict claims such as the one made by the renowned Islamic thinker and rector of Decoband, Shibli Nu'mani:

If an Asiatic converts to Christianity, he does not obtain the rights (*huquq*) of the European community (*qaum*), even though he may have the same religion; even on the plane of religious rights, he cannot he equal (*ham-sar*) to the Europeans. In contrast, the "communitarian identity" (*qaumiyyat*) of the Muslims is not bound to the country, nor to the race (*nasal*), nor to lineage, nor to any other criterion-it is only bound to religion. Whether one is Persian (*ajami*), Indian (*hindi*). European or Asiatic, as soon as one enters the Muslim community, by the sole fact of conversion, one immediately (daf'atan) becomes the equal (barabar) of other Muslims sous le rapprot de all rights; As soon as he has pronounced the profession of the faith, a tanner (*Camar*) can take a place in the first row in the mosque, thus putting himself on a rank equal to that of the |Onoman| Sultan 'Abd al-Hamid Khan; the Sultan cannot then claim to dislodge him from that place (cited in Shams-i-Tabriz Khan, 1983, 58-59).[11]

Gaborieau points out that this ideal picture of Muslim society fails to correspond with reality, Nu'mani aimed to fight Western scholars with their arguments. He wished to show that while conversion to Christianity did not guarantee the Asiatics racial equality with Europeans, such was not the case within Muslim society. Muslim society, in Nu'mani's romantic view, was even ahead of the Christian West. However, Gaborieau points out that equality did not fall to the lot even of Nu'mani himself:

> *His immense learning was recognized the world over: but he lacked any mystic aura. Most importantly, he was descended from converts; and what is worse, his lineage lacked prestige locally. He was a pseudo-Rajput, in fact, from an obscure caste of peasants. He was perfectly conscious of this stigma. This is what led him, like Iqbal to overemphasize learning and the role of Islam, and to be extremely determined to exact the mark of respect due to him in the capacity of scholar. He never succeeded in gaining admittance into the intellectual and religious establishment of the day. He was not able to establish himself in the two prestigious institutions where he taught. (Aligarh and the Nadwatu'l-'ulamu' of Lucknow) which had been founded by genuine Sayyids and were populated with* Ashraf; *in both cases he had to resign (Metcalf, 1982a, 340-342).*[12]

As we have seen before, scholars such as Ansari regard manifestations of societal inequality within Islamic society as an inheritance from Hinduism. In regions where the demographics have not shifted in favour of Islam, the influence from the ambient Hindu society on the Muslim minority is indeed strong. However, the practice of segregating the lower castes has continued in regions where Hindu political power, and possibly Hindu demographic preponderance, has long vanished. As discussed before, in the case of Bengal, castes like the Lal Begis have been discriminated against long after the majority of the population turned Muslim.

Matters were hardly different at the other end of the Indian subcontinent, in Baluchistan. The Census Superintendent of Baluchistan wrote in 1931 that members of the Chuhra caste or tribe, who identified themselves variously as Hindu Balmiki, Hindu Lal Begi, Musalman Lal Begi, Musalman Balashai, Sikh Mazhabi or simply as 'Chuhra' were 'without exception ... not allowed to drink from wells belonging to real Hindus, Muslims or Sikhs' and were 'not permitted to enter their places of worship'.[13]

The disabilities inflicted on the lower castes in Kerala's Muslim (and of course Hindu) society also continued in the Laccadive Islands, after the islands' link with Hindu society had been served. The caste hierarchies prevailing in the islands have been studied in some detail by Leela Dube, one more contributor to the book edited by Imtiaz Ahmed. The aristocracy, called Karnavars are descendants of Nambudiris and Nayars. They are also referred to by the respectful appellation, Koya, which means a religious dignitary. It was this class that monopolized land-and boat-owning. The Malumis or Urukkars formed the sailor-caste, and the Melacheris (literally, tree-climbers) formed a class of serfs, who earned their livelihood by "plucking coconuts, tilling their lords' lands, rowing their boats." The number of castes or classes varied from island to island, some places having four instead of three. One island, Agatti, was regarded as a Melacheri island.

In view of evidence such as has been adduced above, Gaborieau argues that a hierarchical ordering is quite characteristic of Islamic society. He points out that Hindu society is not unique in holding some occupations in ritual opprobrium:

The influence of the Indian context is often invoked to explain the opprobrium suffered by the barber, the weaver, the butcher, the tanner, the sweeper,[14] etc. These are professions stigmatized as being low and even impure. The last two are even regarded as untouchable. But this interpretation is short-sighted: the Hindu ideology only confirms prejudices formerly more widespread spread throughout the world. The tanner who handles animal carcasses is universally detested; the Hajjam who is the scarifier (and, among the Muslims, the circumcizer), as well as the barber are looked down upon in the Talmud as well as under the Sassanians, among Hindus and among Muslims. The contempt towards weavers also dates to remote times. Here we are dealing with traditions which date back to prehistoric times and can be found very different civilizations (for all these questions, see the important documentation analyzed by Brunschvig, 1962, 46-57.) This fact demolishes the contrary argument, according to which Islam in India is supposed to have rehabilitated the depressed castes - the professions which are cited as examples, the barbers, weavers, and tanners, are precisely those whose inferior status is most explicitly affirmed in the Islamic tradition. The stereotypes attached to them in India are widely attested in Islam and in the most ancient traditions: the barber is greedy and arrogant: the weaver - wretched, stupid and treacherous. The conversion to Islam of those who practiced these professions unquestionably opened for them new economic outlets-and this is precisely the reason for their conversion; their conversion in no way improved their status.[15]

In addition to the material already available in the literature, Gaborieau brings to the discussion the results of his own long years of field work in Nepal. He has seen Muslim Curautes redoing their ritual ablutions if they happened to touch a |Muslim| untouchable by mistake. He has also studied the phenomenon of ritual uncleanness-associated with some professions, and social hierarchy based on profession, at work in Muslim society. One of his examples concerns the Kashmiri Muslims in Nepal who pass for *Ashraf*. Periodically, these high born Muslims send for a barber from India, at great expense. However, the barber becomes wealthy, and turns his back on the profession in favour of something more respectable. He refuses to perform circumcisions, and the need for another barber is acutely felt. A new barber is sent for, and he despised, he faces the same stereotypes, and the cycle is repeated. The stereotypes, applied to barbers and weavers, are an old Islamic tradition.

While individual social mobility is attested, collective mobility is virtually impossible, because thee is a kind of "barrier" separating the *Ashraf* castes from the artisan castes:

> *Nowhere have I sensed this barrier as strongly as in my field work in Nepal. The oldest* Ashraf *of Kathmandu, the Kashmiri, traditionalists and devoted to the cult of the saints, totally refuse all socially significant transactions with other Muslims of low status from the valley, who are collectively called Hindustani and who are recruited from various artisan castes. At the most they sometimes accept, under the rubric of hypergamy, some of their daughters as secondary wives who are never any more than concubines. A primary marriage would be unthinkable. The Kashmiris have always been opposed, even in multiple proceedings in front of Nepalese tribunals composed of Hindus, to having common mosques and even a common cemetery with the Hindustani. This is a clinching argument when we remember that the total number of Muslims in the valley does not ever exceed twelve hundred persons. The Hindustani may well be reformed, instructed in religion and devout, they can never cross the barrier (Gaborieau, 1977a, 52-54).*[16]

Gaborieau's studies of conversions into the Muslim Curaute caste contradict the theory that conversion has taken place in India selectively from the lowest orders. The Curaute admit conversions into their caste from Hindus of higher castes such as Chettri and Gurung. But they do not accept untouchables into their caste.

> *Indeed even conversion effected by the Sufis does not seem to wipe out the stigma of untouchability. Gaborieau points out that the* Ashraf *monopolize the so-called orthodox Sufi brotherhoods (*ba-shar'*), as opposed to the "heterodox" brotherhoods (*ba-shar'*) who are relegated to the level of the lowest castes (Gaborieau, 1986c)*[17]

and also that

> *the heterodox brotherhoods are lower than and subservient to the former, so much so that the musicians (*qawwal*), who pronounce the mystic chants (*qawwali*) and play the drum, are in fact untouchable musicians (as in the Hindu temples) even though they*

*claim affiliation with a Sufi order. The heterodox Sufis and these musicians are relegated to the far corners of the shrines dedicated to Muslim saints.*[18]

A caste-like phenomenon exist in the Punjab with the Chishtis forming a hereditary clan, controlling not only the tomb of their ancestor Baba Farid-ud-din (d. 1265) at Pak-pattan, but also the lands and the cultivators surrounding it.[19] Clan members had justified their hypergamous codes of marriages even in front of British courts. The noted historian Richard Eaton rejected these claims as being contrary to Islamic tradition, and as reflecting the influence of the ambient Hindu culture. Gaborieau disagrees with his famous collegaue, pointing out that such hypergamous traditions are completely in consonance with worldwide Islamic practice. According to Gaborieau, Robert Brunschvig (1962,55) had long ago compared the laws of the Manu Smriti to Islamic tradition:

*If a young girl likes a man of a class higher than her own, the king should not make her pay the slightest fine; but if she unites herself with a man of inferior birth, she should be imprisoned in her house, and paced under guard. A man of low origin who courts a maiden of high birth deserves a capital punishment. (Laws of Manu (VIII 365-366))*

Following Brunschvig, Gaborieau claims that this law is exactly that which the dominant Hanafite tradition of jurisprudence would require,[20] as has been spelled out on in the famous compendium of the Moghul period titled *Fatawa-i-alamgiriyya*. The idea that a woman can only marry a man of equal or higher status has been upheld as late as the twentieth century by scholars even of the eminence of Ashraf Ali Thanawi (d. 1943). The marriage of a woman to a man of lower status can be annulled by the family's request, or by a Qazi's judgment.

Gaborieau calls for a frankness in studying the phenomenon of caste in Indian Muslim society. The Muslims who entered did not seem to be shocked by the institution of caste, and if they were not shocked by it, it must be that they were not unfamiliar with such arrangements themselves. Even writers such as Ansari (whom we have quoted on the first page), who trace the caste inequalities in Indian Muslim society to Hindu influence, admit however that Islam was not egalitarian when it entered India.

> *The idea of equality among Muslims was practicable only in the then prevailing conditions of Arabia. In the course of the expansion of Islam and its contact with other complex cultures the democratic forms of political organization and social equality within the community gradually disappeared.*[21]

He then traces the origin of caste to the "Indo-Iranian community". Ansari declares that though "Islam proclaimed the message of equality and universal brotherhood", "the established and deep rooted institution of social segregation in Persia" eventually won out.

> *Even the reputed Muslim scholars of Persia, like Nasir-ud-Din at-Tusi preached the division of society; his classification of society remained the same as it was during the Sasanian period. In his book.* Akhlaq-i-Nasiri *(which was finished shortly before the fall of the Caliphate), at-Tusi considers that each of the social classes should be kept in its proper place. A seventeenth-century work,* Jami-i-Mufidi, *again retains the same four-fold division of society, but it puts forward a slight change in giving precedence to warriors at the top and reducing the relative rank of priests to that of second in the hierarchy. In addition to these philosophers, the noted statesman of Persia. Nizam-ul-Mulk, in his* Siyasat Nama, *instructs his subordinates to maintain the people in their proper ranks.*[22]

The idea of social hierarchy, Ansari syas, had already become part of Islamic society by the time it entered India in the twelfth century. Over the centuries attitudes only hardened, until at last even untouchability entered Islamic society. The plight of Muslim untouchables is described by Ansari in moving detail:

> *A Bhangi, either Muslim or non-Muslim, is not permitted to enter a mosque no matter how clean he may be at the time. Although in theory a Muslim Bhangi or Chamar is allowed to offer his prayer[s] in a mosque, but in usual practice their entrance into such pious places as mosques and shrines of Muslim saints is socially disapproved and thus it is resisted. Even if they could get into a mosque or shrine, provided they have had a bath and are dressed in clean clothes, they do not usually proceed beyond the entrance steps.*

> *In contrast to the Hindu caste system, Muslim Bhangis are allowed to learn the Quran, but they are not expected to teach it.*
>
> *It is a common practice observed in almost all the households of* Ashraf, *Muslim Rajputs, and the clean occupational castes, that Bhangis, either Muslim or non-Muslim, are generally served food in their own containers. If they do not have their own bowls they are served in clay pots which are not again used to serve clean caste members. Bhangis are given water to drink in such a way that the jar does not touch even their lips.*[23]

However Ansari never explains how caste structures in India can be attributed to Hindu influence alone, if Muslim society had also stratified into hierarchies, before Islam's advent in India. Several such problems in the literature need explanation. Gaborieau again offers perspective:

> *... While we have good contemporary studies of Hindu untouchables, no work was done on Muslim untouchables during the colonial period. The absence of work on this key point deserves reflection. This refusal to consider the reality is understandable on the part of Muslim scholars; the problem of untouchability clashes against their ideological convictions on the ecumenical character of Islam, And what is more, any conversion even of untouchables involves burning political complications. On the part of western researchers, this omission is less excusable: I regard it as a manifestation of the prejudice according to which Muslim social order must necessarily obey a different logic than the Hindu social order, and also by the illusion of believing that the enumeration of castes is done from top down, whereas in reality it happens from the bottom up, starting from the untouchables.*[24]

Gaborieau also explains that advent of Islam did not spell the demise of hierarchical structures in Indian society. The Muslims allowed the hierarchical structures to remain, and were not even shocked by it; not only that, they occupied the apex of the pyramid (in the form of the *Ashraf* castes), without otherwise undermining it.[25]

## CASTE IN THE ISLAMIC WORLD

We have already seen from the examples of the *Ashraf's* practices regarding marriage, or admittance to mystic brotherhoods, etc., the *Ashraf* also retained their own stereotypes and prejudices which cannot be traced solely to Hindu influence.

But that is not the whole story, Even if the caste structure was largely a relic from the pre-Islamic past, new castes also sometimes came into existence. The Maratha Bugtis in Balochistan are an interesting case of what may be a caste forming even under Islamic rule. Theirs is a clan claiming descent from Marathas captives of war brought back by members of the Bugti tribe, who served the armies of Ahmad Shah Durrani (Abdali) after the fateful battle of Panipat.

> *In time they underwent 'Bugti-ization' and became Muslims. Although for all practical purposes they may now be considered Bugtis, and are even in the forefront in education and employment, they were once considered little better than bonded labour. They could not own or by land. Up to two generations ago they could be 'bought' for twenty or thirty rupees. Their women were fair game of Bugtis.*

The Maratha Bugtis took jobs as unskilled labourers, which their tribal overlords disdained. Over the years they have come to occupy higher positions, and their prosperity is resented by the Bugtis.[26] It is interesting to note that this caste-like phenomenon has endured for more than two centuries, even in a region largely devoid of Hindus.

The Maratha Bugtis were not alone in their position as a group living in the Islamic world, with their inferior position determined by heredity. The Haratin[27] or Harratin of southwestern Morocco and Mauritania are "a socially and ethnically distinct class of workers". They are descended from slaves, but are now serfs, "without the privileges of freedom". (One of the people who is trying to help them to become independent is Abdel Nasser Ould Yessa, whose life and work is discussed at the following web site: *http://www.iabolish.org/act/abol/profile/yessa1.htm)*.

The facile practice of regarding all hierarchies in the Islamic world as a substratum from pre-Islamic societies does not always work. Hierarchies (in other words, castes) exist even in places like Yemen and the rest of the Arabian peninsula.

As a perusal of the informative entry on "Bedouin" in the Encyclopaedia Brittanica:[28] reveals. Bedouin society in twentieth-century Arabia was also divided into various groups. While the nomads have been settled after the formation of the modern states, the societal hierarchical and patriarchal structure has been retained. The Bedouin tribes were classified on the basis of the species of animal on which they depended. Camel nomads were highest in prestige. They were spread on extensive territories in the Sahara, Syrian and Arabian deserts. Sheep- and goat-herding nomads, rank below, and live closer the cultivated zones in Jordan, Syria and Iraq. The noble tribes are proud of their ancestry, and are divided into "Qaysi" (northern Arabian) or "Yamani" groups. In addition to the noble elements, the Bedouin society also includes vassal tribes, which are "ancestorless" (i.e., tribes whose heredity in not prestigious). These groups are subservient to the noble tribes and include professional groups such as artisans, blacksmiths, entertainers, etc.

Caste-like phenomena are attested in other regions of the Arabian peninsula, even among the sedentary populations. Paul Dresch has studied the situation in Yemeni tribal society at the beginning of the twentieth century.[29] He observes that two groups of people are widely regarded as not belonging to the tribe, but are still endowed with rights and obligations. The first of them is the *Sayyids*-a group claiming descent from the prophet, and the *Qadis*. (The *Qadis* are also a group defined by heredity. While elsewhere in the Islamic world the title *Qadi* refers to judges, in Yemen it only denotes a member of this class, whether judge or not. The *Qadis* or mashaykh are also said to be descended from the Prophet Hud. The *mashaykh* do not enjoy as much prestige as the *Sayyids*.[30]) Below the tribesmen rank the 'weak' people (*dua'fa*) (sing. *da'if*). Weak people have no prestige. They include people of various trades, some prespectable and some not so respectable.

> *Artisans and merchants in the traditional towns tend to be highly organized into castelike guild groups that are ranked largely according to the nature of their craft. In many areas those who ply so-called respectable trades are sharply differentiated from the bam*

> *khonis or sons of the five, practitioners of the five despised trades of barber, bloodletter, butcher, bath attendant, and tanner. In the Hadramaut artisans who handle clay, such as masons and potters, also fall into the despised group, as do sweepers, fishermen, and some other, depending on locality. Poor farm laborers also occupy a low status, but it is higher than those of the despised crafts.*
>
> *The Akhdam, in many areas the lowest group, are so isolated from society that they have been compared with the untouchables of India. Found especially along the Tihama coast and in southern Yemen (Sana) but also in the Hadramaut, they are often distinguished socially by their negroid appearance and often follow the despised trade of sweeper. The akhdam appear to be descendants of slaves, although not all former slaves occupy such degraded positions. Slavery existed in the territories of the Aden Protectorate until the 1930s and persisted in Yemen (Sana) until 1962.*[31]

The Sayyids in Yemen did not allow intermarriage with other Yemeni castes. This superiority was challenged only by expatriates in Singapore in 1905, and again under the Irshadi movement in Java in 1915.[32]

It would thus seem that the practice of forming hierarchical structures is quite a widespread phenomenon. In fact, not only hierarchies, but the specific practice of untouchability is attested in Burma and Japan. The idea of pollution by contact is attested in Qajar Iran, to cite but a single example.[33] An exhaustive comparative study of all the different phenomena that are usually subsumed under the notion of caste is yet to be undertaken. *Home hierarchichus* is not endemic only to India; *Homo sapiens* everywhere has mostly been *Home hierarchichus.*

Even the institution of caste may have served its purpose in India. A.L. Basham regards the institution of caste as having been directly responsible for the survival of skills, handed down from generation to generation in India, whose counterparts were lost in other courtries.[34] Yet over the years it has become an oppressive institution, and a great obstacle to human freedom and national integration.

While studying caste it is certainly important not to lose one's perspective in the zeal to undermine the caste system. It is counter-productive to demonize one religious community as inherently caste-ridden and inegalitarian, and absolve other hierarchically structured religious groups of their responsibility. Indeed, the exclusive identification of caste with Hinduism has caused the situation in Pakistan and in Indian Muslim society to be largely neglected. Several important facts have gone virtually unnoticed.

Gaborieau points out that Syed Ahmad Khan, spearhead of Muslim thought in the Indian subcontinent in the last century, was an Ashraf working for the welfare of the Ashraf. He used to say that his Aligarh college was not for weavers. The Muslim League's social program was copied off the Congress' program, and made no radical improvements. The Congress however, has been labeled a *baniya* party, and that is how it has been portrayed to generations of Pakistani students. Land reforms in Pakistani Punjab (1959, 1972) have not been as successful as in Indian Punjab, and large landholders still have a disproportionate share of the land.[35] A human rights commentator points out that Bhutto's land reforms were 'cosmetic', because landowners had been previously warded to transfer their lands to their family members.[36] This has not provoked the public outrage that it should have. The same commentator also points out that the ulama have not campaigned for the eradication of feudalism. Thus, even in the year 2002 the situation seems to be no different that which obtained in the early forties, when the peasants of Punjab and especially of Sindh were:

> *"under the spell of the pirs," and "had imbibed the doctrine of* taqdir *(fate) from the constant preachings of the pirs". ... whose message was "He is low forever because God has made him so."*[37]

The advent of Islam has not automatically ensured equality. Indeed, the example of former Prime Minister Bhutto shows that inequality continued to be rampant. Bhutto's family owned, according to his own admission, *hundreds of thousands* of acres of land in Sindh and *for generations*. His ancestor Sheto had obtained tax exemptions and other benefits, including the title of khan, from Aurangzeb.[38] Populists such as Bhutto have been able to get away with the rhetoric of *musawat* (equality), which he held out in his electoral promises, while doing nothing to promote social reform.

In a future article we will look at the issue of the development of vernacular languages on the subcontinent. The idea that Hindu society is inherently more hierarchical has led to the blanket assertion that Sanskrit stifled the growth of regional languages, which needed the stimulus of Islamic society before they could come into their own. This claim is also quite untenable. But here we content ourselves with the remark that in the subcontinent it was again India that took the lead in promoting regional languages. The regional languages in Pakistan have not been able to acquire parity of status with the *Ashraf*-imposed Urdu.[39]

It was left to the outspoken Dr. Ambedkar to point out that responsibility of fighting the iniquities of the caste system on the subcontinent devolve equally on Muslim and Hindu:

> *The existence of these evils among the Muslims is distressing enough. But far more distressing is the fact that there is no organized movement of social reform among the Musalmans of India on a scale sufficient to bring about their eradication. The Hindus have their social evils. But there is this relieving feature about them - namely, that some of them are conscious of their existence and a few of them are actively agitating for their removal. The Muslims, on the other hand, do not realize that they are evils and consequently do not agitate for their removal.*[40]

The situation has changed much since the days when Dr. Ambedkar wrote these words. The battle against inequality on the subcontinent, however, is far from won. There is every indication that the battle will yet prove to be long and costly. As a very first step, it is hoped that intellectuals will rise up to examine the institution of caste with an unbiased mind, and rid us of all illusions in this matter.

## NOTES

1. Muslim Caste in Uttar Pradesh (A Study of Culture Contact), Ghaus Ansari, Lucknow, 1960, Page 66.
2. Ni brahmanes ni ancetres: Colportcurs musulmans du Nepal *by Marc Gaborieau,* Nanterre, Societe d'ethnologie (It must be pointed out that there have been several British scholars who did not take this view. Sir Denzil Ibbetson is one. Gaborieau's point is valid broadly speaking.)

3. Dr. James Wise, "The Muhammadans of Eastern Bengal", *J.R.A.S.B.*, (Calcutta: Asiatic Society of Bengal, 1894), No. 1, p. 32.
4. *Pakistan or The Partition of India*, B.R. Ambedkar, Thacker & Co., Ltd., Bombay, pp. 218-219.
5. Caste among the Muslims of Calcutta, M.K.A. Siddiqui, in Caste and Social Stratification among the Muslims, Imtiaz Ahmad (ed.) (see next footnote).
6. *Caste and Social Stratification among the Muslims*, Imtiaz Ahmad (ed.), Manohar, 1973.
7. M.K.A. Siddiqui, in Caste and Social Stratification among the Muslims ... *op.cit.*, pp. 149-150.
8. Status and Power in a Muslim Dominated Village of Uttar Pradesh, Zarina Bhatty, *in Caste and Social Stratification among the Muslims ... op.cit.*
9. *Ibid.* p. 95.
10. Status Groups among the Moplahs on the South-west Coast of India, Victor S. D'Souza, in *Caste... op.cit.*, pp. 45-60.
11. Gaborieau, *op.cit.*, p. 266.
12. Gaborieau, *op.cit.*, p. 378.
13. Quoted in *Caste in India: Its Nature Furction, and Origins* by J.H. Hutton, Oxford University press, 1963, p. 219.
14. In Pakistan many Christians from farming communities became landless after independence, and had to become sweepers by profession. This has caused them to be further stigmatized, indicating that dignity of labor is not yet widely upheld, even though the region is nearly devoid of Hindus. (*Religious Minorities in Pakistan*, Dr. Iftikhar H. Malik, 2002, Minority Rights Group International, p. 12).
15. Gaborieau, *op cit*, p. 370.
16. Gaborieau, *op.cit.*, p. 383.
17. Gaborieau, *op.cit.*, p. 378.
18. Gaborieau, *op.cit.*, p. 354.
19. Gaborieau, *op.cit.*, p. 291-356.

    Gaborieau also gives us the example of the Nizami clan, which manages the tomb of Nizamu'd-Din Auliya'. This clan claims descent from and intermarries with high-born Sayyid. The clan has inherited the mystique and sanctity attached to the founder of the hospice (Gaborieau, *op.cit.*, p. 375).

It appears that the phenomenon of *Pirs* and *Pirzadas* is caste-like, in that sanctity and prestige are inherited by birth. In Caste in India, J.H. Hutton gives the example of Pir Pagaro in Sindh, who is a "hereditary religious leader descended from a family which entered Sind with the Arabs in AD 711."

20. Gaborieau, *op.cit.*, p. 356.
21. Ansari, p. 28.
22. Ansari, p. 30.
23. *Muslim Caste in Uttar Pradesh (A Study of Culture Contact)*, Ghaus Ansari, Lucknow, 1960, Page 50.
24. Gaborieau, *op.cit.*, p. 393.
25. Gaborieau, *op.cit.*, p. 387, p. 415.
26. *Marginality and Modernity: Ethnicity and Change in Post-Colonial Balochistan*, Paul Titus, (ed), Oxford University Press, Karachi, 1996, pp. 54-55.
27. "Haratin" *http://www.britannica.com/eb/article?eu=40019.*
28. *http://www.britannica.com/eb/article?eu=14268.*
29. *Tribes, Government, and History in Yemen*, Paul Dresch, Clarendon Press, Oxford, 1989, p. 117.
30. *Area Handbook For The Yemens*, Richard F. Nyrop, et al., 1977, p. 74.
31. *Area Handbook For The Yemens*, Richard F. Nyrop, et al., 1977, p. 77.
32. *Tribes, Government, and History in Yemen*, Paul Dresch, Clarendon Press, Oxford, 1989, p. 27.
33. *Iran and the Muslim World: Resistance and Revolution*, Nikki R. Keddie, Macmillan Press Ltd, 1995, p. 147.
34. Certainly this is true of music in the lands west of India. Until very recently recording music has not been possible. The musicians in Baluchistan, Iran and Afghanistan happen to be hereditary caste-musicians (Doms, Jugis, Loris) all with Indian caste counterparts. These musician castes will be studied in a future article. It will be seen that they are in all probability descendants of Indians brought as slaves or serfs. These castes completely dominate the folk music scene in Baluchistan and Afghanistan.
35. *Pakistan: Nationalism without a Nation?*, Christophe Jaffrelot (ed.), Manohar, New Delhi, 2002, pp. 59-60.

36. *Religious Minorities in Pakistan*, Dr. Iftikhar H. Malik, 2002, Minority Rights Group International, p. 7.
37. *Politics in Pakistan: The Nature and Direction of Change*, Khalid B. Sayeed, Praeger Special Studies, 1980. p. 7.
38. *Zulfi Bhutto of Pakistan: His Life and Times*, Stanley Wolpert, Oxford University Press, 1993, pp. 3-4.
39. As late as the 1901 census, it was only the *Ashraf* who claimed Urdu as their mother-tongue, even in the Gangetic belt. The others spoke one of many regional languages which have all been declared 'dialects' of Hindi/Urdu. (In fact, an authority on the Muslim League estimates the population of *Ashraf* to be about 7 percent of the total Muslim population, based on the number of people claiming Urdu as their language. See *The All India Muslim League*, Muhammad Saleem Ahmad, 1988, Ilham Publishers, Bahawalpur.)
40. *Pakistan or The Partition of India*, B.R. Ambedkar, Thacker & Co., Ltd., Bombay, pp. 223.

Dileep Karanth dskaranth@yahoo.com

# 10

# THE DILEMMA OF MUSLIM POLITICS

*Shamsul Islam*

Where do Indian Muslim stand today in the race for development and well-being, to arrive at any conclusion in this regard, would be a difficult and tedious task. Muslims in general feel that inspite of India completing 58 years of its independence their problems still remain the same as they were on the eve of independence. In fact this state of affairs is true not only in regard to the largest minority community, but it holds good in respect of all common men relating to any religion or community of this country. The hopes and aspirations aroused by the country's independence amongst the masses, gradually changed to a farce. The slogans of bread, clothing and shelter could not materialize and this bitter truth came to fore that instead of all this making available to the masses whatsoever was already being enjoyed by them is getting dilapidated. So it is not very wrong to say that whatsoever has been happening to the Muslims in independent India, the same has happened with the poor masses also of this country in general. But at tha same time this fact, that due to certain special circumstances, Muslims also as a community, had to suffer a lot, cannot be overlooked.

People and organizations indulging in Hindu communal politics have continuously spitted venom against Muslims and have been raising questions with regard to their Indian-ness and patriotism. When newly appointed President of BJP, Raj

Nath Singh declares that he would carve out a Bharat guided by the philosophy of Hindutava, it simply means that Bharat of his imagination won't have any place for Muslims and other minority communities. If BJP President knows and understands the principles of Hindutava propounded by Savarkar, which RSS people believe to be the root of Indian nationalism, then India of his imagination could only be a Hindu Rashtra where Minority communities won't actually have any place in it. Because of such utterances, Muslims feel Damocles sword to be perpetually hanging over their heads which has compelled them to feel insecure. The violence of Gujrat in the year 2002 has further aggravated the feeling of fear and insecurity prevailing amongst the Muslims. It is also a fact that whenever there were Congress Governments in power, be it either at the Centre or the states, the too did not take any steps to emancipate the Muslims out of this fear-psychosis, rather they were instrumental in aggravating it. It is why that even after so many years of independence, so far as the questions of loss of lives and properties of Muslims is concerned, there has never been much of a difference because of there being a Congress or a BJP government in power.

But are Indian Muslims today faced with this only problem? Taking it so, would actually mean ignoring or lessening the magnitude of challenges which Muslims are faced with. Those who consider security and safety of Muslims to be their only problems, pay no heed to the factual truth that inspite of the fact the toiling masses, Dalits, women folk and tribals of this country have been perpetually suffering from cruel oppression, still the process of achieving their fundamental rights and internal intellectual thinking was not allowed by them to dwindle. Presently, the most important problem of Indian Muslims, which is a problem more of their self-proclaimed leaders rather than theirs (Muslims), is that they never allowed internal democracy to flourish in this religious community. In fact, in this country the people proclaiming to be the leaders of Muslims, both religious and political, have all along deceived them. They have been instrumental in demolishing whatsoever positive and demoractic thinking had been existing in them, by instilling a sense of insecurity into them. A living instance of how the common Muslims have been deceived by their own leaders is the recently passed enactment by the Parliament regarding reservation in private educational institutions. Under this, the policy of reservation can now be implemented in private educational institutions, meaning thereby that the downtrodden people of this country would now be able to avail the facility of reservation in those institution also which are under private management. But under this legislation there is a provision according to which this facility cannot be availed of in educational institutions managed by the minority community. It is important to note that, leaving leftist parties, all other parties supported this legislation. Many such educational institutions are being run by Muslims also and as per this law, giving reservation in them would not be compulsory, People sympathizing with scheduled castes and tribes were hopeful that at least institutions run by Muslims won't shut the door of reservation to them, because people at the helm of their affairs have all along been supporting the demand for reservation for all Muslims. The greatest paradox of this legislation is that, on the one hand, the leadership of Muslims has been demanding for reservation in all the fields in this country and, on the other hand, for the institution controlled by themselves wants to align with a system other than the law of reservation which is in force in the country. This dual policy has once again exposed the Muslim leadership.

Had this leadership been the least concerned with the condition of the Muslims masses and with the injustice meted out to them, they would never have allowed such injustice to occur with the other downtrodden people of the country in their own educational institutions. By not accepting such exemption, they could have given an important message to the Dalits of the land that they are all fully with them in their struggle for securing justice, because their own community also aspires for equality and justice in the Indian society. Though this legislation has been got through by the Congress, the desire of the Muslim leadership, which is fully nobles-based and made up of upper castes, to continue as distinguished class, was also instrumental in its passage. With the help of this legislation this leadership has once again made it to be realized that it has nothing to do with the interest of the common Muslim folk. Dr. Ambedkar had, much before independence of the country, in his book titled 'Pakistan', spelled out this painful fact that the elite class of Muslim leadership never allows the common Muslim folk to get united with the untouchables and Dalits, whereas their problems are almost similar. By not accepting reservation in Muslim educational institutions the Muslim leadership has once again proved that it has not changed the least.

***(English Translation of Article by Shamshul Islam***
***Published in Daily Hindi 'Sahara'***
***Dated 21st Jan. 2006 )***

# 11

# POWERFUL CLASSES CANNOT TOLERATE SHARING POWER AND PROSPERITY WITH THE DEPRIVED ONES

*Saiyid Hamid*

It is for the past two weeks that agitation has been going on throughout the country against reservation in admissions in educational institutions for the deprived classes. Students have been leading processions. Male and female students have sat on hunger stike, and Doctors have stopped working. Patients arrive from far and near and return disappointed. If at all attended to. they get only cursory treatment. At times procession get un-ruly and become victimes of lathi-Charge. This further provokes the agitation. Why all this? It is due to the fact that the Ministry of Human Resource Development, which oversees the subject of Education, has decided to grant 27% reservation in institutions of higer and professional learning to OBCs. This reservation relates to Mandal Commission Recommendations, as its second instalment. In the beginning there was a grievance that reservation would lead to a reduction in seats for the general candidate, to the extent of reservation. Govt, however, proposed a solution to this apprehension by announcing an increase in seats of institutions of higher and professional learing, to the extent of reservation, so that seats available to general candidates, from year to year do not get reduced. It was very much hoped that this would help find a solution of the problem. But when assessed it was found out that an increase in member of seats, infrastructure and teachers would cost some 8000 crores of rupees. This estimate was worked out by the Group of Ministers whom P.M. had entrusted the job of finding out a solution of the problem. Calculations revealed that seats would actually require to be increased by 50% But the Driector IIM Ahmedabad has altogether expressed apprehension on the practical aspectsof the proposed expansion.

Our readers would have assessed from the above situation that our educated well-to-do and influential class is willing to share its wealth, power and prosperity with none else. It would be rememberd that when Mandal Commision recommen-dations were fristly implemented then also wild disturbances were created against it. Thus people loudly praising our democracy get contented only by paying verbal tributes to it and its laudable principles. They pretend that they are grieved by the wretched condition of the poor and backward classes and that they are anxious for them but when probed into, them-selves they are not found paying any price for it. They know that the gap between them-selves and the deprived ones has increased to a painful extent but they are not at all prepared to share their prosperity and their prospects with the poor and deprived ones. What an insensibility and what a state of painlessness is this?

This attitude of ours is a mournful commentary on human nature. Provided negative forces be not at work, man, under influence of greed and lust passes whole of his life amassing wealth and in pursuit of power. Exploitation of the deprived ones, knowingly or unknowingly, becomes, his cherished pastime. Those in possession of wealth derive undue advantage of the abject poverty of the havesnot as if nobility is exacted from heritage. Many of even those who are pious and religious treat the wordly and sinful people with contempt. Those who enjoy power don't fear in oppressing the weak. Those who believe themselves to hale from a superior race, donot let the other races raise their heads. Wherever people of one language are in majority they don't hesitate in usurping the rights of the people of the other language. In India casteism has taken the whole of the society in its grips. People of superior castes, which includes Brahmins, Kshatriyas and Vaishyas and who are hardly 15% of the population of India, don't take the rest 85% favourably. It does never come even into their imaignation that they can some day stand in parity with them, and it does never occur in their minds that initiating steps for alleviating the plight of the deprived people is the responsibility of their fellow countrymen, specially of their own superior classes and of the Govt. of the land.

India was fortunate enough that the framers of its constitution were large hearted and believed in justice and equality. They made provision in the Constitution for alleviating the miseries of the two classes and the Government in turn, did implement these provisions obligingy. As such 15% and 7.5% reservations were enforced respectively for the Scheduled castes and Sched. Tribes in services and educational institution and also in legislative bodies. Besides the above educational stipends were arranged for them, they were assisted in preparing for participation in competitive exams, and treating Dalits as untouchable, was made illegal. However, on demanding the facility of reservation by the other deprived classes, it was told that the doors of merit were open to them and that nobody stopped them from seeking jobs on the basis of merit. But they seldom remember that deprived ones can hardly secure admissiom in good educational institution. The whole of the country witnessed great turmoil when with a view to ameliorating the lot of the backward classes, the present Government made a porvision of 27% reservation in admission for them into higher and professional intitutions. Evidently all these demonstrations and agitations are expressions of selfishness and apathy. These people, who for centuries have been monopolising power and prosperity are not prepared to bestow the least of their wealth rights and power to those who for immemorable times have been continuing as deprived and oppressed. All indications from these fortunate ones seem to suggest that "hold on government, exclusive use of the higher institutes of learning, wealth and prosperity have all been our monopoly for centuries and we are not prepared to share these with others". Out of hyprocrisy they also seem to suggest that "if other backward classes get mandatory benefit of higher education the standard of these institutions of higher learning would fall down and in science and technology, whatever global distinction has been earned by India would get erased". Let somebody ask these anxielyful self centred people whether in this universe, which is basd on justice, should the idea of equality be abondoned for ever and whether these deprived people (since the distant past and persently also) don't have the right to dream of a prosperous future and move forword in this direction.

There is none to speak for the deprived and the weak. Pen and brush both are in the hands of prosperous section of the society, they issue statements as they desire and paint such pictures as they like. One would observe that no mention is ever made of the well-being and upliftment of the "OBCs" in the discussions persently going on as if there is no importance of half the population of India. Importance if at all, is only of the superior classes who have grown up in an atmosphere of prosperity and awareness and who have been born with silver spoons in their mouths and also who believe that the right of every sort of development is theirs only and the rest of the population of this land is born only with a fate to remain devoid of the benefits of development and be looked upon contemptuously.

If the criticizers of reservation who treat themselves to be the sole inheritors of prosperity, comfort and development are prepared to put themselves in place of the OBCs, they leave their comfortable homes and its clean and serene atmosphere and go to live in the habitations of OBCs, only then they wil be able to feel how this atmosphere suppresses the capabilities and spirits. The decision on 'Quota' is also criticized on the pretext that it is a cheap vote catching method. Possibly this aspect also might have influenced the central government. What to say of possiblity this migh have been the dominant aspect. But while judging the decision of people at the helm of affairs of power, instead of doubting their intentions it need be seen that whether it is in the interest of the country and humanity or not.

The first and foremost historic decision in context of Mandal Commission was taken by sri Vishwanath Pratap Singh. There were some political stimulants also behind this decision. But his decision proved revolutionary. This second decision in context of Mandal Commission, is also going to prove revolutionary and historic one.

It would have been beauteous and all pervasive if the prosperous and influential sections had by them-selves suggested that OBCs also need be provided with opportunities for higher education so that they also march forward, side by side, along with the caravan of country's progress.

However, now that they have lost the opportunity of winning hearts and earning gratitude, they should at least, refrain from demonstrations expressing narrow-mindedness, selfishness and ill humour. Traditionally the medical profession has been known as a noble and compassionate profession. But now for sometimes back few of the doctors have started erasing this image. The demonstration which they have been leading against OBCs would adversely affect the feeling of compassion, justice and humanity. The steps that Government have taken are in the larger interest of humanity and justice. The road for reversal is now blocked and what-ever steps are further going to be taken, should lead onwards.

*The writer is presently Chancellor of*
*Jamia Hmdard, New Delhi*
*Translation from "Rashtriya Sahara-Urdu"*

# 12

# CASTE DISCRIMINATION IN CIVIL SERVICES EXAMINATIONS PERPETUATES RESERVATION IN JOBS

## *Department of Personnel Treat General Seats as Seats Reserved For Non-reserved Categories*

***Sharad Yadav***

Whenever there is talk about reservation, the bogey of merit is raised by opponents of this policy. But the question arises: do the opponents respect the merit of candidates from the Other Backward Classes (OBCs) and the Scheduled Castes (SCs) and the Scheduled Tribes (STs)? Emprical studiast suggest they do not. Almost six decades have passed since Independence but all important institutions of India, barging Parliament and Legislative Assemblies ans Councils have been under the strong command of these self-styled votaries of merit. With some exceptions, they have abused their position to denigrate the merit of the people who have been given the costitutional right of reservation - so that privileges enjoyed by some people under the caste system are de-reserved.

The Union Public Service Commission provides glaring examples of how the merit of candidates belonging to SCs, STs and OBCs is denigrated. The UPSC is a eonstitutioal body. It commands high respect in India but in cullusion with the Dapartment of Personnel and Training(DoPT), it has been denying the rithts of meritorious candidates belonging to reserved categories. It has been indulging in unconstitutional activities despite the clear-cut policy of the Government of India on reservation. The Supreme Court and High Courts have interpreted the policy in many judgments. There is no scope for any ambiguity regarding this policy but the UPSC has continued to deny meritorious candidates of reserved categories the rigt to joun the civil services as general category candidates.

This has resulted in a denial of jobs to hundreds of successful candidtes belonging to reserved categories; and almost the same number of candidates belonging to the non-reserved category has got jobs, without being declared successful by the UPSC at the time of declaration of results. This is happening despite many judgments of the higher judiciary against the practice. People controlling the UPSC and DoPT are so strongly motivated against the candidates of reserved categories that they can go to any extent in their adventure to block the entry of reserved categories in the civil services.

Under the reservation policy, 49.50 per cent of the seats is reserved. The remaining 50.50 per cent is open to al. Candidates who qualify for the civil services by dint of their merit alone should be enlisted in general open categories. After all there is no bar on SC and ST candidates fighting elections for general seats. Many leaders, including Kansi Ram and B.P. Maurya, have fought and won from general seats. General seats do not mean seats reserved fro people belongng to non-reserved categories. Similarly,general open seats in the civil services are not reserved for people belonging to non-reserved categories. The Government of India has not reserved hundred per cent of the seats of the civil services. In fact it cannot do so. There is a 50% ceiling placed on reservation by the Supreme Court. But in effect, the UPSC and the DOPT are implementing reservation policy to ensure 50.50% reservation for the unreserved categories that are supposed to for just 15% of the India population.

For the last civil services examination, around 214 of 425 seats were general open merit seats. Out of the first 214 candidates, 50 were from reserved categories. Forty of them were from OBCs. But the UPSC refused to allow reserved categorycandidates to enlist themselves as general candidates. Twenty seven per cant of 425 is 117: this is the exact number of candidates be longing to OBCs who were declare successful. Even those in the top 10 were classified as reseved category candidates!

By doing this, the UPSC has denigrated meritorious candidates from the reserved categories. It has also denied jobs in the civil services to an equal number of reservd category candidates. In fact, 157 candidates from OBC categories should have ben selected: 40 on the basis of merit and 117 on the basis of the 27% reservation extended to them.

People belonging to SCs and STs in the early days of the Republic lacked education. Their number was not sufficient to fill the vacancies declared for them. Later on they picked up but there were all-out efforts to deny them their right to reservation under one pretext or another. If we analysef the data on successful ST and SC candidates, we discover they have done better in the written test, where the examiner does not know their caste. In the intervaiews they have been given fewer marks because people in the interview board know their caste.

It is shocking that candidates belonging to reserved categories are interviewed separately. They sit for the written examinaions alongside non-reserved category candidates, but when the time of interview comes, they are segregated. The interview board is well aware of their social background and discriminates against them while giving them interview marks. An analysis of the results reveals a big gap between the average interview marks given to reserved category candidates amd non-reserved category candidates. One successful candidate of the 1996 civil service examinations, who was denied a job, has calculated these averages on the basis of infromantion available with him. Since he fought for his job in the Supreme Court and won, the data he offers can be relied upon in the absence of authoritative data provided by the UPSC. According to this candidate, the average interview mark in the non-reserved category is around 200, while the average for reserved categories candidates is 140. I believe that if there were no caste discrimination, the number of successful OBC candidates in the general merit category would have been much higher than 40. Unfortunately, even these 40 candidates were not de clared successful in the general merit category.

The concept of excluding the creamy layer sounds progressive. Indeed the bnefit of reservation should be made availabel to people from less privileged OBC families. In princile this is all right. But the design of those opposed to OBC reservation is to keep the creamy layer out of the reservation ambit and deny the benefit of reservation to less privileged individuals. These individuals have no means of fighting the might of the UPSC and the DoPT. They have no money to engage lawyers to fight legal battles. It is quite easy to deny them their right. So they are denied jobs despite getting letters from the UPSC informing them of their successes. My information is that thus far 390 successful candidate have been denied jobs in the civil service. Some of them, who have had resources, thanks to being in other services, have challenged the DoPT sucssesfully. But what about those who have not moved the courts ? why can't the courts take suomoto notice of such gross denial of justice?

Babasahib Bhim Rao Ambedkar was for separate electorates for Dalits. He wanted proportionate reservation for them but also demanded that their representatives should be elected from an electoral college comprising Dalits exclusively. Separate electorates for Dalits were termed the communal award.Gandhi ji and many other leaders thought such an arrangement would divide India; he went on a fast and Dr. Ambedkar withdrew his demand. The policy of reservation was put in place so that those hailing from reserved categery could contest elections from unreserved seats also.

The same rule applies to jobs. But the UPSC has turned the policy of reservation in a policy of communal awards.I cite below some judgement of Indian courts that are been consistently violated by the UPSC and the DOPT:

**(a) Indira Sawhney vs. Union of India,1992 Supp. (3) SCC 217**

"In this connection is it well to remember that the reservation under Article 16 (4) dose not operate like a *communal reservation.* It may well happen that some members belonging to, say, Scheduled Castes get selected in the open competition field on the basis of their own merit; they will not be counted against the quota reserved for Scheduled castes they will be treated as open competition candidate."

**(b) Union of India vs. Virpal Sighn Chauhan (1995)6 SCC 684**

"While determining the number of posts reserved for SCs and STs, the cundidates belonging to the reserved category but sellected on the rule of merit (and not by virtue of rule of reservstion) shall not be counted as reserved category candidates."

**(c) Rithesh R. Shah's case (1996)3 SCC 253**

"In other words while a reserved category candidate entitled to admission on the basis of his merit will have the option of taking admission to the colleges where a specified number of seats have been kept reserved for reserved category..... while computing the percentage of reservation he will be deemed to have been admitted as a open category candidate and not as reserved category candidate."

In a Delhi High Court judgment of April 29, 2003, the division bench made the following observation: The decision of the Apex Court in Rithesh R. Shah's case (supra) as also the proviso to rule 16 clearly prohibit deprivation of the benefit of the reservation only because some reserved category candidtes had also been selected on merit inasmuch as they were not to betreated as reserved category candidates except for a limited purpose, namely for the purpose of allocation of service, but thereby OBC candidates cannot be deprived of their right to obtain allocation of any service."

The interesting question arises: who is perpetuating reservation? If people from the SCs, STs, and OBCs get representation according to their population, the scheme of reservation will come to an end. But who is deprivig the meritorious from getting jobs as general category candedates?

*(The author, a Member of the Rajya Sabha, is president of the Janata Dal (United) and a former Union Minister. He was educated to be an electrical engineer).*

***(Courtesy "The Hindu" Daily)***

# 13

# SC STATUS FOR DALIT MUSLIMS AND CHRISTIANS

*Yogendra Sikand*

Some weeks ago, newspapers reported the case of a Dalit woman, Rima Singh, whose husband, Mukesh Kumar, had converted to Islam and taken the name of Muhammad Sadiq. The woman had recently been elected as a sarpanch on a reserved seat in a Village in Uttar Pradesh and wanted to follow her husband and become a Muslim. However, if she did so, she would have to resign from her post, because as the law stands today, Dalit Muslims as well as Christians, are not considered Scheduled Castes (SCs) by the state. A bench of the Supreme Court issued a notice in response to the writ petition filed by the couple asking the Government of India to explain why Dalit Muslims are denied reservation benefits.

The continued denial by the state of SC status to Dalit Muslims and Dalit Christians despite consistent demands on the part of these communities is a patently anti-democratic and anti- secular stance and a gross violation of the fundamental principles of the Indian Constitution. Receiving official SC status is not simply to do with reserved government jobs and representation in state legislatures and Parliament, although these, too, are important. Dalit Muslims and Christian leaders point out that SC status brings various other benefits, which they are denied simply because of their religion. These include special development programmes, scholarships and hostels for students reserved seats in educational institutions, special laws against atrocities on Dalits and so on, all of which do not apply to Dalit Muslims and Christians.

In 1950, a Presidential Order was passed declaring that the status of Scheduled Caste for official purposes was applicable only to those Dalits who professed to be 'Hindus'. Under pressure from Ambedkarite and Sikh organizations, this was later amended to include Dalits who profess Buddhism and Sikhism. The law restricting SC status to Dalits who profess the Hindu religion, and now Sikhism and Buddhism, has been critiqued by numerous Dalit ideologues, who argue that this is essentially a means to inflate Hindu numbers and create the notion of a Hindu majority and, based on the logic of Hindu majoritarianism, to justify and strengthen the hegemony of the 'upper' castes, who claim to be representatives of the all 'Hindus'. They point out that, technically, all the major Hindu or Brahminical scriptures consider the Dalits as out-castes, outside the four-fold varna system, ranking below even the Shudras, and hence as non-Hindus. This argument is supported by the numerous refrences in the Brahminical scriptures to 'Chandals', Doms, and other such 'low castes, using extremely derogatory language to describe them. Hence, Dalit critics argue, technically, Dalits can not be considered Hindus, and the rule that restricts SC status to those Dalits who claim to profess the Hindu religion is bad not only in law but also in theology.

As many Dalits activists see it, the religious bar to SC status is a means to prevent Dalits from converting to other religions in search of emancipation from caste Hindu hegemony and for gaining self-respect based on a new religious and cultural identity. It is thus, they argue, a means to promote caste Hindu domination. Historically, they point out, in India conversion to non-Hindu faiths, including Buddhism, Sikhism, Christianity and Islam, has been a means for Dalits and other oppressed castes to challenge caste Hindu oppression. That this has indeed been the case is obvious from the fact that the majority of India's Buddhists, Sikhs, Christians and Muslims are descendants of converts from these castes. Seeking to stop conversion as a means of social protest by placing a religious bar, they argue, is not just anti-secular. It is also a means to stem Dalit revolt and, by Hinduising the Dalits under caste Hindu tutelage, it works to further solidify their dependence on the Savarna castes. Conversion to a non-Hindu and egalitarian religion, as Dr. Ambedkar himself realized and insisted, was a principal means for the Dalits to challenge caste Hindu oppression and to fashion a new identiy based on self-respect, which the Hindu religion denies them.

Defenders of the religious bar seek to justify the restriction of SC status to Dalits who profess the Hindu religion by claiming that this is because the Hindu religion alone sanctions untouchability, unlike, egalitarian faiths like Christianity and Islam. Hence, they say, only 'Hindu' Dalits should be treated specially by the state. This argument is specious, to say the least. for one, it goes against the repeated claims by caste Hindu, apologists, including both Gandhians and Hindutva ideologues, that the Hindu religion has no room fro untouchability. Yet, ironically, when it comes to extending SC status to Dalit Muslims and Christians these very same apologists use the argument that since Hinduism sanctions untouchability, only 'Hindu' Dalits should benefit from such status.

Defenders of the religion clause also claim that only Hindu Dalits face social discrimination because the Hindu religion sanctions it, and that, therfore, they alone should benefit from SC status. This argument is too faulty. It is completely blind to the fact that Dalit Christians and Muslims also face the discrimination, from both their co-religionists as well as from caste Hindus. In the case of Dalit Muslims, this discrimination may be even more acute than what non-Muslim Dalits face, given fhe fact of widespread anti-Muslim sentiments and violence directed against Muslims, in which most of the victims are probably of 'low' caste origin. Caste prejudices directed against Dalits run so deep in Indian society that the mere fact of conversion alone does not remove it. In fact, today, given the enormous clout of the anti-conversion and Hindutva lobbies, a Dalit who converts to Islam or Christianity will probably be worse off than prior to his or her conversion, being subject to harassment, boycott and sometimes even physical attacks. All the more reason, then, for such Dalits to also receive SC status.

Given the fact, that a section of 'Hindu' Dalits have received special status for decades and benefits from the state flowing from that status, it is obvious that their conditions are better than most Muslim and Christian Dalits are equally, or even, in a sense, more deserving of SC status in order to help them come up at least to the level of 'Hindu' Dalits. The argument that the religion bar is obviously unfair and untenable is further strengthened by the fact that there is no such bar mandated in case of the Scheduled Tribes. Surely, then, the patently anti-secular and anti- democratic religious bar against which Dalit Muslim and Christian leaders are protesting needs to be removed forthwith.

***Courtesy : Milli Gazzette***

# 14

# RESERVATION IN IITS AND IIMS INCLUDING UNIVERSITIES SHOULD BE WELCOME BY ONE AND ALL

***Voice of Budha***

Even though the announcement regarding reservation in IITs and IIMs and centrally-aided Universities for the OBCs should have been taken as a welcome step by everyone, yet unfortunately a small minority is opposing this step because they do not appreciate the far-reaching consequences this step will have for the over all development of the country.

Lakhs of people from amongst those who have been talking of merit and competence became Doctors, Engineers and Business Managers and left for America and European countries for more cosy and lucrative jobs. Others got jobs in India and were confined only to their individual families. In such a situation, how has their merit and competence helped in the development and progress of the country ? Nor have these gentlemen made any innovative research or development in the fields of Science and Technology.

On the other hand, there is every likelihood that if more and more people from the SC/ST/OBC community become Doctors, Engineers and Business Managers, they will not go abroad whereby the country will stand to gain because their services will be available to the country. Secondly, they will be able to inspire other people of their community who are still backward and steeped in orthodoxy. Thirdly, it will bring about social harmony in the society otherwise there will be an undeclared civil-war like situation all the time among different castes and creeds. We can take the example of Bihar where because of widespread disparities and extreme inequality, the society and State are always in a state of turmoil. Higher education, industrialization, business and investment have come to a grinding halt because the society and the State are always in a state of turmoil. If reservation is viewed in this perspective, the people who are opposing the reservation policy should be the first to support this policy because it will improve law and order situation and bring about social harmony. If the UP and Bihar like situation is allowed to spread to other parts of the country, where will the IIT/IIM graduates and Business Managers work ? The answer is simple that these graduates on whom the government has spent lakhs of Rupees will go abroad for employment.

HRD Minister Shri Arjun Singh should not be blamed personally for this decision because all the constituents of the UPA government are jointly responsible for the same. Media has targeted Shri Arjun Singh and has held him personally responsible so that Mandal Commission like situation could be re-enacted. In all fairness if anyone is to be blamed it is the UPA as such.

Even now more than 50% of seats in IITs/IIMs and centrally aided Universities are open to people who want to prove their mettle in terms of merit and competence. In America, in Hardvard University alone, there is reservation for more than 50% seats in the Medical Faculty. In the midst of this reservation, there have been more than three dozen nobel prize winners. In our country, there is no reservation in the area of sports, but we have not been able to win a single gold medal in the Olympics from out of a population of more than one billion. Again the captains of industry in our country have also not been able to create a single international brand which the country could boast of. The currency of a small country like Singapore is very strong at the international level whereas the Indian currency is rated very poor. Is reservation responsible for this poor show ?

In its historical judgement on 12.08.2005, a Constitution bench of the Supreme Court abolished reservation in the privately managed un-aided minority and non minority educational institutions. The then Hon'ble Chief Justice of the Supreme Court of India, Shri R.C. Lahoti announced that the Government can not enforce reservation in minority and non minority educational institutions which are not getting any aid from the government. The Indian Justice Party and the All India Confederation of SC/ST Confederations strongly opposed this decision and organized protest rallies throughout the Country. The Government passed 104th Constitution Amendment Bill to deal with the situation arising out of this decision.

People who are opposing reservation in IITs, IIMs, and centrally aided Universities for the OBC coummunity may review their stand and accept it whole heartedly as it will ultimately benefit them also.

***Courtesy : "Voice of Buddha"***

# 15

# SYNOPSIS OF PARLIAMENT DEBATES ON 104TH CONSTITUTIONAL AMENDMENT

**ARJUN SINGH**

Now, I would like to come to the other point which has caused some apprehensions in the minds of our friends from the other backward communities castes. I must inform the hon. House that as a humble member of the Congress Party, ever since I started my career, I have to the extent it was possible for me, supported the issues which would bring backward classes into mainstream of Indian politics. It is in that pursuit that in 1982, in Madhya Pradesh a separate Commission for Backward Classes was set up.

Perhaps, before the Central Government passed the Mandal Commission, the Madhya Pradesh Government passed the Mahajan Commission Act giving the backward classes the rights, to which Mandal Commission subsequently entitled them. So, it is not something which you can grow conveniently. Certain things come out of conviction. I want to say that the provision regarding the OBCs in this Amendment, when some doubts were raised by some collegues, we tried to see how we could accomodate them.

The hon. Prime Minister referred the issue for advice to the Law Department and after the Law Department clearly said that the terms used in 15 (5), which were taken from article 46, a Directive Priciple, is the only way which can use the terms that can be used in the Constitution as of today. If we were to use the word OBC as such, there would have been confusion. I would like to assure the house, certainly Members cutting across all parties-who belong to the backward classes-that has accrued to the country after this Bill is passed, in terms of admission and in terms of other advantages which the backward classes should get. Yes, there will be certain procedures and certain other steps would have to be taken, as the hon. Members said here this morning. Those steps will be taken. You rest assured that we will not leave these things halfway. This question does not arise.

Then, Sir, one query has been raised and I can not but respond to it because it has pointed out that you are saying that this Amendment will bring these rights to the OBCs in the private unaided colleges. But, how is it that these rights do not accrue to them today to many of the Central institutions? It is a very pertinent question. I do not want to duck it. I would like to assure this hon. House that after the passage of this Amendment, the question of rerservation in the Central Institutions, this problem will be addressed frontally and in a holistic manner. The enabling provisions of this Amendment, infact, make our task simpler and indeed define our stand and intention on this issue.

**V. NARAYANSAMY**

Sir, I rise to support the Constitution 104th) Amendment *Bill brought to this House by the Minister of Human Resources* Development. It is a very historic Bill. The hon. Minister has responded to the request of all the hon. Members of this House, cutting across party lines, to nullify the Supreme Court's Judgements, in the Inamdar case followed by TMA Pai's case, which took away the reservations that were given to the SCs, STs and OBCs in th unaided private educational institutions. Sir, at that time, when the hon. Members of the House raised the issue in this House, the hon. Minister gave an assurance that he would consult the leaders of all the political parties, and the various sections of the people who were involved in this, before taking a decision. Ultimately, after due consultations, after discussions with the leaders of various political parties and the Members of Parliament, particularly, the SCs, STs and Others, who are affected by this, this Bill has been brought in this August House. This Amendment is another landmark in nullifying the judgement of the Supreme Court, in restoring the rights that have been accrued to them, the reservation that has been given to the Backward Classes, SCs and STs in this country. There is the commitment of the UPA; in fact, if you go through the UPA's agenda, that is, the common Minimum Programme, its prioritoy is welfare and interests of the weaker sections, namely the SCs, STs, Minorities and OBCs. So, there are two issues. About linguistic minorities, some apprehensions have been expressed. I want the hon. Minister to address this issue.

Finally, I come to the deemed university. There is also apprehension in the minds of the Hon. Members. In the name of the deemed university, the reservation part is not being implemented by some universities With these words, I support the amendment moved by the hon. Minister. Sir, the hon. Minister is championing the cause of the OBCs, the SCs, the STs and the minorities. First, he brought this amendment in Madhya Pradesh. He has been fighting for the cause of the weaker sections of our society. I compliment the hon. Minister for bringing forward this amendment.

**V. HANUMANTHA RAO**

I welcome this Constitution (One Hundred and Fourth Amendment) Bill, 2005 brought forward by Shri Arjun Singhji to provide reservstion for the Scheduled Castes, the Scheduled Tribes and the socially and educationally backward classes, that is, the Backward Classes, in all the educational institutions. aided and unaided. It is a landmark decision of the UPA Government to amend article 15 of the Constitution by adding article 15 (5). I congratulate Shri Arjun Singh for this very speedy action of introducing the Bill provide greater access to all the reserved categories in professional colleges, etc. These weaker sections of the society survived because of the great vision of social reformers like Mahatma Phule of Maharashtra, Vemana of Andhra Pradesh, Sri Narayana Guru of Kerala, Periyar Ramasamy Naicker of Tamil Nadu, Basavanna of Karnataka and Baba Saheb Ambedkar.

The terminology "Backward Classes" has come to stay to refer to socially and educationally backward classes and several State Governments, while notifying lists of backward castes or communities under articles 15 (4) and 16 (4), use the term " Backward Classes ".

Therefore, it is our request to the Government to take appropriate steps later to include this terminology in the Constitution, and, in the meantime, to issue necessary clarifications to all the State Governments and other relevant authorities to the effect that socially and educationally backward classes include all backward classes notified by the State and Union Territory Governments and the Central Government. Such a clarification will ensure benefits to the recognised Backward Classes and not others. The O.B.C. MPs Forum has already represented to the hon. Minister for Human Resources Development to amend the Constitution to include the term " Backward Classes"

Secondly, there is no separate machinery to oversee the implementation of reservation for the Backward Classes. It is appropriate that the National Commission for Backward Classes, which is a national level body, is empowered to inspect wherever needed and monitor the implemenatation of the rule of reservation for the Backward Classes, like the SC and ST Commissions, which are exercising these functions. Thirdly, it is a great anomaly that while this historic amendment is being introduced to provide for reservation to the SCs and STs, and the Backward Classes in the private aided and unaided educational institutions, but the Central Government has not so far issued orders providing reservation to the Backward Classes in the educational institutions under the Central Government.

I earnestly request the Minister to issue immediate orders for providing reservation in all Central educational institutions including the IITs and management colleges, etc. in the interest of social justice to the Backward Classes for which executive orders are enough. This will be appriciated by the Backward Classes very much as it has been their long pending demand.

**ANANTH KUMAR (BJP)**

If social justice is part of the national interest, then, its implementation should happen not only in the non minority institutions but also it should happen in the minority institutions.

**SHRI DEVENDRA PRASAD YADAV**

In this Bill, alongwith SCs and STs, OBCs have also been protected in admissions to aided and unaided educational institutes. I support this Bill in its revised form. The history of the country has been thousands of years old. Some people have always been occupying the education, educational institutions, history, literature and wealth of this country. *The people whose population is less are providing reservation to those who are in majority.* In the Statement of Objects and Reasons the word "OBC" has been incorporated but it is missing in the main Bill. Even after the Supreme Court verdict on Mandal Commission's Report in 1992, "OBC" has not been incorporated in the original Bill. I would like to know whether it has been implemented even in the Government run educational institutions over the last 13 years. Private educational institutions can say that if Mandal Commission could not be implemented in Government institutions over a period of 13 years, then how can they do it ? If as per Supreme Court verdict the word "Creamy Layer" can be adopted everywhere in the Government machinery then why not the word " OBC". I want the hon. Minister to clarify. There must be some measures that the 52 per cent OBC people do not have to face.

**SHRI RAM KRIPAL YADAV**

Through this Bill Government has provided proper safeguard to the Scheduled Castes, Scheduled Tribes and other backward castes who have been suppressed for years. The way this Bill has been introduced will not be helpful in providing proper protection to the persons belonging to OBC section. *My party demands that reservation be provided on the basis of population. All classes will get reservation as per the percentage of their population. There is a need of amendment in the Bill introduced here and it should be carried out.*

Unless reservation is provided in the education sector, how these people will make progress? therefore, education is the need of the hour. Regarding capitation fee it has been pointed out that the poor, the Dalits and persons belonging to backward classes can not have enough money to afford this. Government should provide concessions to them in this regard.

**DR. CHINTA MOHAN**

This is a very progressive Bill. This 104th Amendment in the Constitution is a very praiseworthy and laudable. After globalization, so many private colleges have come today.

**SURESH KURUP (KOTTAYAM)**

As I have mentioned earlier, this Bill is only a small step which will help to overcome a portion of the unrealistic judgment of the Court. As such, it is welcome. If the Government has any intention to implement the assurance given in the Common Minimum Programme that nobody will be denied the opportunities for professional education just because he is poor, the Government should bring a comprehensive legislation regarding all aspects of the unaided professional colleges in the country.

**DR. M. JAGANNATH (NAGAR KURNOOL)**

Fianally, on behalf of TDP and on my own behalf, I support the Bill with a suggestion that there should be a provision for reservation for Scheduled Castes, Scheduled Tribes and OBCs, even in the linguistic minority, aided and unaided private institutions. Unless it is provided, it is not a comprehensive Bill.

**DR. SEBASTIAN PAUL (IND)**

I support the Bill with the mixed feeling of anguish and satisfaction. The 104th Amendment will deprive justice to dalits and backward classes. The exclusion of the minority educational institutions, referred to in clause (1) of Article 30 of the Constitution, from the scope of the amendment, will defeat the very purpose of the amendment. The net result of the amendment will be substantial denial of educational opportunity to students belonging to the socially and educationally backward classes, and Scheduled Castes and Scheduled Tribes. Article 30 allows minorities to run educational institutions to propagate their ideas, beliefs, scientific thinking, etc. This right would not be violated if they were to be forced to accommodate students, many of them belonging to their own communities, under the proposed quota. The minorities should be asked by this supreme House to have a concern for the poor and the deprived. The minority status is for protecting the rights of the minority and not to protect the vested interests of the leaders of the minorities.

## P. MOHAN (CPI-M)

The amendment seeks to protect and safeguard the rights of the socially and educationally backward classes. Capitation fee, exorbitant fee structure and self styled functioning in certain minority institutions must be looked into. Education is in the concurrent list of the Constitution. Hence there is a need to allow the states to have their own say in this matter. Certain educational institutions among the new crop of minority institutions established by virtue of minority status available in the name of religion and language are run on commercial basis. Such institutions must be regulated and proper arrangements should be made to provide reservation ot SCs, STs and OBCs.

## MOHAN SINGH (SP)

Government of India have introduced this Bill in the House in view of the sentiments expressed by all the political parties in the wake of the judgment of Supreme Court. Keeping in view the social circumstances of the country Mahatma Gandhi had pleaded for the principle of reservation. The Constituent Assembly constituted under the chairmanship of Dr. Rajendra

Prasad and in the guidance of Dr. Baba Saheb Ambedkar framed constitution of the country. Our Constitution is capable of dealing with not only the democratic challenges but it redresses social and educational grievances of its people.

Today when higher education is getting very expensive, a number of State Governments provided reservation to the children of Scheduled Castes and Scheduled Tribes in admission to all classes quite long ago, but it is not so in the educational institutions imparting specialized education which are mostly in the private sector. The fees charged by the big institutions aided hundred per cent by the Government of India are so high that despite all these provisions the poor and SC/ST children can not afford to seek admission therein. After this Bill is implemented such children will get admission in these specialized institutions of the private sector, but they should get financial assistance from the Government so that they could finish their education. Time and again this issue is raised as to why there is no provision of reservation in the minority institutions. Under section 30 and section 31 of the Constitution of India the constitutional right to run the minority institutions has been given to the people belonging to minority classes.

**RAJESH VERMA (BSP)**

The hon. Minister has respected the sentiments of crores of our countrymen by bringing this Constitution Amendment Bill in the House. But only by providing reservation we can not give justice to the weaker sections of the society. The fees charged by the private educational institutions are so high that the people of the weaker sections of our society are not in a position to deposit their fees even after getting reservation. This needs serious consideration. I request the hon.Minister to remove the small lacunae in this Bill. He has expressed his intention to include OBCs also. I would like to ask him to make it clear before the House and include OBCs in the purview of the Bill. I also request the hon. Minister that the UGC norms should be so modified as could ensure a uniform system in the whole country.

## ANANT GUDHE (SS)

India is a poor country and the poor people do not have any caste nor any religion. But when they go to take admissions in private colleges they face denial in the absence of money. Can we provide admission to those students in such private colleges after passsing this Bill ? I feel that this Bill is not enough to cater to their objectives. Therefore, any student who want to acquire higher education, be they belong to minorities or poor and if they face any problem in regard to higher fees then this should be entirely borne by the Central Government. We can achieve the objectives of the Bill if we incorporate this provision in the present Bill.

Whenever, Constitution Amendment Bills are introduced in the House it is said that it is a matter of national integrity. Whether this national integrity only confine to giving speeches in the House ? Why not we provide reservation for everybody in minority educational institutions? Why we did not incorporate this provision in this Bill? Therefore, my suggestion is to bring SCs, STs and other backward people, whose income is very meagre, under the purview of this Bill. Only then we can give social justice to all the needy people and also to attain our objectives.

## BALVANT ALIAS BAL APTE (BJP)

Sir, insofar as minority institutions are concerned, their right under article 31 is controlled by the provision of Article 29 (2) and the State can provide both for their regulation as also for reservation in such minority institutions. Sir, the Statement of Objects and Reasons of this enactment expressly mention article 31. Probably, a little more homework would have enlightened that article 29 (2) and it controls it.

## JANARDHANA POOJARY (INC)

Sir, I rise to support this Bill.

They will have to give reservation, and if they don't give, if they misuse it, then the Government should be open taking corrective action, whatever mistakes they are going to commit. Sir, we have got Mandal Commission. So many steps have been suggested by the Mandal Commission. Is the hon. Minister going to give benefits of Mandal Commission? *Is the Government aware of the fact that every single advantage, that has accrued to the country after the Mandal Commission, would accrue to the country in real terms after this Bill is passed in terms of admission and in terms of advantages which backward classes should get?* And, if there are many procedural defects, those defects could be corrected and if the procedure has to be adopted, that could also be adopted and remedial measures could be taken. Then, Sir, as I said, hon. Minister is a committed man, I would request him that he should not leave these things half way.

**SITARAM YECHURY (CPI-M)**

Sir, I rise in support of this Constitution Amendment Bill. And the reason why I rise in support of this is that two essential elements, which, in my opinion, constitute the essence of the Republican character of the country, are the questions of equality and secularism as my learned elder has said earlier. But in our country's context, equality and secularism can not be separated from each other. And that is precisely why I think we must recollect today that during the last days of the Constituent Assembly, Babasaheb Ambedkar had warned all of us saying, " that the Constitution that we are adopting gives 'one man, one vote', but the economic and social structure that we have in our country does not give 'one man, one value'. And unless you convert this 'one man, one vote, one man, one value', the entire political structure that we have built, even that is perilously threatened." This warning was given more than 50 years ago, but, unfortunately, we have still a long way to go on this. Reservation for the Scheduled Castes, the Scheduled Tribes and the OBCs is only a part measure in our opinion, though, we support it fully, but it is not the final solution for the upliftment of these sections without whose upliftment, we can not preserve even the political democracy we have, forget the question of equality. Therefore, I rise to support this principle of reservations in these private institutions from the point of view of the fundamental tenets of our Constitution. I think that is the basis on which this Amendment has been made.

**P.G. NARAYAN (AIADMK)**

The present Constitutional Amendment does not shed light on whether the State Governments will be empowered to enact laws to earmark a certain percentage of seats and enforce their reservation policy in respect of this earmarked percentage. We insist that the States should be given full powers in this regard.

I demand reservation for OBCs in IITs, IIMs, NIIT, AIIMS and JIPMER and in the Central Government Law Universities and Centrally funded educational institutions. Already this issue is pending before the Chennai High Court. This is the proper time for the Government to act on this matter. I hope the hon. Minister will respond to this important burning issue when he replies to the debate.

**RAVULA CHANDRA SEKAR REDDY (TDP)**

The other aspect is that, right from the begining, my Party has been committed to reservations not only for the Scheduled Castes and the Scheduled Tribes, but also for the Other Backward Classes. We are also interested in reservations for minorities in educational institutions. Our Party tried to bring forward a legislation when we were in power in the State.

Sir, the objective of the present Bill is to promote the advancement of the socially and educationally backward people of the country. The matter of admission of students belonging to the OBC, SC and ST categories in unaided private educational institutions is laudable. The amendment undoes the injustice done to the people of these categories by the recent judgment of the Supreme Court wherein the reservations prevailing earlier in private and unaided educational institutions were set aside.

**RAM NATH KOVIND (BJP)**

That report has already been submitted. *I urge upon the Government, and appeal to the Government, to come forward and get this Bill passed as quickly as possible.*

**DR. CHANDAN MITRA (NOMINATED)**

I would say that if the intention is to benefit the Scheduled Castes, the Scheduled Tribes, the OBCs and other backward communities, the quota that has been sought to be introduced—which is fine; we welcome it—must be introduced across the board and selective discrimination should not be done because it will not benefit any of the three communities, if it leaves out more than half such institutions outside its purview.

**SATISH CHANDRA MISRA (BSP)**

Sir, on behalf of the Bahujan Samaj Party, I am standing here to support this Bill as it aims to ensure giving social justice to the Scheduled Castes, the Scheduled Tribes and the backward class people. *Sir, unless social justice is given, there is no question of giving political and economic justice to them.* If proper education is not given to these people, they would be deprived of proper economic justice as these people would be deprived of good and proper jobs and livelihood. They will also be deprived of political justice because unless proper education is given and they are properly educated about the inequality with others, they would not be knowing their own rights, legal and Constitutional rights, which are given to them and they can not fight for the same.

**M.P. ABDUSSAMAD SAMADANI (ML)**

Sir, regarding these minorities, I would like to appreciate the bold stand taken by the Government. I would also like to congratulate the hon. Minister, Shri Arjun Singh, for the very effective step of keeping away the minorities from the purview of the Constitution (Amendment) Bill.

**ROBERT KHARSHING (NCP)**

Yesterday, under the leadership of Shri R.S. Gavai, about 20-22 Members of Parliament from both the Houses, of different political parties, including the Congress, BJP, NCP, RPI, etc. cutting across party lines, met the hon. Prime Minister to express our protest against this Bill, as it stands now. While we thank the Government for the good intentions behind this Bill, we strongly feel that this Constitutional Amendment Bill has reduced reservations for SCs and STs to zero in minority institutions.

**R.S. GAVAI (RPI)**

Sir, with all wisdom, I support this Bill. I request all hon. Members to just pass the Bill because some parties are divided on two issues. What is the loss we will have if the Bill is not passed ? If the Bill is kept in cold storage, that means, we have a net loss and it shows that we dont want to pass it. Whatever apprehensions are to be discussed with the hon. Minister—I think the hon. Minister is for the cause of the weaker sections and have a social obligation to uplift the backward classes—I hope he will hear those and do the needful.

**SANJAY RAUT (SS)**

As far as Maharshtra State is concerned, there is a provision under sections 7 of the University Acts par with the provisions of articles 15, 19 and 46, and as such universities are open to all irrespective of sex, creed, class, caste, place of birth, religion or opinion. Reservations to SCs, STs and Backward Classes are implemented in Maharashtra State.

**N.K. PREMACHANDRAN (RSP)**

Sir, I rise to support, this Bill as the main objective of the Bill is to provide reservation to the socially backward classes, especailly the Scheduled Castes, the Scheduled Tribes as well as Other Backward Classes. Since the objective of the Bill is absolutely within the scope of the Constitution, I fully support the Bill. *If this Constitutional Amendment has to achieve its objective, definitely, a comprehensive legislation in respect of the admission criteria, in respect of the fee structure, in respect of the running of the college, has to be brought so as to solve the problem in totality.* Otherwise, this Constitutional Amendment would not serve the purpose. With these words, once again, I would like to take this opportunity to congratulate the Government in giving reservation to the deprived section of the society.

**PROF. SAIF-UD-DIN SOZ (INC)**

Sir, I must congratulate the Government and the hon. Prime Minister. The hon. HRD Minister has worked very hard and brought this measure before this House. In fact, I know, and many people know that th UPA Chairperson personally takes a lot of interest in the legislative business, particularly the business which brings up the downtrodden section of the society. It is a majour question of social justice, and it is a noble cause. I think, the hon. HRD Minister has come forward with legislation after legislation, and rightly so, and this is an unprecedented situation. He deserves congratulation and appreciation from all sections of the society. *I raise a question that if the downtrodden people, the Scheduled Castes and the Scheduled Tribes, the OBCs and the minorities do not join the political mainstream, how can we strengthen the edifice of the Indian unity ?* We want to have the Indian unity and strength in larger measure. That can happen only if the weaker sections join the political mainstream. Therefore, it is a measure of strengthening the system of social justice.

**PROF. P.J. KURIAN (KERALA)**

But allow certain reservation to the weaker sections, which is a social obligation. It is not control, I feel. But it should not be seen as control. *I would have been happier if minority institutions were also brought under the purview of this Bill.*

**SHARAD YADAV (JD-U)**

I would request that exact figure of institutions of linguistic and religious minorities vis a vis other institutions should be provided. Mandal Commission have prepared list of backwards in various communities. *I would say that the backward sections of Minority Communities must also get the benefit of reservation.* I would say that we will have to carry on this system until the caste system is not eradicated from our country. We will have to keep a close watch on the rights of Dalits and downtrodden. People feel that their burden should be shared by all sections equally and in a justifiable way. There is no need to change the religious and linguistic character of an institution but you may allow the backward section of that community to take admissions in such institution. Untill such an amendment is brought forward, Hon'ble Minister should convene an all party meeting to discuss this issue.

## PARLIAMENTARY FORUM OF OBC MPS & HISTORIC LEGISLATION

*The Constitutional (104th amendment) Bill, 2005* passed in both Houses of Parliament (21st December in Lok Sabha & 22nd Dec. in Rajya Sabha), which further amended Article 15 and included clause (5) to provide reservation for OBCs, SC and STs in unaided educational institutions other than minority educational institutions is a historic legislation. The amendment was necessitated due to the Supreme Court judgement delivered on 12/08/2005 nullifying the reservation policy in private colleges, Within four months, the government could bring an amendment and get it passed with support of two-third Members of Parliament with all major parties supporting the amendment is a history. Special mention has to be made about the commitment exhibited by HRD Minister Arjun Singh.

Actually, the government intended to introduce the Bill on 14th December but has to defer it, due to the clarification sought by the OBC MPs. The Parliamentary Forum of OBC MPs, in its third meeting held at Delhi on 13th December became a significant meeting in the history of OBC people, in that the leaders cutting across party lines, expressed in clear terms that the words "OBCs" (other backward classes) should clearly be mentioned in the bill so that there is no legal hurdle in the future.

While the government deserved all praise for bringing the amendment to provide reservation in unaided colleges, further improvement and effective mechanism has to be built up in regulating the fee, capitation fee etc. In the name of linguistic minority institutions, colleges have been opened and totally commercialized which shuts the door to the ordinary citizens.

The Centre and States while formulating the legislation have to ensure that the private educational institutions are monitored in terms of reservation policy, the fee structure and capitation fees so that the OBCs, SC and STs do find it helpful in entering these institutions.

***Courtesy : Voice of OBC***

# 16

# WEAKER SECTIONS AMONG MINORITIES, ESPECIALLY MUSLIMS AND CHRISTIANS OF DALIT AND OBC ORIGIN, SHOULD GET THE BENEFIT OF RESERVATION IN UNAIDED MINORITY EDUCATIONAL INSITUTIONS

*Iqbal A. Ansari*

Minority Educational institutions have been exempted from the purview of the Constitution (104th) Amendment Act that enables the state, under Article 15 (5), to provide reservation of seats in unaided educational institutions for socially and educationally backward classes or Scheduled Castes and Scheduled Tribes. This legislative measure seeks to harmonise the claims of citizens' right to freedom with the obligation of the state to fulfil the promise of social justice to weaker sections. Does the exemption amount to privileging minority status? The right of the unaided minority institutions not to be subjected to any regulatory measures, other than those aimed at promoting the educational standards of the institution and the interests of the community concerned, has been judicially upheld right from the Kerala opinion (AIR1958CS956) to the T.M.A. Pai Foundation judgment of the Supreme Court and in the subsequent clarifying judgements.

It is the lack of proper understanding of the legal philosophy guiding these firm directions of the judiciary that makes sections of the intellectual and political class in the country view such exclusion as minority appeasement.

The vulnerability of the minorities arising from their inadequate share in power and decision-making and disadvantages caused by widespread discrimination and intolerance against them (and not necessarily any educational backwardness) requires special constitional and legal provisions to enable them to secure effective equality along with preserving their distinct identity. The necessity of such speceal measures for the minorities to ensure substantive equality to them has been recognised by all international instruments on minorities.

The right under Article 30 should not be taken as an affirmative measure on a par with the provisions under Article 15. The two stand on different footings. It also needs to be taken into account that social situations of minorities and majorities not only differ from country to country, but also from one minority to another within a country such as India. The Parsis, for example, are an affluent microscopic minority, who do not face any problem of discrimination or exclusion. Christians, except Dalit sections among them, are educationally advanced and are not uniformly subjected to discrimination.

The Sikhs have lately been facing problems of identity, but have the advantage of their bulk constituting a majority in one State. They are again not routinely subjected to discrimination.

## UNIQUE CASE

The case of Muslims as a minority is unique. Large sections of the power-wielding majority generally treat them as a suspect community held responsible for the perceived wrongs of history, including Partition.

The over-blown projection of identity issues of Urdu with its 'foreign' script and Muslim personal Law, which is supposed to be causing 'alarming' increase in their population, provide further justification for their exclusion, even periodic demonisation, and open boycott.

Coupled with this reality is the fact that the bulk of present day Indian Muslims are of indigenous Scheduled Caste and other Backward Class origin, whose social occupational structure has continued to perpetuate their educational backwardness.

The National Policy on Education (NPE) 1986, recognised Muslims along with neo Buddhists as being educationally most backward on an all-India basis, and included in the Programme of Action a whole range of schemes for their educational uplift. Most of it, however, remained unimplemented for lack of a conducive political-bureaucratic climate, especially in the States, as well as for lack of financial backing, and doubts about the legal validity of community specific measures.

This non-implementation did not become a significant public issue, in spite of the V.P. Singh Government's effort to highlight the gap between the successive Congress Governments' promises and performance for Muslims, largely because of the preoccupation of the Muslim elite during the period with the Mandir-Masjid issue.

The decade following the Ayodhya debacle has withnessed Muslim urge for education as an instrument of developmet. But their experienc of the earlier four decades had been one of bureaucaratic obstruction in getting recognition and aid for their institutions and uncertainty of preferential admission of Muslim students under the pretext of secularism. The professional educational institutions recently started by Muslims, along with other minorities, have been facing problems of recognition, affiliation, and government management share of quota.

Given the historical, political and sociological dimensions of the Muslim educational situation, the Supreme Court's ruling in the T.M.A. Pai Foundation case upholding the right of minorities to preferentially admit students of the community without any limitation in unaided institutions and with out the rigid ceiling of 50 per cent in aided institutions should receive ungrudging universal social-political support.

While endorsing such 'magnanimity,' it needs to be kept in view that Muslims, though the largest minority, have so far not been the major beneficiaries of Articale 30 (1) s scheme of minority empowerment. Any minority educational survey will reveal this reality.

The fact that their largest educational institution, the Aligarh Muslim University, has been denied the rights available to minorities under Article 30, especially the right to preferentially admit students of the community, should convince all honest observers of the educational scene that Muslims are not being appeased and that they are not enjoying any 'privilege' denied to others.

On the contrary, their now increasing urge for secular education needs universal support, as a measure of their modernisation and integration.

## ADDERSSING CRITCISM

However, the concerns raised during the debate in Parliament on the Constitution Amendment Bill to provide reservation for socially and educationally backward classes of citizens, are genuine and need to be addressed. One set of criticisms relates to abuse of the right by members of religious and linguistc minorities simply for profiteering. The other rightly points out that at least the weaker sections among minorities, especially Muslims and Christians of Dalit and OBC origin, should get the benefit of reservation in unaided minority educational institutions. There is no justification for either minting money in the name of minority rights, or monopolising now-expanding educational opportunities under Aricle 30 (1) by the already advanced and affluent sections among minorities.

It requires audit of the perfomance of all religious and linguistic minority institutions, to ascertain the extent, nature and modalities of profiteering and to find out which minorities and sections of minorities have benefited from the empowerment under Article 30 (1).

The findings may indicate that though many minority educational institutions are rendering service to all communities, like most Christian and some Muslim and Sikh institutions, they have no uniform policy of any special provision for admission of their own weaker sections. There soon may arise a need to reserve a quota for Dalits and OBC s among minorities in aided as well as unaided minority educational institutions under law. There is also a strong case for extending the benefit of reservation to all citizens of Dalit origin including Christians and Muslims, as are available to Dalits following indigenous religons.

Regarding the admission of non-minority students of any class including Scheduled Castes and Scheduled Tribes, it must be clearly borne in mind that imposition of any fixed quota for un-aided as well as aided minority educational institutions will not be valid legally or socially. However minorities must realise that social engineering for national integration, as well as the agenda of social justice, both require admitting a fair mix of students from all communities, sections and classes.

The law only prohibits inposition of any fixed quota for any category other than minority. It does not come in the way of a minority autonomously developing policy for preferntially admitting students on the basis of class and the community to fulfil the obligation of integration and social justice in their own free domain.

On the same grounds, the demand of under-represented minorities, such as Muslims, for provision of preferntial admission in State educational institutions, though without fixing any fixed quota under law deserves consideration.

*(The writer is a retired professor of the Aligarh Muslim University.)*

**Courtesy : " The Hindu" daily**

# 17

# GOVT. HAS RIGHTLY COME TO THE CONCLUSION ABOUT THE AUTHENTICITY OF THE NATIONAL SAMPLE SURVEY:

**This was made clear by Govt's reply in the civil writ Petition (No. 265 of 2006). Relevant extracts from the Counter affidavit filed on behalf of Govt. are reproduced**

***Editor***

## COMMON COUNTER AFFIDAVIT ON BEHALF OF RESPONDENT NOS. 1-7

I, Sunil Kumar S/o Dr. A.M. Kurup, Age 52 years, working as Joint Secretary and being the Authorized Signatory on behalf of the Union of India in respect of Respondents at Nos. 1 - 7, do hereby solemnly affirm and say as follows:

1. That I am the Authorized Signatory of the Respondents above named and am duly authorized and competent to make and affirm the instant Common Affidavit for and on behalf of the said Respondents.
2. That I have read a copy of the writ petition tiled by the Petitioner herein and have understood the contents thereof. I affirm and state that the averments made in the writ petition filed by the Petitioner are incorrect and contrary to the records.

3. That the writ petition filed by the Petitioner challenging the proposal for reservation of seats in institutions of higher education is not maintainable in law.

**4. BIDEFFACTUALBACKGROUND**

4.1 The Constitution (Ninety-third Amendment) Act, 2005 has, by inserting a new clause (5) in Article 15 of the Constitution, enabled the State to make special provision, by law, for the protection of the rights of the Scheduled Castes (SCs), the Scheduled Tribes (STs) and socially and educationally backward classes of citizens in all educational institutions, including aided or unaided private educational institutions, except minority educational institutions established under Article 30(1) of the Constitution.

4.2 The provisions of Article 15(5) aim at advancement of weaker sections including the Socially and Educationally Backward Classes of Citizens (SEBCs), also referred to as Other Backward Classes (OBCs), in matters of admission to educational institutions. Thus the Union and the State Governments are competent to enact comprehensive legislation in keeping with local conditions, covering all matters, including reservation of Seats for weaker sections in all educational institutions coming under their respective domain.

4.3 The attention of the State Governments has been drawn to take suitable action to effectively implement this provision. The imperative to implement the reservation of seats for the students belonging to the SCs, STs and the SEBC/OBCs in the centrally maintained and aided educational institutions and including the institutions deemed to be Universities so declared under Section 3 of the University Grants Commission Act, 1956, has been engaging the attention of the Central Government and while no final decision has yet been taken, the Central Government is considering various options in regard to implementing the provisions of Art. 15 (5). However, any such policy of reservations would have to be made by an appropriate law for the purpose which, in regard to admissions in educational institutions under the Central Government, can be made only by Parliament.

## 5. PRELIMINARY OBJECTIONS

5.1 It is submitted that the present writ petition is liable to be dismissed in limine with costs, in as much as the Petitioner has failed to consider that there is as yet no final decision in regard to a policy of reservation in matters of admission in institutions under the Central Government and that any such decision can be implemented, in terms of the requirement of Article 15 (5), only by an appropriate law to be enacted by Parliament. The contours of a policy in regard to reservation are still being examined within the Central Government. This is admitted even by the Petitioner, who categorically submits at various stages of the writ petition that the Central Government's reservation policy is only a proposal. Moreover, even if a draft legislative Bill is finalized, the same would be subject to debate and passage in Parliament. The present writ petition seeking to challenge a proposal, even before it is fully formulated, is therefore premature and improperly asks this Hon'ble Court to intervene in the Executive's prerogative to examine and formulate public policy options, as also in the privilege of Parliament as the legislature to make appropriate laws for the purpose.

5.2 It is submitted that the Petitioner has wrongly premised the writ petition on figures for ST/SC, OBC, and Muslim citizens computed by the National Sample Survey Organisation (hereinafter referred to as the "NSSO"). By definition, the mandate of the NSSO is simply to draw a "sample survey" across various cross-sections of society. The NSSO regularly collects, compiles and disseminates statistical information on different social-economic facets of the country through nation-wide surveys conducted in the form of successive 'rounds', normally of one- year duration. The NSSO has full authority to formulate its programmes, including choice of subjects for survey, the "sample" design to be adopted, the form in which data are to be collected, processed, analyzed and published. The NSSO however does not seek to replicate or carry forward or question or modify the objective achieved by a National Census conducted through decennial Census operations of the Registrar General of India, namely, to provide a detailed 'head count' of the various constituents of society in India. In other words, the NSSO data does not provide an accurate account of the actual number of citizens belonging to all the various castes/classes. This is evident from the fact that the NSSO data relied upon by the Petitioner was the result of the fifty-fifth round conducted during July 1999 and June 2000 covering only about 120,000 households (approximately 71,000 from rural India and 49,000 from urban India spread over 6,000 villages and 4,100 urban blocks) across the country. The NSSO data was not for the purposes of a head-count of different caste or class populations cannot therefore be relied upon to challenge any policy of reservation under consideration by the Central Government.

5.3 The Petitioner has miscalculated the figures drawn by the NSSO from its sample survey and misjudged the impact of the NSSO survey data quoted in the present writ petition. It is submitted that the results quoted by the Petitioner in the instant writ petition are not directly found in the published 55th report of the NSSO. As a result, the NSSO had to re-tabulate household level data to check the veracity of the averments. Such revision led the NSSO to conclude that during 1999- 2000, ST, SC and OBC citizens comprised 8.9%, 19.6% and 35.8% of the total population respectively, besides revisiting other data.

5.4 This also demonstrates that the Petitioner failed to consider the element of disadvantage in all sample surveys. Social surveys deal with human populations which are not only heterogeneous but also tend not to be well mixed. Further, it is well accepted that the social surveyor has little effective control over his/her sampling units. He/she may get people who refuse to be drawn into the sample, or who are not available at the time of the survey. In such cases, the social surveyor may have to rely on secondary data to compensate for the absence of first-hand recording. Such disadvantages make a sample survey an inaccurate reflection of the constituent elements of society as compared to a national census which insists on a head count, and is therefore, more reliable.

5.5 Moreover, nowhere does the NSSO data, relied upon by the Petitioner, contradict the views that reservation of seats of 27% in higher educational institutions would be appropriate for the SEBCs or the OBCs regardless of faith, in addition to and apart from the reservation for the SC (15%) and the ST (7.5%) already existing since a long time. In fact, *arguendo,* even if the figures and interpolations drawn by the Petitioner are taken at face value, they reinforce the view that reservation of seats for the SEBCs/OBCs has become imperative, now more than ever before, to strengthen their social and educational status and to remove the inequality being suffered by them. By studying the need for, and the implications of a reservation policy, the Central Government is merely discharging its duty to ensure action providing for the legitimate and long-delayed rights of the SEBCs/OBCs, of whom an integral part are the SEBCs/OBCs belonging to religious minorities. Such measures are designed to eliminate existing and continuing discrimination, to remedy the continuing effects of past discrimination, and to create systems and procedures to prevent future discrimination.

5.6 It is submitted that the Petitioner has wrongly claimed that the proposed reservation policy would benefit only Hindu SC/STs and SEBCs/OBCs, at the cost of Muslims and Dalits, and that only the 'creamy layer' amongst them would directly benefit. The central list of SEBCs/OBCs notified in 1993 and subsequently, includes a number of communities from among the Muslims, Sikhs and Christians as well, belonging to the socially and educationally backward classes. The proposed reservation policy is being debated within the framework of the Constitution of India which proscribes discrimination only on grounds of religion, caste, sex or place of birth. Accordingly, any reservation policy formulated by the Central Government will ensure that only members of castes/communities identified as socially and educationally backwards classes derive benefit from such a policy regardless of religious faith.

# 18

# 93rd CONSTITUTION AMENDMENT

*Anwer Ali*

The stir against reservation for Other Backward Classes (OBCs) in educational institutions, including Central Professional Institutes such as Indian Institutes of Technology (IITs) and Indian Institutes of Management (I.I.Ms) including medical colleges and institutes of excellent education and training was un-called for and illogical. It has now melted into nothingness. The 93rd Consttutional amendment in Constitution is a fait accompli. P.M. Manmohan Singh has declared in unequivocal words quota issue as settled, "there was no going back on the reservation issue."

The 93rd amendment in Constitution inserting sub-clause (5) in Art. 15 on 20th Jan 2006 was consensually passed by all political parties. This newly inserted sub-Article reads as follows.

"Nothing in this Article or in sub-clause (g) of clause (1) of Article 19 shall prevent the state from making any special provision, by law, for the advancement of any socially and educationally backward classes of citizens or for the Scheduled Castes or the Scheduled tribes inso far as such special provisions relate to their admission to educational institutions, includig private educational institutions, whether aided or unaided by the state, other than the minority educational institutions referred to in Clause (1) of Article 30".

This was a direct consequence of Supreme Court Judgment in P.A. Inamdar case (August 12, 2005) which declared that state could not impose its reservation/quota regime on: (i) minority (ii) and non-minority un-aided private educational institutions, including professional colleges and institutes; the court found the entire quota regime as unreasonable restiction in exercise of "the fundamental right of freedom of profession, trade and business" guaranteed by Art 19 (i) g of the Constitution. P.A. Inamdar case is a clarifactory judgment of the two previously delivered judgments - viz; T.M.A. Pai Foundaton case (Oct. 31, 2002) and Islamic Academy Case (August 14, 2003). To summarize the rational of the cases:

(i) There shall be no quota regime in private un-aided educational institutions and minority established and administered educational institutions. The SC held that neither could the policy of reservation be enforced by the State nor any quota or percentage of admissions carved out to be appropriated by the State in a minority or non-minority unaided educational institutions. The Judges said: "The State cannot insist on private educational institutions which receive no aid from the State to implement State's policy on reservation for granting admission on lesser percentage of marks, i.e. on any criterion except merit." they were of the opinion that "a limited reservation of seats, not exceeding 15 percent, in our opinion, may be made available to NRIs depending on the discretion of the management".

(ii) Regarding admissions, the court held that the court said up to the level of undergraduate education, the minority unaided educational institutions enjoy total freedom. However, different considerations would apply for graduate and postgraduate level of education as also for technical and professional educational institution. Such education cannot be imparted by any institutions unless recognized by or affiliated with any competent authority created by law, such as a University, Board, Central or State Government or the like.

(iii) Regarding fee structure to be charged from the students, in the Pai foundation case, the court declared that every institution was free to devise its own fee stucture subject to the limitation that there can be no profiteering and no capitation fee can be charged. According to the Constitution bench in the Islamic Academy case, a provision for reaonable surplus can be made to enable future expansion. The relevant factors which would go into determining the reasonability of a fee structure are (i) the infratructure and facilities available, (ii) the investment made, (iii) salaries paid to the teachers and staff, (iv) future plans for expansion and betterment of the institutions etc. (v) And regarding management of the colleges; the Judgment in the Pai Foundation case is unanimous on the view that the right to establish and administer an institution, the phrase as employed in Article 30 (1) of the Constitution (Right of minorities to establish and administer educatioal institutions), comprises of the following rights: (a) to admit students; (b) to set up a reasonable fee stucture; (c) to constitute a governing body; (d) to appoint staff; and (e) totake acton if there is dereliction of duty on the part of any of the employees. A minority educational institution may choose not to take any aid from the state and may also not seek any recognition. Such institutions connot indulge in any activity which is violative of any law of the land. they can admit all students of their own communty.

Therefore in pith and substance and in reality education, to great extent, was made a trading merchandise protected by art 19 (i) g of the Constitution. The commercialisation of education is apparent from the allowance made to the management of colleges for carving out seats, not exceeding 15% for NRIs (with no consideraton of merit and creation of free domain for minority education tycoons. So the political classes as a whole unanimously passed 93rd amendment.

The issue of reservation as provided by newly added sub-clause (5) or Art. 15 in the Constitution now stands finally settled, the central government is devising a bill to be passed in the coming monsoon session to implement the constiutional mandate of Art. 15(5).

But a very serious feature of sub-slause (5) of Art 15 is that it provides exemption tō minority educational institutions referred to in clause (1) of Art. 30 of the Constitution from its operation/Prima facie, it appears that this exemption was provided to the minority institutions as they enjoy "a special right to establish and administer educational institutions. of their choice" as provided by a Art 30 Perhaps, it was thought that imposing quota regime on minority institutions would be violative of Art. 30 of the Constitution being unreasonable restriction and also against the Principle of secularism enshrined in the Constitution. It is submitted that this view is superficial and violative of the principle of social justice which is the basic structure of the Constitution, as constitutionally recognized in Art. 15 (5); and also violative of Art. 15(1). To be more candid, Art 15 (1) mandates the State not to discriminate against any citizen on grounds of religion, race, caste, sex or place of birth or any of the three.The exemption phrase in Art. 15 (5) (supra) discriminates on the ground of religion (and language) and that is too under the protective umbrella of Art 30 i.e. right of minorities to establish and administer educational istitutions of their choice, Prima-facie, Backward, Most Bckward and deprived sections of a minority community (OBC Muslims, such as Weavers, Telis, Nais, Saqqas, Nilgars, Khakrobs et al and DalitChristians and Mazhabi Sikhs are deprived of the benefits of social justice policy of the State in the institutions established and administered by the elite and forward classes of their religious breathren.

As well said Art 15 (5) has given constitutional recognition to the principle of social justice, that is empowering the weaker and deprived classes of the society. But exemption phrase added to Art. 15 (5) ignores the stark social reality that Muslim minority (and to a great extent the Christians) is not a homogeneous social monolith. It is, like its Hindu counter-part, caste/class ridden, vertically divided on caste and class lines. Indian Muslim society is also based on caste hierarchy; on its apex are socially and educationally (and also economically) advanced classes/castes-i.e. Syeds, Shiekhs, Mughals and Pathans (called Asrafs) and at the base of this social pyramid are artisans, poor labourers and socially educationally bckwards and most backwards called Ajlafs/Arzals. This social fact is recognized in Kaka Saheb Kalelkar report, Mandal commission report (part I p. 55) and Mandal's judgment of Supreme Court (p. 83). The fact of existence of other Backward Classes and Educationally Socially Most Backward Classes (below poverty line and double poverty line) in Muslim society was confirmed in scholarly works of eminent social scientists like professor M. Imtiaz Ahmad and Prof. Rajni Kothari and other eminent sociologists). Successive census reports show the Indian Muslim society as largest minority community (13.4% of the Indian population) and also show that majority of Indian Muslims are socially and educationlly backwards (approx. 85% of Muslm population) who are indigeneous scheduled castes and depressed/deprived calss origin.

The sad unfortunate historical social reality is that the social/occupational struture of weak and deprived classes of Muslim society (since Qutubdin Aibak 1206 A.D.) continued. They had no reach to education even after embracing Islam and their social educational backwardness was perpetuated so deep that they are still sulking in the quagmire of social educational backwardness. The National Policy on Education (N.P.E.) 1986 has also recognized backward/most backward classes of Muslims. as being "most educatuonally backward" but they had no acces to benefits on programme of Action of NPE, partly because beaurucratic inaction and partly because the Muslim elitist class had no inclination or desire to improve the social educational status of their weaker coreligionists.

A plain reading and analysis of Art. 30 will lead to the irresistible conclusion that "the fundamental right to establish and administer educational institution of their choice" is constitutionally conferred on the community and not on self selected individuals in the garb of a registered society or trust. Laws of education throughout India abhors and bans monopolizing educational institutions in the hands of a few/ or in closed family circles ; they also provide that no educational institution can be establised/administered for profit motive. The Supereme Court has also time and again,warned against profiteering in education. Education should always be grassroot collective community affair. *(Aligarh education movement in North, Anjuman Islam movement in South and DAV education movement of Arya Samaj can be alludede to)* But what is happening in practice is that private minotity educational institutions are established and run for profiteering. Socially educationally backward classes of Muslim and other minorities are not getting any benefit, their educational needs are not addressed in the minority institutions. There is no legal/moral justification for either minting money in the name of minority rights and for monopolizing of now expanding educational opportunities under Art. 30 of the Constitution by the elitist affluent and forward classes of minority community. Examples can be cited to prove that the much publicized Muslim minority educational institutions with high sounding sentimentally attractive Islamic religious names in South India and in the North at Deobad, Lucknow, Delhi, Aligarh and elsewhere are charging exorbitant capitation fee from the aspiring students with costly fee structure (the only appreciable exception is Hamdard University where no capitation fee is charged and the fee structure is less costly) There is complete lack of transparency in these so called minority educational institutions in matter of admissions and financial transactions. Ostensibly most of these minority institutions receive no grant in aid from the state exchequer but receive petro-dollars from West Asia and Euorup and USA and funds from government aid agencies and Zakat from philanthropists. Weaker and deprived sections of Muslims are not getting any benefit from the minority educational institutions. There can be no justification of minting money. It is submitted that the phrase added to Art. 15(5) conferring exemption to minority institutions will create segregated education system benefiting financially and edcationally only the elitist forward castes of Muslims.

It reminds one Adam Smithians principle that "the state ought not to meddle with the education of the rich" (Muslims). This exception has also provided a handle to Hindutva forces for centrifugalising simple minded Hidus on the slogan of 'Muslim appeasement,' widening communal divide.

In the proposed bill for implementation of social justice programs under Art. 15(5) there should be effective provisions for auditing of performance of all religious/minority educational institutions to ascertain the extent, nature and modalities of profiteering and also effectivly monitor and find out which section, caste or classes of minorities are reaping benefits from the empowerment process under Art. 30 of the Constitution. There should be permanent statutory machinery for the purposes of performance auditing and financial screening.

The proposed law should also provide admission policy in minority instutions and there should be mandatory guidelines for admissions of students specifying not less than 30% out of 50% of admissions from weaker sections of the particular minority. (50% open category + 20% general minority + 30% OBCs and MBs Muslims = 100%) To be lucid there need to reserve quota for Dalits and O.B.Cs. of indigenous origin among minorities in state aided as well as unaided minority educational institutions under the proposed law. There should be mandatory reservation for the classes/castes of indigenous (Dalit) origin (Christians and Muslims) as is available to non-Christians and non-Muslim Dalits. The proposed bill should mandatorily ensure the compliance of the guidelines given by the Supreme Court in Islamic Academy case barring capitaion fee and allowing "reasonable surplus." *The over sight committe* headed by Veerappa Moiley should also cosider the educational needs of Muslim OBCs and MOBCs and MBCs below poverty line and double poverty line. There is a general strong need to reserve specific quota for Dalits and OBCs among minorities in aided as well as un-aided minorities educational institutions under law. There is a strong case for extending benefits of reservation to citizens of all Dalit origin, of Muslims and Christians as is available to Dalits bracketed as Hindus.

It may be noted that social engineering for national integration and the program of social justice require that all sections of the community shall be provided access to admissions. The law only prohibits imposition of any fixed quota for any category other than minority. It does not bar a minority to devise and develop a preferential policy of admisions of students of their community on the basis of percentage of a backward/deprived classes in a minority community to fulfill the obligtions of social justice in this autonomous area. Proposed law should address this important issue of reservation of deprived and depressed Muslim minority students in Muslim (minority) instiutions. Minority status of an institution under Art. 30 is not an open gereral license for profiteering and money minting and for conferring eductional benefits on affluent, socially advaced elitist classes of the minority community. It does not confer freedom to block admissions of minority OBCs and MBCs.

It is the right and duty of the state to provide education for all the common citizens, with no discrimination; this means the deprived and weaker sections of the society must have reach to the sources of educatuon and Knowledge from primary to the higher education to the scientific and technical education.

The state should not ignore the soci-educational interset of the socially educationally backward/depressed classes of the Indian Muslim society. If you leave the multitude of Mulims un-educated, depriving them from modern education, there is serious risk that misplaced religious sentiments embedded in ignorance irrationality and superstition may produce the most dreadful consequences of ghettoisation.

# PART - II

# PART - II

# 19

# EXEMPTION OF MINORITY EDUCATIONAL INSTITUTIONS BY 93RD CONSTITUTION AMENDMENT IS AGAINST THE INTEREST OF SOCIALLY AND EDUCATIONALLY BACKWARD SECTIONS OF MINORITIES

*Ashfaq Husain Ansari*

Prime Minister Dr. Manmohan Singh assured CPI leader D. Raja that the UPA government is committed to resevation to OBCs and the bill in this regard would be brought in the monsoon session of Parliament. It may not be out of place to mention that during the winter session of Parliament, the Constitution (104th amendment) Bill 2005 was passed by both houses of Parliament. The Lok Sabha passed it on 21st December and Rajya Sabha on 22nd December, 2005. It further amended Article 15 and added clause (5) to provide reservation for OBCs besides SCs and STs in unaided and aided educational institutions, of course other than minority educational institutions. This is no doubt a historic legislation. The amendment was a direct consequence of Supreme Court Judgment in what is known as P.A. Inamdar case delivered on 12-8-2005 nullifying the reservation policy in minority institutions as well as non-minorty unaided private institutions, including professional colleges and institutions of higher learning. The court found that reservation of seats in these institutions is not justified and violates Article 19 (1) g of the

Constitution. UPA Govt. at the centre with in four months brought the necessary amendment and got it passed with the support of more than two-third membrs of both houses of Parliamant. All major parties supported the amendments which is a history in itself. It could happen only because the UPA along with allies are committed to the principle of social Justice, particularly reservation to the socially and educationally backward sections of the community in admission to eductional institutions and jobs in public organations including public funded establishments. Besides the commitment of UPA government and its allies the significant role played by the OBC MPs is also to be noted. The OBC organisations also generated necessary pressure in their own way.

The statement of objects and reasons of the Bill (No. 160 of 2005) specifically mentions in Para 2:

> *"It is laid down in Article 46, as a directive principle of State Palicy that the state shall promote with special care the educational and economic intrests of weaker sections of the people and protect them from social injustice. Access to education is important in order to ensure advancement of persons belonging to Sheduled Caste, Sheduled Tribes and the socially and educationally backward classes, also referred to as OBCs."*

But further in para 3 and 4 it states :

> 3. *"Clause (1) of Article 30 provides the right to all minorities to establish and administer educational instulutions of their choice. It is essential that the right available to minorities are protected in regard to institutions established and administered by them. Accordingly institutions declared by the state to be minority institution under clause (1) of article 30 are omitted from the operation of the proposal."*
>
> 4. *"To promote the educational advancement of the socially and educationally backward classes of citizens i.e. OBCs or of the Scheduled Castes and Sheduled Tribes in matters of admission of students belonging to these categories in unaided educational institutions referred to in clause (1) of article 30 of the Constitution, it is proposed to amplify article 15. The new clause (5) shall enable the Parliament as well as the state legislatures to make appropriate laws for the purpose mentioned above."*

The Constitution (one hundred and fourth amendment) Bill 2005 now becomes part of the Constitution after being passed by both houses of Parliament and after getting the presidential assent. It is now known as 93rd Constitution amendment. The amended Constitution (93rd Constitution amendment) after inserting sub clause (5) reads as under.

Article 15 (5)

> *"Nothing in this article or in sub clause (g) of clause (1) of clause 19 shall prevent the state from making any special provision by law for the advancement of any socially and educationally backward calsses of citizens or for the sheduled caste or the scheduled tribes in so for as such special provision relates to their admission to educational institutions, including private educationial institutions, whether aided or unaided, by the state, other than the minority educational institutions referred to in clause (1) of Article 30."*

Minorities in India, be it Muslim, Christians or Sikhs are mainly from two categories. Most of the minorities are converts from Hindu religion. They are called indigenous Muslims, Chiristians or Sikhs. They are mostly converts from Scheduled Castes or low caste Hindus. Very few of the Muslims claim that they are direct decendents from Arab, Iran, Turkey and Egypt. Very few Christians claim their European orgin. Almost all Sikhs are converts from Hindu relegion. Few converted Muslims claim that they are converts from upper caste Hindus. So is the case with Christians and Sikhs. But these converts remain socially and educationally backward from generations.

Mandal Commmission's conclusion are very clear on this count. It says:

> *"There is no doubt that social and educational backwardness among the non-Hindu Communities is more or less of the same order as among the Hindu Communities. Though caste system is peculiar to Hindu society yet in actual practice it also pervades the non-Hindu communities in India in varying degrees. There are two main reasons for this phenom-enon, first, caste system is a great conditionor of the mind and leaves an indelible mark on a person's social consciousness and cultural moves. Consequenly even after conversion the ex-Hindus carried with them their deeply ingrained ideas of social hierarchy and stratifications. This resulted in the*

*Hindu converts inadvertantly acting as Trojon horses of caste system among highly egalitarian religions such as Islam, Christianity, Sikhism etc. Secondly, non-Hindu minorities living in predominantly Hindu India could not escape from its dominant social and cultural influences. Thus both from within and without caste amongst non-Hindu communities received sustenance and stimulous."*

Besides the Mandal Commission's assertion on this count the Encyclopaedia Americana International Edition describes this divison amongst the Muslims:

*"All important communities including the Muslims, Christians and Sikhs have some sort of caste schemes. These schemes are patterned after the Hindu system, since most of these people origionally came from the Hindu stock. The large scale conversion that have been going on for centuries have modified Indian caste society."*

Similarly Encyclo-paedia Britannica describes this phenomenon as under :

*"Among Muslims it is pointed out, a distinction is made between Ashraf (supposed to be decendants of Arab immigrants) and non Ashraf (Native converts). Both are divided into sub groups. particularly the non-Ashrafs who are converts from Hindusim. It is pointed out that they practice caste system (including Endogamy) in a manner else to that of their Hindu counterparts."*

On the pretext of Article 30 clause (1) of the Constitution and the P.A. Inamdar and other judgements of the Supereme Court, the UPA government under the pressure of socially and educationally advanced Muslim leaders who dominate not only the UPA but almost all the political parties, agreed to exempt minority institutions from reservation ambit. It is an open secret that 90% of the minority institutions in India are established and managed by the elite sections of the minorities who are socially and educationally advanced. By exempting the minority institutions from the reservation ambit the 93rd Constitution amendment contradicts the statement of objects and reasons of the bill itself.

It contradicts what is laid down in Article 46 as a directive principle of state policy. By excluding minority institutions the state has failed to promote with special care the educational interest of the socially and educationally backward sections of the minorities. They also failed to protect this section from social injustice. They also failed to provide access to education in order to ensure advancement of persons belonging to scheduled caste and scheduled tribes and also the socially and eductionally backward classes particularly among the minorities.

Leaving aside the scheduled caste and scheduled tribes and non-minority OBCs what will happen to socially and educationally backward sections of the minorities whom the Constitution Review Commission of Justice Venkat Challiah has specifically defined as "bulk.":

> *"Backward classes belonging to religious minorities who have been identified and included in the list of backward classes and who infact constitute the bulk of the population of religious minorities should be taken up with special care along with their Hindu counter-parts in the developmental efforts of backward classes."*
>
> *Padama Vibhusan Justice Venkat Challiah, charmain National Commission for Review of Working of the Constitution.*

These bulk of the minority community will not get their due share commensurate to their population in the institutions run by. the minority community who come under the category of institutions *"other than the minority educational institutions referred to in clause (1) of article 30."*

Prof. Nadeem Hasnain eminent social scientist and anthropologist has rightly said: said:

> *"Significantly for sometime now a section of Muslim leadership has been demanding a separate quota in reservation for Muslims as a whole despite the fact that Muslim OBC,s constitute an overwhelming majority of the entire Muslim population of India are already covered under the existing provision for the OBCs."*

He further adds:

> *It is unjust because some groups with-in each religious community are traditionally forward and socially and educationally and economically advanced as compared to the rest of their population as well as in the absolute sense of the term. The Sayyed, Sheikh and other Ashraf castes of north India the Thangal, Arakkal, Koya and*

*Keyi of Kerala Muslims and Jat among the Sikhs, the Syrian among the Kerala Christians and so on are the advanced higher castes. Thus the argument that an entire religious community is socially and educationally backward negates the sociological reality and goes against the principle of social justice."*

Prof Nadeem Hasnain further adds:

> *"The response of the leadership of Muslim OBC's is also very meaningful and significant. They are strongly apprehensive that if Muslims, as a whole as a religious community are extended reservation, the relatively better off castes shall be cornering and gobbling up most of the opportunities for educational and economic advancement. The efforts for the empowerment of Muslim OBC's along with Hindus, Christian and Sikhs OBC's have exploded the myth (perpetuated largely by the Muslim elite) that the entire Muslim cemmunity is monolith devoid of any economic, social and cultaral complexities."*

Prof D.L. Sheth has rightly said:

> *"The new demand for Muslim reservation is simply a strategy to introduce through the backdoor the principle of communal quota into the Constitution."*

Inspite of the clear cut warnings of the eminent sociologists and anthropologists, the UPA government under the pressure of Muslim elite (Ashraf) leadership has exempted the minority educational institutions from lthe purview of reservation "negating the sociological reality and the principle of social justice. The entire minority community professing any religion, Islam Christianity or Sikhism is not socially and educationally backward and hence the entire community or the educational intitutions established and administered by the minorities cannot be exempted from reservation provisions.

The elite of the minorities particularly Muslim Ashraf leaderhip feels that by keeping the educational intitutions run by the minorities "referred to in clause (1) of Article 30 of the Constitution outside the provisions of the newly added clause (5) of Article 15 of the Constitution is a victory for the minorities. But the fact of the matter is that minorities consist of Muslims Christian and Sikhs and overwhelming majority of Muslims, Christians and Sikhs are socially and educationally backward and they could not compete with socially educationally and economically advanced sections of their own community. Moreever this fact is also to be noted that minority educational institutons are mostly established and adminstered by the elite (Ashraf) well to do sections of the minorities. The socities or the trusts which are managing these institutions belong to the socially, educationally and ecconmically advanced sections of the minorities. Keping these institutions outside the reservtion ambit will go against the directive principle of state policy enshrined in Article 46 of the Constitution. It will not promote *"special care to the educational and economic intrest of the weaker sections of the people"* and will neither protect them from social injustice.

No doubt *"access to education is important in order to ensure advancement of persons belonging to the scheduled caste, sheduled tribes and the socially and educationally backward classes also referred to as OBCs."*

Now the most pertinent question is what will happen to OBCs of the minorities who constitute aroud 80% of the minorities. There is no guarantee clause which could eusure the representation of socially and educationally backward section of the minorities now exempted by the newly added clause (5) of Article 15. No doubt cluse (1) of Article 30 gives the right to establish and administer educational institutions to minorities. But minorities include all categories, particularly its overwhelming majority who are socially and educationally backward and are included in the Central and State list of OBCs.

The forthcoming bill slated for the mansoon session of the Parliament should take care of the intrests of the socially and educationally backward sections of the minorities who are deprived by the provision of the 93rd Constitution amendment. Reservation of at least 50% of the seats in minority institutions for the 80% socially and educationally backward section of the minorities will do some justice to them, other wise These sections of the minorities will have no option but to knock the door of Supreme Court for justice to socially and educationally backward sections of the minorities We hope that ultimately good sense will prevail upon the UPA leadership, particularly

Human Resources Development Minister Arjun Singh while giving final touches in drafting the Bill.

Although during the debate on Constitution, 104th amendment bill (now 93rd amendment of the Constitution) most of the members of both houses of Parliament had not taken the concluding sentence of Para (5) of the bill which says ........ "other than the minority educational institutons referred to in clause (1) of Article 30" seriously but the addition of this concluding sentence is not so simple. Exclusion of minority institution means the exclusion of institution itself and not the minority students. A minority institution is the institution established and administered by minorities. It has nothing to do with the strength of the institution. A minority institution excluded from the reservation ambit may have 20% or less minority students. There is no binding on the composition in the strength of the institution but the exemption is permitted to the full strength of the students. It means that in the name of minority institution non-minority students who may be 60% or more of the total strength will reap the benefit of exclusion from reservation ambit. So may be the case of appointment of staff Mostly institutions excluded from reservation formula can not refuse admission to non minority students. It should be made clear that exemption from reservation fromula is to the minority students and not the institution. For rest of the students who do not belong to the minority, the reservation principle will be same as it is in practice in non-minority institutions.

Minority consists of both socially and educationally backward sections and those also who are socially and educationally not backward. Generally around 80% of the minorities are from socially and educationlly backward sections and around 20% are from socially and educationlly forward section. Socially and educationally backward sections need affirmative action or reservation in admission because they can not compete with the socially and educationally forward sections of the community. Reservation in admission for the OBC and Dalit Muslim students has to be provided whether the institution is a minority institution or otherwise. In the name of minority institutions, OBC and Dalit minorities cannot be kept away from the reservaion formula in admission to these intitutions.

Before giving final shape to the proposed bill the Ministry of Human Resource Development, particularly Mr. Arjun Singh, should see that in the case of minority institution socially and educationlly backward sections of the minorities who constitute around 80% amongst the minorities, are not denied admission in minority institutions. He will also have to see that the exemtpted minority institutions will not become commercial capitation institutions for non-minorities. While drafting and introducing the reservation bill incorporating the 93rd Constitution amendment it is the responsibility of the government to see that all sections of the minorities particularly the socially and educationally backward sections amongst them (The OBCs) should get admission in the minorty institutions commensurate to their population.

The Kerala Government has recently unanimously passed the bill incorporating the 93rd Constitution amendment to the Constitution. After getting the assent of the Governor it has now become Act. known as "Kerala Professional Colleges (Prohibition of Capitation Fees, Regulation of Admissions, Fixation of Non-exploitative Fees and other Measures to Ensure Equity and Exellence of Admission in Professional Education) Act 2006". One of the important clauses of this act is defination of minority institution . The criterian for minority institution is rightly defined. It has rightly defined that only those institutions will be given the status of minority institution where the strength of minorities is not less than 50%. To make it more effective this Act should have also taken care of socially and educationally backward sections of the minorities by reserving at least 50% of the seats in minority institutions for the OBCs and Dalits of the minorities. Then and only then it will do justice to socially and educationally backward sections of the minorities in minority institutions.

The Kerala Act will really become a Model Act for Centre and other States if it incorporates the reservation clause for socially and educationally backward sections of the minorities.

# 20

# MINORITY CHARACTER OF ALIGARH MUSLIM UNIVERSITY

*Ashfaq Husain Ansari*

The Aligarh Muslim University was formally established through "THE ALIGARH MUSLIM UNIVERSITY ACT, 1920 (40 OF 1920). An Act to establish and incorporate a teaching and residential Muslim University at Aligarh" (14th September 1920).

The Act begins with :

> *"WHEREAS it is expedient to establish and incorporate a teaching and residential University at Aligarh, and to dissolve the Societies registered under the societies Registration Act 1860 which are respectively known as the Mohammadan Anglo-Oriental College, Aligarh and the Muslims University Association and to transfer to and vest in the said University all properties and rights of the said societies and the Muslim University Foundation Commitee."*

Thus Aligarh Muslim University was established after dissolving the Mohammadan Anglo-oriental College Aligarh and The Muslim University Association which were registered under the Societies Registration Act 1860. It is also an undeniable fact that at this stage some non Muslims of the area also associated with the establishment of these societies during Sir Syed's lifetime. Some of the eminent non-Muslims who donated liberally were Maharaja Mahendra Singh of Patiala, Raja Shambhoo Narain of Benares, Raja Jai Kishan Das and Raja Kishun Kumar.

The 1920 Act (40 of 1920) was amended several times before and after independence and more so after the adoption of the Constitution of India but the framers of the amendments never took seriously the position taken by the Supreme Court through the land mark judgement of Aziz Basha V/s. Union of India of 1968. The Aziz Basha judgement took the view that Aligarh Muslim University Act 1920 has not given the status of Minority Institution within the meaning of article 30 of the Constitution of India. Instead going through the meaning of Constitutional amendment the Union Government and its Education Ministry at that time headed by Mr. B. Shankara Nand were not serious in providing the Minority character to The AMU through necessary Constitutional amendment, the reasons better known to them. During the discussion in the Parliament on the AMU Amendment bill 1981 several members including myself who participated in the debate pointed out that by deletion of the word "established" and other amendments will not "restore" the minority character of the University. By deleting the word "established" will not hide the facts mentioned in the two registered societies documents. While dealing with the powers of the University it added clause in 5 a, b and c. particularly clause 2C which states "(C) to promote especially the educational and cultural advancement of the Muslims of India". But for the promotion of educational and cultural advancement of the Muslims of India an Act cannot give the power to overrule the constitutional provision of Article 29-2, 30-1 and 15-4 and 16-4. These Articles do not give powers to a university to reserve seats in admissions or employment to persons of a Community for whome the University was established under the Act of Parliament. Establishment of a University under an Act of Parliament or establishment of an institution or society under the Societies Registration Act is altogether different when an institution is established under an Act of Parliament, may be with the name of Hindu, Muslims, Sikh and Christian, its scope is different from the institutions, organisations established by the Societies Act. So even after the deletion of the word "established" the AMU Act of 1981 remains the same as it was there under the 1920 Act. So by adding the clause 5-C the AMU Amendment Act 1981 could not provide the power to reserve seats for Muslims. These clauses have to follow relevant Articles of the Constitution dealing with the fundamental rights including the Articles dealing with reservation and social justice that is why Allahabad High Courts operative part of the judgement has very clearly mentioned:

> *"However this Court is also conscious of the fact that reservations as has been applied in admissions for Muslim students only is totally unconstitutional and in the teeth of Article 29 of the Constitution"*

It further stated :

> *"The court accordingly allowed the petitions, holding that the judgement of the Supreme Court in the case of Aziz Basha still holds good even subsequent to the AMU Amendment Act 1981 (Act No. 62 of 1981) AMU is not a minority Institution within the meaning of article 30 of the Constitution of India. Therefore the University cannot provide any reservation in respect of the students belonging to a particular religious community."*

The main thrust of the Allahabad High Court Judgement is on two counts. On the first count "that reservations, as has been applied by AMU for Muslim students only, is totally unconstitutional and in the teeth of the Article 29-2 of the Constitution" It means if the AMU admission policy is not for reservation of seats for Muslim students only the learned judge would not have objected to it. But the learned judge forgot that AMU is also a Central university and Central universities, be it AMU or BHU or JNU or IIT's and IIM's, all are either Central universities or Central Institutions and Central Institutions are till now out side the reservation net.

On the second count, Justice Arun Tandon is of the firm opinion that as per the Aziz Basha V/s Union of India Judgment of the Supreme Court of India of 1968 AMU is not a minority Institution and since the AMU amendment Act of 1981 (Act No 62 of 1981) has not amended the Constitution accordingly, the AMU minority character is not "restored", hence the AMU is not a minority institution." Threfore the university cannot provide any reservation in respect of the students belonging to a particular religious minortiy."

The learned judge further adds :

> *"Subsequent to the enforcement of the University Grants Commission Act 1956 a private University can be established provided such university is granted recognition as deemed university by the University Grants Commission. Therefore to that extent minority citizens may establish a minority university subject to it being declared deemed university by the University Grants Commission".*

On both the counts the learned judge of the Allahabad High Court raised the Constitutional points about which even a former Vice Chancellor of Aligarh Muslim University also expressed doubts in the recent article in an Urdu Newspaper *"University was given its Historical character not the minority character"* He further stated in his own style that he failed to understand that why the Government of India has done what he called in Urdu *"Is mamle mein dandi Kiyon Mari"*. He further expressed doubts that the Amendment Act was not clear.

No doubt Article 29-2 and 30-1 of the Constitution of India have given the right to establish and administer the educational institutions for the minorities but this right to establish and administer the educational institutions was and is never absolute. Reservation of seats in admission and appointment of staff including non teaching staff have been discussed by several benches of the Supreme court for more than two decades.

The Aziz Basha judgement was delivered by the 5 judges Constitution bench of Supreme Court in 1968. Thereafter on the pressure of AMU students Union which spearheaded a nation wide movement for "restoration" of the minority character of Aligarh University the Congress Government at the Centre under the Prime Ministership of Smt. Indira Gandhi brought the AMU Amendment Act 1981 posing that this Amendment Act will negate the five Judges Constitution Bench judgment of 1968. But as per the Allahabad High Court Judgement of 4th October 2005, the said Amendment Act of

1981 has not changed the character of Aligarh Muslim University as held by the 1968 Constitution bench judgement of Supreme Court. Inspite of the so called restoration of minority character by the AMU Amendment Act of 1981, the University Academic Council and its Executive Council have not thought of reserving 50% seat for Muslim students particularly in its PG courses. The AMU Executive Council and its Academic Council sat with the AMU Amendment Act 1981 for more than 20 years. During this period it only formed one committee after another and after that, one fine morning the VC, the Academic Council and Executive Council came out with its admission scheme which provide 50% reservation to Muslim students in 36 courses out of 289 courses over and above seats for internal students. It may also be noted that universities are autonomous in character and there is no need to get the approval of the Government of the decisions of University Academic Council and Executive Council but AMU VC thought it necessary to get the approval of the Government.

The definition of Minority Institution is not so easy as it is understood generally by the leaders of the minority community. Whether Aligarh Muslim University still remained a minority institution even after the 1968 Supreme Court five judges Constitution bench judgment is a question to be examined in details but more important is to define the word minority itself.

After a long wait of 13 years the Government of India moved the Aligarh University Amendment Act 1981 but even after this Amendment Act the AMU Executive Council and Academic Council with hesitation decided to treat that as if the minority status of the university was 'restored' and hence consented to approve the 50% reservation for Muslim students besides the 25% reservation for internal students.

Minority educational institutions in India, particularly institutions of Muslim minorities are generally established by the elite sections of the Muslims who were either Zamidars or bureaucrats and businessmen. Social stratification among the Muslims is almost on the same line as is there in the Hindus. This social stratification is confirmed by the Census Reports of

1901 on-words. Encyclopedia Britannica & Americana also confirm it. Muslim Ulema from Mufti Shafee Deobandi and Maulana Ashraf Ali Thanvi to Maulana Ahmad Raza Khan of Bariilvi School all confirm this division between Ashraf and Ajlaf-Arzal.

The Constitution of India also recognizes this divide between socially and educationally backward sections and those who are socially forward. The Supreme Court while confirming the Mandal Commission report very clearly categorised this division and enlisted them in the socially and educationally backward section of minorities. Even the Constitution Review Commission headed by Padam Vibhushan Justice Venkat Challaiah confirmed this categorisation in the following words:

Under chapter 10-11-1 after dealing with the disadvantage sections he said.

> *"In this context it is also to be noted that the bulk of the religious minorities consists of castes and communities which are included in the list of socially and educationally backward classes. They are mainly counterparts of Hindu Backward Classes and to some extent of Hindu scheduled castes."*

> *"At present the political representation of Minority Communities in legislature specially Muslims has fallen well below their proportion of population.* ***The proportion of BC's among them is next to nil."***

> *"Backward Classes belonging to religious minorities who have been identified and included in the list of backward classes and who in fact constitute the bulk of the population of religious minorities should be taken up with special care."*

Besides this the leader of now what is called Muslim Reservation Movement Mr. Zafaryab Jeelani also accepts this division.

In the name of minority status of a University or institution the socially and educationally backward category of Muslims who constitute bulk of the minorities be it Muslim, Christian or Sikh and are included in the list of backward classes will be deprived of their due share in the admission and Jobs in teaching and non-teaching staff of these institutions and if a way could not be found for proper representation of these deprived sections of the minorities be it Aligarh Muslim University or any other institution established by the minorities, the backward classes among the minorities who are included in the list of backward classes will have no option but to take up the matter with the Supreme Court through a SLP. Being an aggrieved party it may also oppose reservation in admission granted to Muslims without providing due share to socially and educationally backward sections of the Muslims who are included in the list of backward classes and whose population ratio among the Muslims is more than three fourth of the Muslim population.

The representation of socially and educationally backward Muslims in every sphere of life is almost nil. Begin with the Aligarh Muslim University itself, how many Vice-Chancellors of AMU were from this category of Muslims till date? The overwhelming dominance of its Executive council by what is called the Ashraf category of Muslim is also a fact which could not be denied. Almost same is the position of Registrars of this University. Now coming to the Presidents of its students union. It will not be an easy job to find out a union president who is from the "Backward classes belonging to religious minorities, who have been identified and included in the list of backward classes, who in fact constitute the bulk of population of religious minorities" Almost same is the position of this category of Muslims among the teaching and non-teaching staff.

In this context now examine the position of socially and educationally backward Muslims who are identified and included in the list of Backward Classes in the judiciary. At present no Muslim Judge is there in the Supreme Court. But no one cares to take up the matter with the present UPA Government. Out of 524 judges of High Courts only 27 are Muslims and out of the 27 Muslim judges not more than 3 visibly belong to non-Ashraf category of Muslims. (Source Muslim World Law Review Jamiat Law Institute journal issue one) the sequnes are only upto April 2005.

Leaving aside Vice-Chancellors of Aligarh Muslim University among the Muslim Vice-Chancellor through out India including Jamia Millia Islamia and Jamia Hamdard not more than three VC,s from what is called "*Aqwame Razila*" is visible. The visibility of Muslim Governors from 1947 onwards is almost nil. Every where "*Aqwame Sharifa*"s domination is visible.

From 1st to 14th Lok Sabha around 7500 members were elected but out of this only around 400 Muslims in all could be elected and out of this 400 Muslim members of Lok Sabha around 340 are from elite or Ashraf Muslims and only around 60 are from Ajlaf-Arzal category. The population ratio between Ashraf and non-Ashraf is three fourth and one fourth (Even Syed Shahabuddin recognises it) It comes to that 75% non-Ashraf Muslim Population is getting 15% representation while 25% Ashraf population is getting 85% representation. Same is the story every where be it Aligarh Muslim University, Supreme Court or High Courts, Parliament and State legislatures. In All India and State civil services a little change is visible after the reservation dicta was adopted consequent to 1992 Supreme Court Judgement.

Before concluding I would like to restate that socially and educationally backward Muslims who in fact constitute the bulk of the population of Muslims and according to a conservative estimate their population among Muslims is not less than 75 per cent will fail to get commensurate representation in a university or other minority institution. Government of India and Supreme Court should also consider this aspect with all seriousness.

To conclude finally only a Comprehensive Constitutional amendment could remove the contradictions between different Articles of the Constitution particularly Articles 29, 30 and 15 and 16 otherwise fruitless exercise of the Supreme Courts from five Judges bench to seven Judges bench and from seven Judges bench to nine Judges bench and from nine Judges bench to eleven Judges bench will go on without coming to any final conclusion.

In the light of above facts the 'restoration' of minority character means the restoration or bringing back the dominance of Ashraf category of Muslims not only in all the effective positions of AMU and other minority educational institution, established even by an Act of Parliament or State legislature or by the Societies Registration Act of Centre and State Reservation of seats in admission for Muslims in PG or other classes be it 50% or above, without any scheme for providing reservation to socially and educationally backward sections of Muslims "who are identified and included in the list of backward classes" will be against the sprit of the Constitution of India. Government of India should also take notice of this aspect before filing a SLP to the Supreme Court or a revision petition before the High Court.

In this connection it will not be out of place to mention few facts about the mind set of Sir Syed Ahmad Khan the founder of Aligarh Movement. The world famous anthropologist Marc Gaborieau writes in his book about Sir Syed Ahmad Khan.

> *"Syed Ahmad Khan spearhead of Muslim thought in Indian sub-continent in the last century was an Ashraf working for the welfare of the Ashraf. He used to say that his Aligarh college was not for weavers".*

In his book *"Asbabe Baghawate-Hind"* Sir Syed openly hated *"budzat Julahe"*. Further Sir Syed Ahmad Khan in a letter to Badruddin Tayyab Jee the first Muslim Congress president advising him to disassociate himself from the presidentship of Congress party because Congress is a Hindu organisation is also on record. He is also on record that his Aligarh College is for Ashraf only. These facts are also confirmed by no less a person than renowned socialist thinker Late Madhu Limay.

It seems that Sir Syeds thinking about the division of Muslim community between Ashraf and non-Ashraf and his favour towards what the Ulema called *"Aqwame Sharifa"* and his harted for *"Aqwame Razila"* still dominates in Aligarh Muslim University. Reservation of seats for Muslims be it 50% or more in practice means taking away the share of socially and educationally Backward Muslims guaranteed by the Constitution of India and relevant judgements of Supreme Court.

Will *"The Aqwame Sharifa"* provide necessary safeguards to what they called *"Aqwame Razila"* that they will get commensurate share not only in admission in course of minority educational institution including Aligarh Muslim University but also in jobs of its teaching and non-teaching staff? The minority status means right to administer a minority institution by all section of minorities and minority includes the socially and educationally backward sections of the minorities (here it means Muslims) who are included in the list of backward classes and whose population ratio among the Muslims is more than three fourth of the Muslim population. It is but natural that if an agreement is reached between the "*Aqwame Sharifa*" and "*Aqwame Razila*" neither the Supreme Court nor the Government of India will have any objection to it. "*Aqwame Sharifa*" should also see that their "*Aqwame Razila*" brethren also get representation in the governing bodies i.e. Court and Executive Council commensurate to their population.

*A general debate has stirred up on the revival of minority character of the Muslim University Aligarh and on reservation in admission in 36 Professional Courses for its students. At one side Sangh Parivar is looking at it with their own eye glasses and has taken the matter to the Court of law and at the other side the leftists have sighted it with their point of view. The Ministry of Human Resources Development of the Govt. of India is sitting aloof putting the whole responsibility on the Vice-Chancellor. When an M.P. asked for clarification of the matter from the HRD Ministry their superior Officers sailed clear stating that whatever has been done it is the sole doing of the V.C. and that no office Memorundum has been issued by their Ministry. As for the revival of the minority character of the AMU neither any amendment has been incorporated in the 1981 Act in this respect nor a Memorandum has been issued. Yet the executive Committee of the AMU on its own fine morning revived the minority chacter, Under this minority status the Executive Committee and the Academic Council have reserved 50% seats in 36 out of 289 courses for Muslims. Over and above it 25.00% and 5.00% seats have been set at the discretion of the V.C. for internal students.*

*Matter, like Aligarh Muslim University, Urdu and Babri Masjid have, for quite some time, emotionally occupied the psyche of the Muslims of India. On these matters the attention of Muslims is vastly focussed. Added to it is now the reservation to Muslims issue too. A section of the Muslims which is very small in population, has come on roads taking up these emotional issues and demands 10.00% reservation for Ashraf Muslims alongwith "Other Muslims". It is surprising that some serious people who are considered versed in law and Constitution have, in search of new emotional issues, stood up with this issue. They know well that issues of Babri or Urdu no more can cause explosion. Hence they have seized with both hands the opportunity to join campaign for reservation to all Muslims. The Sangh Parivar is also convinced that the issues of Babri Masjid Common Civil Code and Article 370 were no more of any effect to its vote bank. The Kashmir and Indo-Pak relations have taken a different turn. Under this background the Sangh Parivar was looking for some issue. Hence, Muslim appeasement bypassing the Hindus has taken an importance of great potentiality. With this common view point extremists and reactionaries of both sides have not only taken this emotional issue to roads but are knocking at the doors of judiciary. Emotion has its own importance and utility yet at times emotions do screen wisdom.*

It is still not clear whose action, that of Parliament or Govt. has revived that minority character of Aligarh Muslim University. But Secret cannot last long because the matter has already been referred to the Court and now the Administration of the Muslim University alongwith the HRD Ministry shall have to elucidate to the Court as to when the order or the office Memorandum was issued on this matter and also since when the minority character was revived; and if this right was available under the Act of 1981 whose hindrance came in the way of granting reservation to Muslim students. Whose negligence was responsible that the job could not be accomplished so far ? To what extent the University is responsible and how far the HRD Ministry shares it ? These things must be exposed.

Revival of minority character and reservation to Muslim students in admission is a separate issue for legal and Constitutional dissension. From High Court to Supreme Court many a judgement has been pronounced. Concurrence of the Apex Court is yet to come on issues like the nature of the institution, extent of administrative power of the Management, what are the rules and laws for the appointment of teachers and for admission of Students and how for the State and Central

Govts. could interfere. Some times 5 member Bench pronounces a judgement which does not clarify the issues, then the matter is referred to 7 Member Bench. Even then the matter remained unexplained and was sent to the 11 Member Constitution Bench in 1977. The Constitution Bench of 11 Members too could not clear the contradictions and complications. In turn the case went to a 5 Member Bench for pronouncing clarification. The Complications and Contradictions, however, did not go and as for now the Constitutional and legal position of minority educational institutions remains still unresolved legally and Constitutionally. Against this background the case before the Allahabad High Court can be seen. It is feared that this case will too go to the Supreme Court. We will see if any solution of vexed problem comes out or becomes prey to more complications.

Legal debate and discussion will go on in the High Court and Supreme Court. There is a social aspect as well which has never occurred in any discussion whatsoever. Muslim minority or for that matter Christian or Sikh minority all are divided in two sections. One section of minorities is that which is included in list of Backward classes while the other section is out side. No one derives that be it Muslim minority, Christian or Sikh minority all have social classification and this classification has beenaccepted by our Constitution. Mandal Commission specified it in its Report and the Supreme Court too has, in very clear terms, specified through its 9 judge Constitutional Bench. Recently the Constitution Revision Commission under Justice Venkat Chalaiya has also confirmed it in a very clear manner. This Commission has said in Para 10-11-2 of its Report, "(c) Now it requires serious consideration as to what rules and regulations are being framed for admission or recruitment of teachers and employees to the minority institutions for this (B.C.) section particularly Muslim B.Cs. these sections of the minority forms more than three fourth of the total minority population. These sections of the minority are not only socially backward but there are no two opinions about their educational and economic backwardness. After reservation of 50.00% seats in admission to students Aligarh Muslim University and other minority educational institutions will have to consider what treatment with be meted out to such sections which are included in the list of Backward Classes. Are they in a position to compete with the students who belong to educationally and socially advanced class. The relief granted to them by the Constitution is being snatched away in the name of minority institutions. This should not be forgotten that these sections are very important part and parcel of the Minority Community and the Constitution and the judiciary have specified them to be within Minorities. Their right can not be deried in the 50.00% of reservation in Muslim University. The Executive Council needs give serious consideration to the representation in admissions of these Sections. Prime Minster Man Mohan Singh should also send special directions in this respect to his HRD Ministry because this very Ministry has granted approval to the admission scheme of A.M.U. Though in the list of O.B.Cs, the Backward section is more than three fourth of the total population of the minority, particularly Muslim minority yet the AMU needs to move necessary amendments in its admission Scheme in order to provide reservation of two-thirds out of 50% seats in admission to these Backward Section of Muslims so that students of these sections may get reservation benefit near to their proportion in population.

If the vice-chancellor of the AMU, the Executive council and the Academic Council do not grant separate seats to the students of these Backward Sections of Muslims, it will be naturally concluded the 100 year old prejudice of Sir Syed Ahmad Khan, the founder of the University, still persists. No one can deny that Sir Syed founded this institution to cater to the educational need of Muslim Ashraf (elites) and he never tried to hide this fact. Madhu Limye has cited it in reference to his own collection of articles and the renowned anthropologist Mark Gaboriean has put it in very clear words, *"Sir Syed Ahmad Khan who was a leading person of Muslim Thought in the Indian Sub continent was such on Ashraf who worked only for the benefit of Ashraf. He used to say that his Aligarh College was not for julahas."*

If the V.C. and the Executive of AMU are still under the influence of such views then nothing is to be said. But Congress led U.P.A. Govt. and more particularly the Chairperson of UPA, Shrimati Sonia Gandhi and the Prime Minster Man Mohan Singh must pay attention.........The University is still under the influence of Sir Syed's conclusion so they will never give importance to it. But Congress and UPA should not ignore it and way has to be found out for the share of reservation to the Backward Muslims alongwith Dalit Muslim and those enumerated in the B.C. list in proportion to their population. other wise reservation would only mean reservation for Ashraf leaving the bulk of population of the Backwards in the lurch.

# 21

# MUSLIM RESERVATION IN ANDHRA PRADESH

*Ashfaq Husain Ansari*

The Andhra Pradesh Government on the basis of recommendations of Commissioner of Minorities Welfare issued orders vide G.O. Ms. No. 33 Backward Classes Welfare Department dated 18-11-2004 providing 5% (five per cent) reservations in educational institutions and employment in the state over and above the reservations presently available to the Backward Classes and some sections of the Muslim Minorities to be treated as Backward Classes under Category "E" inaddition to the existing A,B,C,D Categories.

This G.O. no. 33 was however challenged in the High Court of Andhra Pradesh, Hyderabad by writ Pittion's Nos. 12239, 12552, 12653, 13059 & 13113 of 2004. The Honourable High Court of Andhra Pradesh "after Considering the fact and circumstances of the case has viewed that the impugned G.O. Ms. No. 33 is unsustainable". In one of my articles on the subject of Andhra Muslim reservation my observation was clear:

> *"Now coming to Andhra Pradesh G.O. No. 33 it may not be out of place to mention that it is based on a report by the 'Commissioner for Commessionarate of Minorities Welfare dated 05-07-2004', and This report was not placed before the Andhra Pradesh Backward Classes Commission, the only required statutory authority as per Supreme Court nine Judges Constitution bench judgement of Nov. 1992, for inclusion of any Community in the OBC Category"*

As required the Hon. High Court directed the State Government to reconstitute the State Backward Classes Commission which was not functioning for more than two years and place before it the impugned G.O. Ms. No. 33 with necessary materials. The State Backward Classes Commission after examining the same shall submit a report within four months for taking necessary action by the Government and the Government has to pass appropriate orders within a period of three months thereafter, considering the dicta laid down by the Supreme Court in Indra Sawhney Case.

The A.P. Backward Classes Commission was reconstituted Vide G.O. Ms. No. 57 and assumed charge on 22-11-04, and submitted its report on 14-06-05 to the Government. After considering the recommendations of the A.P. Commission for Backward Classes the Governor of Andhra Pradesh promulgated "Andhra Pradesh Reservation of seats in the Educational Institutions and appointments of posts in the public services under the State to Muslim Community Ordinance 2005" Thereafter the Government of Andhra Pradesh has notified that the Muslims residing in the State (other than Dudekula, Laddaf, Pinjari/Noorbash and Mehtar) as Socially and Educationally Backward and include them in the list of Backward Classes under separate Category "E" (which shall be in addition to the existing "A", "B", "C" and "D" Categories). Accordingly a notification was issued for publication in the extraordinary issue of A.P. Gazette dated 25th June 2005" to provide 5% (five per cent) reservation in educational institutions and employment in the state over and above the reservations presently available to the Backward Classes under Category "E" in addition to the existing A, B, C, D Categories.

In Andhra Pradesh the groups, castes and percentage of reservations under existing categories A, B, C and D are as under:

| **Groups** | | |
|---|---|---|
| (A) | (38 Castes)Aboriginal Tribes, Vimukta Jatis Nomadic & Semi-nomadic Tribes | 7% |
| (B) | (21Castes)Vocational (occupational groups) | 10% |

| | | |
|---|---|---|
| (C) | (1 Caste)Harijan Converts from Christianity) | 1% |
| (D) | (33 Castes)Other Backward Classes | 7% |
| | Total 93 Castes | 25% |

Now with this Notification of 25th June 2005 5% reservation for Muslim Community is added to the existing 25% OBC reservation bringing the total OBC reservation to 30% (thirty per cent) (21 per cent reservation for SC and ST already exist there surpassing the limit of total reservation of 50%) Besides surpassing the 50% limit which is provided under the 'dicta' of Supreme Court Indra Sawhney Case. The report of A.P. Backward Classes Commission is not made available even after the right to Information Act was passed recently by the Parliament on the pretex that it will be made public only after placing it before the A.P. Assembly. The report is said to be based almost on the earlier "in depth study on the Socio-Economic and Educational Conditions of Muslim Community in the State" it is presumed that "this in depth study" could not provide the basis for declaring a Community on the whole as Socially and Educationally Backward. No doubt 65% of the Muslims of A.P. may be living below the poverty line and also the literacy rate of Muslim Minorities as per the in depth study is only 18% But, the 2001 census figure is quite contradictory. According to the census report of 2001 the literacy rate of Andhra Pradesh Muslims is recorded as 68% and that of Christians it is 75.3 and for the Hindus it is just 59.4. At present there is no barometer to gauge the social Backwardness of a community. But going through the history of Andhra Pradesh one can find easily that dominant part of the present Andhra Pradesh was part of the princely State of Hyderabad and during the rule of Nizam dynesty particularly elite Muslims of Hyderabad were Socially and Educationally more advanced in comparison to Muslims of other regions. The Muslims of Hyderabad princely State were and are Socially and Educationally more advanced than the Muslims of the neighboring States who were not part of the princely State of Hyderabad. One may agree that the general Muslim population of the present state of Andhra Pradesh is poor in comparison to the Noble elite population of the princely State. The inclusion of these elites in the list of Socially and Educationally Backward Classes could not be justified by any unbiased survey. For further in-depth study on this count one may scrutinise the list of Muslim MPs and MLAs of this area and will find that from the Nizam period down this day no Backward Muslim could find a place in the Lok Sabha or Assembly. The educational position of Muslims is evident from the 2001 Census Report and if the majority of the population of a state is not educationally Backward all the population of the community cannot be treated as socially Backward. The elite or Ashraf Muslims of Andhra Pradesh particularly of that part of the Andhra Pradesh which was part of princely region of Hyderabad cannot be decleared socially backward. Hence the decision of A.P. Government in declaring all Muslims of Andhra Pradesh as socially and Educationally Backward could not be justified.

Now let us examine how far the A.P. Government gave consideration to the dicta laid down by the Supreme Court in Indra Sawhney Case.

The first dicta is what Justice Sawant, the concurring judge of the Nine judges Constitution bench judgement has very clearly defined in para 552.

> *"552-The backward class of citizens referred to in Article 16(4) is the socially backward class of citizens whose educational and economic backwardness is on account of their social backwardness. A caste itself may constitute a class. However in order to constitute a backward class the caste concerned must be socially backward and its educational and economic backwardness must be on account of its social backwardness.*
> *The economic criterion by itself cannot identify a class as backward unless the economic backwardness of the class is on account of its social backwardness."*

Not a single person or organisation has yet contradicted this criteria of identification of Backwardness of a caste or class or community. Justice Sawant has very clearly explained that "the economic criterion by itself cannot identify a class as backward unless the economic backwardness of the class is on account of its social backwardness." In the same paragraph Justice Sawant begins with "The backward class of citizens referred to in the Article 16(4) is the socially backward class of citizens whose educational and economic backwardness is on account of their social backwardness". So social Backwardness is the first and foremost criteria for judging an individual group or community as backward, that means that if an individual or a group or a Community is not socially backward they cannot be declared backward even if they are educationally and economically backward. In the same judgement Justice Pandian also one of the concurring judge has further elucidated in paragraph 92.

> *"92- As per the statistics given in the Report of the Second Backward Classes Commission in Tamil Nadu out of 27,05,960 people belonging to Muslim minorities 25,60,195 are included in the list which works out to 94.61% of the total Muslim population of the State. Si milarly, among Christians, out of 31,91.988 of the total population 25,48,148 are included in the backward list which worksout to 79.83%."*

It means that even if 94.61 per cent of the total Muslim population or 79.83 per cent of the population of Christian community are qualified to be included in the list of Backward Classes, the whole community cannot be declared backward.

The people who propagate that whole community can be declared backward or brought in the list of backward classes should minutely study these paragraphs of Indra Sawhney Judgement. They may point out that in the same judgement it is there that a whole community in a region or state may be declared backward if the whole community is socially and educationally backward. It is clear from the paragraph quoted above that even if in a community 94.61% is socially backward the whole community cannot be declared backward.

Individuals and organisations who are in favour of reservation of Muslim community as a socailly and educationally backward community often quote the example of Karnataka and Kerala state governments. According to them Karnataka and Kerala state governments include all Muslims in their list of Backward Classes. But the fact of the matter is that Karnataka list is not yet cleared by the Supreme Court and judicial scrutiny. While scrutinising the Karnataka and Kerala list The National Commission of Backward Classes added the word "other Muslims excluding" in both the Karnataka and Kerala list. Those excluded in the Karnataka list are mentioned on page 20 and serial No. 125. "Other Muslims excluding Kacchi Memon, Nayayat Bohra, Bhuraya, Borha, Saiyed, Sheikh, Pathan, Mughal, Mahad Yoma, Mohadi Konkani and Gomti Muslim, Similarly on Serial No. 46 of the Kerala list it is mentioned "Other Muslims excluding" Bohra, Kachi Momon, Nayayats, Turkan, Dakhni Muslims". Thaugal and Koya are already out of the list of Backward Classes in Kerala.

Besides this more than 76 per cent reservation in the Karnataka Backward Classes list could not be cleared by the constitutional procedure of putting them under the protection of 9th shedule of the Constitution. These are the truth of reservation of Muslims as a community in the state of Karnataka and Kerala. Can one imagine that all Muslims of a state, be it, Karnataka, Kerala and now Andhra Pradesh are socially Backward, and if all Muslims are not socially Backward they cannot find place in the list of Backward Classes of these States or any other State of India, however educationally and economically Backward they may be.

One should judge the notification of Andhra Pradesh Government in the light of the facts mentioned above. The Andhra High Court has already referred the matter to a five member bench. Let us wait and see the process of Judicial scrutiny from High Court to Supreme Court.

# 22

# RESERVATION FOR MUSLIM BACKWARDS: A REJOINDER TO SYED SHAHABUDDIN

*Ashfaq Husain Ansari*

"Reservation for Muslims is constitutional and socially necessary in national context" is the caption of the "frank rejoinder" by my learned colleague, former Member of Parliament, former IFS and President of All India Muslim Majlise Mushawrat and now a leader of Congress Party, Syed Shahabuddin. My thanks are due to Mr. Anis Chishti, the editor of "Alp-Jan" a reputed English language quarterly on minority affairs published form Delhi, who reproduced the introduction of the book titled "Basic Problems of Backward Muslims" edited by me and also the article of Prof. D.L. Sheth, which is also reproduced from the same book. Actually the article of Prof. Sheth was reproduced by me from Times of India published more than five years ago. The book "Basic Problems of Backward Muslims" was also sent to Syed Shahabuddin in April itself at his East end Apartment, Mayur Vihar I, address. But I do not know what provoked him for the "frank rejoinder" in English and Urdu news papers. However, my thanks are due to my learned friend for not only highlighting the issue of Muslim reservation but also highlighting my point of view, of course with his own interpretation. So far as the head line of Milli Gazette is concerned it could have been more appropriate and acceptable if it was "Reservation for Muslim Backwards is constitutional and socially necessary in National Context."

From Syed Shahabuddin's "frank rejoinder" I came to know that my article really hurt him too much otherwise he would not have charged me for launching "such a pernicious and divisive campaign against the Muslim community". I have never rejected to the idea of Muslim unity, but certainly I am not for any unity at the cost of present benefits provided to the Backward Muslims through OBC reservation. He rightly observed "He seems to think that reservation in public employment for the Muslim Community as a whole will be harmful to the interest of the backward sub-communities because they will lose what they are getting under the Mandal regime and they will be marginalised by the so called 'Ashraf'. So they would be losers in balance." He further states "This is practical wisdom, no doubt, because a bird in hand is always better than two in the bush. If this was at the back of his mind his diffidence in joining the common cause of the community would be well understood". He claims to have understood my mind but I fail to understand his mindset when he reads "something more to it than what appears at the surface".

My article in question consists of three parts. Syed Shahabuddin has reacted only on part one, Part two deals with the Dalit Muslims i.e. about those Muslims whose Hindu counter parts are included in Scheduled castes but Muslims and Christians are debarred from inclusion in the scheduled castes list not by the regular Articles of the Constitution of India but by "Presidential (Scheduled Caste) order of 1950". The third part is the opinion of NCRWC headed by Justice Venkat Challiah. But my learned friend altogether ignored the other two parts.

Regarding his "Religious Minorities as Backward Classes" subsection, I have to say only this much. He discusses about the well authenticated records of the Constituent Assembly debates and the first draft of the Constitution. Prof. Iqbal Ahmad Ansari also quoted the verbatim report of the debate in his article on Andhra Muslim Reservation in the Milli Gazette and elsewhere. With this regard I would like to repeat what I have said earlier that debate of the Constituent Assembly, Parliament or State legislatures are, after all debates, but what matters Constitutionally is the out-come of the debate, the Constitution or the Acts of Parliament and State legislature. My learned Advocate friend very well understands this practical proposition.

"Aasman Doobe Huway Taron Ka Matam Kab Talak...." Later on Syed Shahabuddin claims that "The Supreme Court in the Indra Sawhny Judgement clearly states that a religious community may also be categorized as a Backward Class. He further states that Venkata Challiah Commission which has sated that grant of reservation to the "Muslims, Hindus, Sikhs or Christians" if they constitute Backward Class" does not require amendment to the Constitution. There are no two opinions on this count. Nine Judges Constitution bench Judgement is also of the same opinion. The real point of difference is on "if they constitute a Backward Class". Muslims like Sikhs, Christians and Hindus are broadly divided into Backward and non-Backward classes. The elite section and Ashraf section of Muslim Ulema claims that there is no cateogorisation between Ashraf and non-Ashrafs i.e. Ajlaf and Arzal, among Muslims. They should know that the word Ashraf, Ajlaf and Arzal are not derived from Sanskrit or Hindi language. They are Arabic words and are in usage from earliest period. It indicates that the division between Ashraf, Ajlaf and Arzal was, and is in practice in Arab Society. Sheikh-ul-Islam Mohammed bin Abdul Wahab in his book 'Deen Ke Teen Aham Usool' also confirms this. Indian Muslim Ulema, Maulana Ashraf Ali Thanvi, Mufti Mohd. Shafee and also Maulana Ahmad Raza Khan Bareilvi not only confirm this division but use pernicious and derogative words for all Ajlaf and Arzals, (See Nehayatul Erab fee Ghayatun-Nasab extracts published in Zindagia-Nau, August, 2000).

Now, Syed Shahabuddin himself should decide who has divided the Muslim Community-The Muslim Ulema or an ordinary person like me.

Syed Shahabuddin's admission that 'Backward Muslims of U.P. constitute at least 75% of 16% i.e. 12% of the state population' while recognising the 75% of Muslims as backwards he wants to know from me as to what percentage of them are getting benefits in U.P. Services. It is nobody's claim that Backward Muslim are getting 50% of seats i.e. 6% in U.P. Civil or police services. He knows the position better than any one else because he was founder editor of Muslim India, a monthly Journal of Research, Documentation and Reference. I would like to know from the founder editor the position of Muslim representation on the whole in both Houses of Parliament and state legislatures and out of the total representation of Muslims in these bodies what is the percentage of representation of Backward Muslims whose percentage of population, according to him is, 75% of the total Muslim population. He should tell the world frankly that more than 75% of the seats in these decision making bodies are captured by the Ashraf Muslims and only remaining less than 25% of seats are filled by the category of Muslims who are Ajlaf and Arzal or non-Ashraf. He should also state the position of representation of Ansaris out of this less than 25% representation of Backward Muslims. No Ansari could be elected in 11th, 12th and 13th Lok Sabha. Only one Ansari could enter the present Lok Sabha out of 36. Muslim Representation of Ansaris in state legislatures was also less than 5% of the total Muslim population. Non-Ansari Muslim backward repres entation was always better than Ansari representation in these bodies. But I have never raised the issue of Ansari representation. I always raised the issue of Backward Muslims under representation, but Syed Shahabuddin and persons of his mind set always paint this picture that Ansaris are grabbing all the facilities of O.B.C. while other Backward Muslims are deprived. While giving a certificate to Ansaris "They were pampered for their nationalist record while the so called Ashraf who largely associated themselves with the Muslim League politics and later with the Pakistan Movement were left high and dry". No doubt the historical facts came from his per but for the purpose to express his heart felt but biased feeling about the Ansaris and with ulterior motive of dividing the Muslim OBCs. He accused me of "drumming up support for the Muslim OBCs because he wants the relatively forward Ansaris to lord it over the other Muslim OBCs. In the end his real ulterior motive comes out of his bag, drumming separate quota for other Muslim OBCs excluding these Ansaris". Although earlier he posed a question "If Mr. Ansari wants a separate quota for Muslim OBCs, say of 6% in U.P. I would support him". No doubt every OBC Muslim desires separate OBC quota for all OBC Muslims but will oppose tooth and nail the motive of Syed Shahabuddin to divide the OBC Muslims. After all he belongs to ruling class and ruling caste, and ruling class believes and practices the policy of divide and rule. It is for the OBC Muslims to give befitting reply to the lord of ruling Muslim elite class by uniting themselves.

I leave it to the readers of Milli Gazatte to decide who is perniciously launching the division of Backward Muslim Category. His (Syed Shahabuddin's) main ambition now is to create division among Backward Muslims and rule.

In fact Backward Muslims are not opposed to reservation to Ashraf section of Muslims but they are certainly opposed to "bundling of the unequals" together. If the Constitution approves provision of reservation under separate category other than OBC for forward or Ashraf Muslims, their backward brothers will support it whole heartedly. Syed Shahabuddin himself opposes the "bundling of unequals" theory and he will agree that Sheikhs, Syeds, Mughals and Pathans and socially educationally and also economically superior to the Ajlaf and Arzal groups of Muslims. Let my learned friend who is also a legal expert suggest any way out for reservation of Ashraf Muslims under separate category which could be provided to them, other than OBC.

About Muslim reservation of Kerala, Karnatak, Manipur and Tamil Nadu. I have already explained it in my above referred book. There is no reservation for all Muslims in Karnatak and Kerala. In Tamil Nadu only Tamil speaking Muslims are included in backward list excluding one Urdu speaking. In Manipur, all Muslims are not included in backward list. In Kerala the word used is "All Muslims excluding" and those excluded in Karnataka are "Kachi Memos, Navayat, Bohra, Bhunaya, Borha, Saiyad, Sheikh, Pathan, Mughal, Mahad

Yoma, Mohadadi, Kokani or Gomti Muslim". In Kerala those excluded are, "Bohra, Kachchi Memon, Nayayats, Turkan and Dakhni Muslim" (Source National Commission of Backward Classes).

Inspite of all his venomous writing Syed Shahabuddin will not be able to achieve his cherished goal of creating division and misunderstandings among the Backward Muslims. No doubt Ansari Muslims are the target of all his attack in his "frank rejoinder" but his main object is to create division among the OBC Muslims who are included in the list of OBC category. The fact of the matter is that Muslims are categorised in two broad divisions. This division is confirmed by Encyclopaedia Britannica and Encyclopaedia Americana and also not only by Muslim Ulema but also by Prof. D.L. Sheth and Prof. Imitiaz Ahmad, the nationally known sociologists. Even Syed Shahabuddin himself confirms this division and categorisation.

Through his last sentence while dealing with my article he wants to play the heinous game of dividing the OBC Muslims. I do not know what made him understand that Ansaris are the main beneficiaries of the OBC Muslim quota. The fact is just the reverse. I am placing positive facts for his perusal. Let us first examine the position of representation of Ansaris in the lower house of Indian Parliament. The authentic date is as under. From 1st to Fourteenth Lok Sabha 396 Muslims of both the Ashraf and non-Ashraf categories were elected, out of which only 14 were Ansaris. 1st and 2nd Lok Sabha had no Ansari representation. In each of the 3rd, 4th, 5th and 6th Lok Sabha only one Ansari could be elected while 7th Lok Sabha had 5 as the highest ever number of Ansari representation and 8th had only 3 Ansaris. In 9th Lok Sabha Ansari representation came down to zero while 10th Lok Sabha had only one Ansari. In 11th, 12th and 13th Lok Sabha Ansari representation again came down to zero. The present Lok Sabha (14th) has only one representation. According to Syed Shahabuddin's own assesment 75% of the Muslim population belongs to OBC category and remaining 25% are from Ashraf category i.e. Sheikh, Syed, Moghal, Pathan. Out of this 75% OBC Muslim population around half of them, or say more than 35% of the

Muslims, consists of Ansaris who according to him are the main beneficiaries of the OBC quota. But on the other hand the facts of the Lok Sabha OBC Muslim representation and among them Ansari representation are just reserve. No doubt, Muslim representation in Lok Sabha is below the percentage of its population. Out of around seven thousand five hundred members from 1st to 14th Lok Sabha only about four hundred Muslims could get elected. If for calculation sake Muslim population is counted as 12%, then only 6.25% of Muslims got elected in the Lok Sabha. Out of this only 14Ansari and around 46 OBC Muslims could get representation in 1st to 14th Lok Sabha, roughly the figure comes to 60 OBC Muslims out of 400 all Muslim elected to Lok Sabha. That is to say that out of 75% OBC Muslim population only 15% could get representation in Lok Sabha and 60% representation is cornered by 25% Ashraf or non-OBC section of the Muslims.

Before concluding it may not be out of place to write a few lines about the census Report 2001. No doubt "Muslims are in a state of socio economic decline" but the important factor to note is that more than 75% Muslims belong to OBC category whose socio-economic condition is worse than the scheduled castes Tribes and the figures derived by census report includes this category. The scenario would he entirely different if the condition of remaining Muslims (Non-OBCs) is looked into separately.

Now I leave it to the readers to decide which section of the Muslims are grossly under represented and which section of the Muslims is over represented among them. Almost same is the position of representation of Muslims in general in state legislatures, public services, in admissions, in educational institutions, and in decision making bodies of Government and political parties. Finally I conclude with a quotation from NCRWC headed by justice Venkat Challiah which was part of my article published by "Alp-Jan" and which hurt my learned colleague Syed Shahabuddin very much:

> *"At present the political representation of minorities especially Muslims in legislature has fallen much below the proportion of their population. The proportion of BCs among them is next to nil.*

Backward Classes belonging to religious minorities, who have been identified and included in the list of backward classes and who in fact constitute the bulk of the population of religious minorities should be taken up with special care along with their Hindu counterparts in the developmental efforts for the backward classes."

# 23

# RESERVATION FOR BACKWARD MUSLIMS —REJOINDER TO PROF. IQBAL A. ANSARI

*Ashfaq Husain Ansari*

"Reservation for Muslims of backwardness and discrimination" is the caption of the article of my learned academician friend Prof. Iqbal Ahmad Ansari appeared in The Milli Gazette dated 1-15 November 2004. The Learned Professor has dealt at length with different aspects of reservation with reference to Mandal Report, The Supreme Court nine judges Constitution bench historic judgement, and justice Venkat Challiah's NCRWC Report. Since in his article he has honoured me by taking my name at four or five places I am morally bound to elucidate my point of view so that there may not be any misunderstanding. Before going into little details I would like to make it clear that interpretation of a Report or Constitution itself differs from individual to individual. It is general practice of the honourable judges of the bench, High Court or Supreme Court, to concur or dissent to the same judgement. Even Mandal Commission Report incorporates a dissent report and even in the Nine Judges Supreme Court historic judgement, Justice SR Padian and P.B. Sawant had differed on many points but concurred on the main Judgement, while Dr. T.K. Thommen, Kuldeep Singh and R.M. Sahai honourable Judges dissented by their separate Judgements. A common man and an ordinary person like me cannot dare to *"expose the ignorance"* of a learned academician.

Para 83 of the Supreme Court Judgement of Mandal Report which he quoted is part of the Judgement on Mandal Report of Justice Pandian one of the concurring judges which reads as under :

> *"83. True the caste system is predominantly known in Hindu society and runs through the entire fabric of the social structure. Therefore, The caste criterion cannot be divested from the other established and agreed criteria in identifying and ascertaining the backward classes."*

Prof. Ansari's case is "Though the bulk of the present day Indian Muslims is of indigenous origin, who continued to suffer deprivation after joining the Muslim fold owing to continuity of their low esteemed occupation after independence". He further states that "this bulk alongwith the Indian Muslims of non-indigenous origin has been collectively facing the disadvantages of discrimination, exclusion and even periodic violence for their being bearers of common Muslim religious identity irrespective of their, class, occupation, biradari, sect and regional linguistic ethinic variations". No body can differ from what he calls his case but where one differs is that "Muslims of indigenous origin suffer from deprivation after joining the Muslim fold owing to the continuity of their low esteemed occupation." This bulk is what Mandal and our Constitution call" socially backward". Most of this section of socially Backward Muslims are also educationally and economically backward, and for this socially educationally and economically backward section of Minorities NCRWC Report has dealt in detail which I need not quote here because I have already quoted them earlier in Andhra Muslim reservation and rejoinder to Syed Shahabuddin. My case is that so far reservation of Muslims under socially and educationally deprived category whom Prof. Ansari categorised "Muslims of indigenous origin" should only be the beneficiaries of OBC reservation. The other Muslims whom Prof. Ansari categorised as "non-indigenous Muslims (He tries to avoid the use of word Ashraf, Ajlaf and Arzal because he understands, the meaning of these words in depth) are part of Muslim community no doubt and "They along with the bulk of indigenous origin of Muslims have been collectively facing the disadvantages ofdiscrimination and even periodic violence. But only bulk of the Indian Muslims of indigenous origin who are socially and educationally backward deserve the OBC advantages and not the "non indigenous Muslims" who are in other words called Ashraf.

About Andhra Muslim reservation GO No. 33, which the Andhra High Court rightly negated Prof. Ansari poses that he has not expressed any opinion but if one goes through his article minutely he has expressed his opinion for reservation to all Muslim in Andhra Pradesh. In the name of his "academic, not political interest" he "expresses the opinion that extending the benefit to all Muslims of the State of A.P. was constitutionally valid. The Andhra High Court has rightly directed the A.P. Government to constitute and refer the issue before the Andhra Pradesh Backward Classes Commission, which is presently not functioning in the state for more than two years, and this Commission is the right constitutional authority to decide which section of the community is socially and educationally backward. The Supreme Court Judgement in Para 92 very clearly mentioned in the case of Tamil Nadu that even a community whose 94.61% of population is included in the backward list could not entitle the whole community for inclusion in the backward list. Para 92 reads as under :

> "92- *As per the statistics given in the Report of the Second Backward Classes Commission in Tamil Nadu out of 27,05,960 people belonging to Muslim minorities 25,60,195 are included in the list which works out to 94.61% of the total Muslim population of the State. Similarly, among Christians, out of 31,91.988 of the total population 25,48,148 are included in the backward list which worksout to 79.83%.*"

It is my case that Prof. Iqbal A. Ansari is "insensitive to the grossly neglected lot of historically deprived backward classes of Muslims". No doubt he may be "the first to raise the demand from his Minorities Council forum for allocation of 6% reservation for Muslim backward classes under the Mandal Scheme". Now let us examine the "Mandal Scheme", My academician friend Prof. Ansari's demand for 6% reservation for the Muslim backwards contradicts the Mandal Scheme itself. According to Mandal Commission derived statistics 52% is the total population of OBCs belonging to all communities and religious groups. Out of this 52%, 8.40% is the population of all non-Hindu OBCs which includes besides Muslims, Sikhs, Christians and others. Mandal scheme recommends only 27% reservation for all OBCs, thus out of 52% only 27% reservation is recommended and allowed by the Supreme Court. The simple arithmetical calculation is that only 27% reservation is allowed out of 52% OBC population then the percentage for 8.40 would come to 4.36% and this 4.36% includes all non-Hindu OBCs. Through this arithmetical calculation after deducting the percentage of non-Muslims from 4.36%, the Muslim OBCs derived figure would be below 4%. I do not know how Prof. Iqbal Ahmad Ansari's. Minority Council demanded 6% reservation for OBC Muslims under Mandal Scheme. Politician have demanded 8.44% and even 10% reservation but an academician should not (see Syed Shahabuddin's demand for 10% Muslim reservation out of 8.5% Muslim population of Andhra Pradesh).

Before concluding I would like to put in my own humble way that Muslim minority is facing two separate problems, one is social and educational backwardness of the bulk of the present day Indian Muslims of indigenous origin. The other problem is of discrimination faced by all Muslims, irrespective of indigenous and non-indigenous categories. Muslim intellectuals, academicians and politicians should deal with both the problems separately.

Muslims of the non-indigenous category who are generally known as Ashraf should not demand their "pound of flesh" reserved for the bulk of indigenous Muslims who are generally called Ajlaf and Arzal. The leadership of the Muslim community as present is in the hands of Ashraf Muslims in political, social and administrative fields. They should fight for their OBC brethren who are in fact socially, educationally, politically and administratively under-represented in all fields. Instead of demanding their share out of the "pound of flesh" reserved for socially and educationally backward section of the Muslims, they should rather fight for their indigenous brethren's cause as per recommendations of the NCRWC and also the directives of the Constitution of India. Their backward brethren will not fail to come forward and fight for any benefit provided by the Constitution and recommended by NCRWC and also the recommendations of (now forgotten) Dr. Gopal Singh High Power committee's report. Dr. Gopal Singh Committee recommended important measures to the government for all weaker sections particularly minorities sans-reservation but it could not be placed even on the table of Parliament as yet.

Prof. Ansari is very much hopeful with the announcement by the UPA Government for the proposed Commission of what he called "on Backwardness for the minorities demand which had been persistently raised by the Minorities Council". But he knows well that it all depends under which Article of the Constitution it is going to be formed and what are its terms of reference. Besides all this the proposed Commission can not take away the reservation benefits already provided to the bulk of indigenous origin Muslims.

# 24

# WHICH MUSLIM GROUP IS UNDER-REPRESENTED

*Ashfaq Husain Ansari*

Andhra Pradesh Government has issued G.O. for 5% reservation of Muslims in Andhra Pradesh. In the latest issue of Milli Gazatte 16-31 August, two articles by prominent Muslim intellectuals and Milli Council members Syed Shahabuddin and Prof. Iqbal A. Ansari are published. Both the intellectuals whole-heartedly support the 5% reservation for all Muslims in Andhra Pradesh. In support of the "Muslim Reservation" they referred and quoted excerpts from National Commission for Review and Working of the Constitution, Mandal commission and Constitution of India. Prof. Ansari's Minorities Council of India submitted extensive memorandum and Syed Shahabuddin after reading the NCRWC report came to the conclusion that the Commission has accepted their point of view about Muslim Minorities. They quoted the relevant paragraphs which I am also quoting for reference.

3-7-1-There was a plea on behalf of some minority communities for an express provision for reservation in favour of minorities both in articles 15(4) and 16(4). The Commission upon due consideration of the representation felt that no special provision was necessary in as much as, under the existing provision of articles 14, 15 and 16, it is open to the State to make reservation if it is of the opinion that such reservation is necessary and justified."

3-7-2-The Commission noted that the ultimate aim of affirmative action of reservation should be to raise the level of capabilities of people of disadvantaged section and to bring them at par with the other sections of the society.

Now let us see how a *"state can come to the conclusion that such reservation is necessary and justified."* The procedure laid down by nine Judges historic Supreme Court Judgement of its Constitution bench is defined under paragraphs 847 and 861. The judgement has given direction which states as under. *"The following directions are given to the Government of India, the State Government and the Administration of Union Territories."*

861-A-The Government of India each of the State Governments and the Administration of Union Territories shall within four months from to-day constitute a permanent body for entertaining, examining and recommending upon requests for inclusion in the list of Other Backward Classed of citizens. The advice tendered by such bodies shall ordinarily be binding upon the Government."

In para 3-7-2- itself the NCRWC has given specific reasons for affirmative action of castes/communities which are included in the list of socially and educationally backward classes. They are mostly counterparts of Hindu Backward Classes and to some extent of Hindu Scheduled Castes."

Now look at what the Commission's recommendation are and how far it accommodates the views expressed in the memorandum of Minorities Council.

10-11-2- The Commission recommends that :

*"(a) Steps should be taken for improvement of educational standards amongst the minority communities. Special programs should be drawn up after the widest consultation with the leaders of minority communities including leaders of BCs, SCs and STs among Minorities from academic Professional, business and socio-political spheres and from low-occupation spheres."*

*"(b) At present the political representation of minority communities in legislatures, especially Muslims has fallen well below their proportion of population. The proportion of BCs among them is next to nil. This can lead to a sense of alienation. It is recommended that in situation of this kind it is incumbent for political parties to*

> ***build up leadership potential in the minority communities including BCs, SCs and STs among them for participation in political life.***
>
> ***"(c) Backward Classes belonging to religious minorities who have been identified and included in the list of Backward Classes and who in fact constitute the bulk of the population of religious minorities, should be taken up with special care along with their Hindu counterparts in the developmental efforts for the Backward Class."***

These are the specific recommendations of the NCRWC under the chapter Minorities. Nowhere the Commission has recommended for reservation of all minorities of Muslims. The Commission is openly sympathetic to the BCs, SCs and STs among Muslim minorities. The Commission is particularly distressed about under representation of Muslim Backward Classes in legislatures, and legislatures include Parliament. Syed Shahabuddin also talks of under representation of Muslims in Parliament and legislatures. No doubt Muslims are under represented in Parliament and State legislatures. But which category of Muslims are actually under represented ? Now the Lok Sabha list of members from first to 13th Lok Sabha is available under one binding. One can examine and find the names of Backward Muslims without much difficulty. No Backward Muslim got elected for thirteenth Lok Sabha. From First to 14th Lok Sabha you will find that never more than five Backward Muslims got elected. More or less same is the position of other elected bodies of State legislatures. The present Rajya Sabha has no Backward Muslim. Representation of backward Muslims was never of more than one or two. Almost same is the case of other decision making bodies. In political parties representation of Backward Muslims from State to Central level is negligible. That is why NCRWC has said "That the proportion of BCs among them is next to nil. Forward or Ashraf Muslims are well represented much above the proportion of their population, be it Parliament, State legislatures, or decision making bodies of Government or political parties.

Now coming to Syed Shahabuddins 5% Muslims reservation for all Muslims in Andhra Pradesh issue, I do not know from where he came to know the population figure of

Muslims in Andhra Pradesh. The Government of Andhra Pradesh Backward Classes Welfare (C2) Department G.O. No. 33 dated 12-7-2004 in its para 3 states as under :

> *"3-According to 1991 census the population of Minorities in A.P. State is 72 lakhs (i.e. 11%) of total population, out of which Muslim population is around 64 lakhs consisting 8.5% of total population."*

This G.O. itself explodes the myth of 12% Muslim population of Andhra Pradesh. On the basis of 12% Muslim population of Andhra Pradesh Syed Shahabuddin finally demands 10% reservation for Muslims in Andhra Pradesh.

About Mandal Commission he states in the same article".

> *"The Mandal Commission calculated that roughly 8.4% out of 52% of the people who consitituted the Backward Classes were Muslims."*

But Mandal Commission Reports States as under :

> *"V-Back Backward Non-Hindu communities - 8.40%*
>
> *E-52% of religious groups under section B may be also treated as OBCs.*
>
> *F-The approximate derived population of other Backward Classes including non Hindu communities is 52%"*

8.40% is the approximate derived population of all Non-Hindu Backward Classes which includes Sikhs, Christians and others and not Muslim BCs only.

Now coming to Andhra Pradesh G.O. 33 it may not be out of place to mention that it is based on a report by the "Commissioner for Commessionarate of Minorities welfare dated 5.7.2004" and this report was not placed before the Andhra Pradesh Backward Classes Commission, the only required statutory authority as per Supreme Court nine Judges Constitution bench Judgement of Nov. 1992, for inclusion of any community in the OBC category.

# 25

# BACKWARD MUSLIMS ARE NOT RESPONSIBLE FOR DIVISION OF MUSLIM COMMUNITY

*Ashfaq Husain Ansari*

It so happened that one of my unknown supporter sent me a photo copy of my intellectual lawyer friend Janab Syed Shahabuddin's reply to my rejoinder published in the Mill Gazette 1-15 January 2005. It is mere coincidence that this issue of Milli Gazette could not be delivered to me by the postal authorities. Hence, I am thankful to my unknown supporter who has sent the photocopy of said article of my learned friend Syed Shahabuddin with the anonymous side note on the same page *"Dear Sir, May like to reply this nonsense. He should be taken up."* I would like to make it clear that I don't consider my learned Friend's reply to my rejoinder published in Mill Gazette as nonsense.

My intellectual friend has written this reply in full seriousness. I have never questioned the very concept of Muslim community. But I do consider that the Muslim community is categorized between Ashraf and Ajlaf-Arzal. To the Ashraf Syed Saheb has given the new name in English i.e. elite but in Urdu he calls them Ashrafia or Ashraf and my other intellectual and academician friend Prof. Iqbal A Ansari calls as nonindigenous Muslims. Syed Saheb considers *"the elite formation is a historical process. There is no sudden beginning and sudden cut off in history. The composition of Muslim elite is changing and Ansaris* (why

Ansaris only? AHA) *will insha allah increasingly represent the Muslim community as a whole and the non Ashraf shall throw the so called Ashraf in the shade"*. For him the Ashraf is so called but for the non Ashraf he does not consider necessary adding any prefix. Not only I but Syed Saheb and persons of his mindset like Prof. Iqbal A. Ansari agree that the political leadership is generally monopolized by the elite or so called Ashraf or in Prof. Ansari's word non-indigenous Muslims. I, Asfaq Husain Ansari or the persons of my way of thinking are not the least responsible for this historical division of the Muslim community. Division of the Muslim community between Ashraf and non Ashraf (Ajlaf-Arzal) or between Muslim of indigenous and non indigenous origin is because of historical formation or process. He more seriously and vehemently begins with in his earlier out burst. "*During my nearly twenty five years of public life I have rarely come across such a pernicious and divisive campaign against the Muslim community as the one launched by Mr. Ansari*" I fail to understand that after such a harsh and vehement attack in his first article he now remembers me with such mild word. May be after that outburst good sense prevailed on him and he concurred with my political understanding.

Now I come to the basic question raised by Syed Saheb "*My basic question was and is that having forsaken the principle of Muslim solidarity why does he try to create a sub category of Muslim OBC's within the OBCs*". My answer to his basic question is that I am not trying to create any subcategory of Muslim OBCs. The OBCs have been in existence much before the Mandal report. The Mandal report itself categorized the non-Hindu OBCs and it has given the figure of population of all non-Hindu OBC's (which includes Muslim, Sikhs & Christians OBC's) as 8.40% of the total population Kanshi Ram and Mayawati along with Muslim leaders of all opinion still misunderstand it to be figure of only Muslim OBC's. I am not angry but I really feel pity for the ignorance of intellectuals, academicians and political leaders. Even after providing figures of OBC Muslim representation in Parliament and the percentage of Ansaris in this figure he again and again repeats what is there in his mind. He should have contradicted the figure of Muslim representation in Lok Sabha which I have provided in my rejoinders to him and Prof. Iqbal A. Ansari. I have also provided in these rejoinders (already published in Milli Gazette) figures of OBC representation and among them the representation of Ansaris also which I precisely reproduce here. No doubt representation of Muslim community in Lok Sabha is much below the ratio of their population. From first to fourteenth Lok Sabha around 7500 members were elected. But out of this only about 400 Muslims could be elected and out of this 400 about 340 are from elite, Ashraf or Muslims of non indigenous category and only 60 are from non Ashraf (Ajlaf-Arzal) or indigenous categories and Syed Saheb should note it that out of this 60 Ajlaf-Arzal or non Ashraf or indigenous category Muslims only 14 are Ansaris. In spite of these facts, the intellectual politician Syed Sahabuddin and persons of his mindset are still laying stress on the same false domination of Ansaris. According the him to population ratio between Ashraf and non Ashraf is three fourth and one fourth. It comes to that 75% non Ashraf Muslim population is getting 15% representation while 25% Ashraf population is getting 85% representation.

Some figures of Bihar are available with me. These figures also confirm almost the same ratio. In Sayed Saheb's home state (which includes Jharkhand also) from 1952 to 1995 only 246 Muslim members could get elected for Bihar Assembly. Out of this 246 Muslims 140 belong to Sheikhs, 35 Syeds 23 Pathans. That is out of 246 Muslim members of Bihar Assembly 198 belong to Ashraf and rest 48 belong to non Ashraf. Out of this 48 non Ashraf or Ajlaf-Arzal 30 are Ansaris, 5 Sher Shahabadi, 6 Kulahia, 3 Rayeen, 3 Mukeri and 1 Malik. United Bihar and Jharkhand have almost same ratio of Muslim population as there in Uttar Pradesh and almost the same ratio of Ashraf and non Ashraf. The ratio of Ansaris among the non Ashraf according to Syed Saheb himself is 65%. In the year 2000 only 30 Muslim could get elected and out of this 11 are Sheikh, 4 are Syed and 4 are Pathan. This means that out of 30 Muslims 19 belong to Ashraf category and only 11 belong to non Ashraf category but of these 11 non Ashraf, only 4 are Ansaris, one

Sher Shahabadi, 1 Rayeen, 3 Kulahiya, 1 Mukeri and 1 Qurashi. This means that out of 30 Muslims in Bihar including Jharkhand Legislative Assembly only 11 belong to non Ashraf category and rest 19 belong to Ashraf category. Here also against 75% Backward Muslim population only 11 Legislators from non Ashraf and against the remaining 25% of Ashraf population 19 Ashraf (Sheikh, Syed and Pathan) got elected. Let us wait and see the out-come of 2005 election. But to Syed Saheb political representation matters very little because it does not suit his formulations. So he demands from me the other figures which are not available. The figures of his choice can be had from the organization he is closely associated with i.e. the Institute of Objective Studies, his own journal "Muslim, India", The Milli Council, Muslim Majlise Mushawrat and other similar organizations. But he knows very well that these organizations may not provide figures which suit his formulations. So to confuse the issue he demands these unnecessary unavailable figures from me.

About 90% of the minority educational institutions are administered by the Ashraf where favoritism in the employment of teachers and in admissions also is the order of the day. These institutions are excluded from reservation and hence are the centre of caste based favoritisms also.

Syed Sahabuddin lays more emphasis on public employment. He undermines political representation in Parliament and state legislatures. I would like to assure him that I am not for creating any deliberate confusion. If there is any such confusion it is of his own creation. The data provided above of Bihar legislature and of Lok Sabha speak themselves. His artificial and deliberate fear on Ansari domination among the OBC Muslims is imaginary as figures speak just the reverse. Janab Syed Sahabuddin himself agrees that "*For historical reason the so called Ashraf among the Muslims have been educationally more advance than the non Ashraf in the community. When universal Franchise came, they were recognized as the social and political leaders of the community and fielded by political parties as candidate for Parliament and Assemblies. The gap is steadily narrowing with spread of education and political awakening among the deprived group of all communities. Indeed this also has the effect of multiplying Muslim candidate, in Muslim concentrated constituencies"*

The learned lawyer politician accepts the fact that Muslim Ashraf may by historical reasons be educationally and socially advance and due to this advancement they were and are grabbing the political representation. I want to add only this much that even today they are socially, educationally and politically more advance in every sphere of life and their social educational and also political advancement was the reason why Constitution debarred them from being included in the list of OBC's. Neither the data of Lok Sabha nor state Legislatures confirm his formulation. Representation of Muslims in general and in particular of backward Muslims on non Ashraf Muslims in Lok Sabha and state Assemblies is on the decline. It is not my opinion only but the NCRWC Commission headed by Justice Venkat Challiah also confirms this fact.

> *"At present the political representation of minorities especially Muslims in legislature und (legislature includes Parliament also AHA) has fallen much below the proportion of their population. The proportion of BCs among them is next to nil.*

After accepting that *"so called Ashraf among the Muslim have been educationally more advanced than the non Ashraf in the Community"*, and also adding afterwards that *"they were recognized as the social and political leaders of the community"* intellectual and leader of the elite or Ashraf Muslim, Syed Shahabuddin questions *"Why does Mr. Ansari resist the idea of Muslim community as a whole being declared a backward class and working unitedly and more forcefully for its recognition as a separate Backward Class"*.

The earlier quoted statements of the legal luminary themselves are in fact the answer. A community or a part of the community educationally, socially and politically claimed to be advanced can not be declared Backward Class. My limited knowledge of the Constitution of India, the relevant portion of the historic *Indra Sawhney V/s Union of India* Judgment clearly state that social and educational backwardness is the main parameter for declaring a community or a part of it as Backward. The above quoted statement of my learned legal luminary intellectual politician friend may now be quoted against inclusion of Ashraf Muslims as Backward Community. I fail to understand what he means by recognition of the Muslim community as a separate Backward Class. I also fail to understand under which Article of the Constitution he wants the Sheikhs, Syeds and Pathans to be declared as a separate Backward Class. If there are any provisions of declaring these subgroups as a separate class neither Ashfaq Husain Ansari nor any section of the Backward Muslims will oppose it.

Before concluding I would ask the learned Syed Saheb to provide the alternate data of even the political representation of Ashraf and non Ashraf in the Lok Sabha and also Bihar Assembly. I would also request him to place before the readers of the Milli Gazette, in particular and others in general the actual data of the position in the Lok Sabha and Bihar assembly of the representation of Backward Muslims (other than Ansari) in these bodies. I have never taken up the position of Ansari representation separately but the data available itself speaks the actual position about the representation of total Muslim, and among them the representation of Muslim OBCs in these bodies and also the comparative data of Ansari representation among the OBC Muslims.

It is for the readers of the Milli Gazette to judge the data provided by me and also to decide as to what extent Mr. Syed Shahabuddin's attack in almost every paragraph of his present reply and the earlier article is biased against the Muslim Backwards in general and Ansaris in particular. I would request him to come forward with his data, if any. Besides political representation he can also come forward with the datas of representation of Sheikhs, Syeds & Pathans in State and All India Civil, Police and Judiciary services, particularly in higher judiciary and also the data of non Ashraf or Ajlaf-Arzal Muslims in these services and also, if available, the data of Ansari's among the Ajlaf-Arzal Muslims. I would also request him to provide the data of decision making bodies of all the secular parties, at least at the national level. Who are the persons there in these parties/bodies and how many of them are OBC Muslims and out of them how many are Ansaris. Because my learned friend's case is that Ansaris are over represented at every stage in every party so that once for all the Ansari phobia of Syed Shahabuddin may come to an end.

In the end I would like to make it clear that we the OBC Muslims, which include Ansaris also, would never accept the formula of Syed Shahabuddin in which he says that "*I do not mind if the entire Muslim quota in government services (or the legislatures) when it comes, goes to Ansaris or to the combination of Muslim non-Ashraf so long as they are articulate and effective*". We want only what the Constitution and relevant Supreme Court judgment have provided to the OBCs. We do not want any alms from the feudal Lords who are still taking pride in giving alms to the deprived section of the community known as Ajlaf-Arzal or non-Ashraf.

All the OBCs including Muslim OBCs are not getting reservation in admissions in central and minority educational institutions and no body from Ashraf has ever raised his voice in favour of providing reservation in these institutions of learning for non-Ashraf under Mandal dispensation. In this connection it will not be out of place to mention that the architect of Aligarh. Movement Sir Saiyed Ahmad Khan is known for his favouritism for upper caste Muslims. He proudly announced during early days that his aim was to provide an institute of learning for the upper caste Muslims. Syed Shahabuddin in some of his writings in Urdu news papers, particularly Rashtriya Sahara accepts this. Sir Syed Ahmad Khan also opposed the move for holding the Indian Civil Service examinations in India because of his fear that non-Ashraf will easily participate in these examinations if held in India. Mohd. Ali Jinah, Muslim league or Dr. Sir Sheikh Mohd. Iqbal were not the proponent of the Idea of two nation theory. Sir Syed Ahmad Khan the founder of Aligarh Movement was the real originator of the two nation theory. He wrote a letter to the first Muslim Congress President Mr. Badruddin Tyyab Ji advising him to disassociate himself from the presidentship of Congress party because Congress is a Hindu organization.

Further, Sir Saiyed Ahmad Khan, the ideal of Syed Shahabuddin and persons of his mindset was openly against the Ansaris and he referred them in his book "Asbab-e-Baghawat-e-Hind" as "Badzat Julahe". The same "Badzat Julahe" (Ansari) are haunting my learned friend day and night. Famous anthropologist Marc Gaborieau in his book has also confirmed Sir Sayed Ahmad Khan's hatred towards non-Ashraf Muslims particularly Ansaris:

> *"Syed Ahmad Khan, spearhead of Muslim thought in Indian sub-continent in the last century, was an Ashraf working for the welfare of the Ashraf. He used to say that his Aligarh College was not for weavers."*

Now, it is for the readers of Milli Gazette to decide who divides the Muslim. Community between Ashraf and non-Ashraf. Sir Sayed Ahmad is not only the founder of two nation theory but also the founder of division of Muslim Community between Ashraf and non-Ashraf and Syed Shahabuddin is his ardent follower.

Muslim Ashraf leadership never raised their voice in favour of Muslim OBCs particularly Muslim Dalits although they claim to be their leaders also. Christian community is divided between Roman Catholic and Protestants besides several other subdivisions in the name of different churches but they are one in raising their voice in favour of providing SC status to their followers. From late Mother Teressa to my friend former External Affairs Minister Edverdo Flario, now a Rajyasabha Member all have been raising their voice in favour of it. All the Christian Members of Parliament, from Flario to Oscar Fernandis recently met Prime Minister Manmohan Singh and Home Minister Shiva Raj Patil to demand SC status to Christian converts from SC. Will the Muslim Members of Parliament follow them in voicing the same demand for their Muslim brethren for deleting the Constitution (Schedule caste) Presidential order, 1950 ?

No body can deny the social and caste stratification among the followers of Islam particularly in India. Eminent sociologists and Muslim Ulemas of all shades accept this. Even Syed Shahabuddin accepts the division between what the calls so called Ashraf and non-Ashraf. No matter his reasoning is according to his mindset. "*For Historical reasons the so called Ashraf among the Muslim have been educationally more advanced than the non Ashraf in the community*". Prof. Iqbal A. Ansari accepts the division according to his mind set as Indigenous and non indigenous Muslims. Syed Shahabuddin further says "*that the composition of Muslim elite is changing and Ansaris, Insha Allah, will increasingly represent the Muslim community as a whole and the non-Ashraf shall throw the so-called Ashraf in the`shade.*" But he forgets that according to Muslim Ulemas of all shades if the prophesy of Sayed Sahab comes true it would be the sign of Qayamat or dooms-day coming close, and Dajjal will appear along with Julahas.

> *"jab tak Ilme deen hazrate Shayukh mein raha aur aqwame deegar (Razila) taabe rahein koyee aafat nahei aayee, magar jab se Qasayee, nayee, teli, lohar, bhisti, kalal, julahc waghaira Molvi, Muddarris, Qazi, Soofi, Hafiz waghaira hone lage masayeb ka daur-daura bhee aane laga, kyoon ki yeh ahadees se sabit hai ki Dajjal per eeman lane wale aksar julahe hoange."*
>
> *(Nehayatul Irab-fee-Ghayatunnasab from Mufti Shafi Deobandi and Maulana Thanvi's book quoted by Maulana Masood Alam Falahi in* "Zindagi-e-Nau" *Urdu monthly of Jamate-Islami-e-Hind).*

# PART - III

(Reproduction of the Thin Volume Earlier Published)

Released on 14th April 2004 at Andhra Bhavan, New Delhi, by Justice (Retd.) Rajendra Sachar. The Function was presided over by P.S. Krishnan, IAS (Retd.) Former Secretary to Govt. of India, Ministry of Welfare & Former Member Secretary, National Commission for Backward Classes, Chairman National Action Forum for Social Justice.

Among the distinguished persons who graced the Function and expressed their views were Mr. (Now late) Suraj Bhan, Former Governor and Chairman National Commission for Scheduled Caste, Justice Ram Surat Singh (Retd.) Chairman, National Commission for Backward Classes, Mr. D. Raja Secy. CPI, Mr. Oscar Furnandies (at that time) Genl. Secretary. ICC, and distinguished Sociologist, Prof. Imtiyaz Ahmad.

# 26

# FOREWORD

***P.S. Krishnan***

India is engaged in the gigantic task of becoming a "developed country" within the next decade and a half, eliminating backwardness which is the legacy of the pre-Independence centuries and the post-Independence decades. To that end, efforts have been and are being mounted to remove perceived road-blocks in the path to advancement and development.

But it is a futile exercise to lop off the withered branches, instead one should strike at the root. The first step for this is to identify the root, the tap-root. Swami Vivekananda, one of the modern and modernising minds of modern India, posits, in an article published serially in 1899-1901, the interesting concept that each nation has a national purpose of its own, around which revolves the life of that nation, which constitutes the source of its strength. He compares it to the ogress of children's myths, who had her soul living in a small bird, and who would never die unless the bird was killed.

As a corollary to this, I would posit the concept that each nation and society suffers from certain characteristic deficiencies or flaws which hold it back. In some cases, it assumes the dimensions of a "fatal flaw" as in Shakespeare's tragic heroes, like Hamlet's indecisiveness ("To be or not to be") Macbeth's vaulting ambition, and Othello's suspiciousness. Nations and societies and their leaders must analyse, understand and diagnose their own flaws and fatal flaws and strike at their root to avert tragedy or stunted growth.

Analysing India and Indian society, or fundamental flaw lies in the major proportion of the population being denied the opportunity of growth to the fullest of their potential and this leading to the Nation and Society being deprived of the benefit of the fullest contribution of every individual and section of the people. In a society in which this happens only on account of direct economic factors, this can be rectified with relative ease, with the application of Reason and Logic, by appropriate economic measures and reforms. But the task becomes infinitely more difficult where deprivation of opportunity for a substantial part—in our case the vast majority—of the population emanates from a rigid social structure, with intergenerational continuity across centuries, "hallowed" by Custom and sometimes giver a pseudo-religious (not really part of any religion) underpinning. For, then emotions, sentiments, encrusted attitudes, fossilised mind-sets come into play. Rationally and logically essential economic and other reforms are not judged and evaluated with reason and logic. Resistance to Reason and Logic becomes almost irresistible. There is no doubt progress, but it is painfully slow, patchy, inadequate and truncated.

This is what has happened in India and in different degrees most of the countries of the South Asian region. Indian and most of the other South Asian societies have traditionally evolved the most rigid Social Structure in their Caste System. It is not a mere ritualistic mechanism of psychological affiliations and satisfactions. It is the most elaborate and thorough instrumentality devised by Man anywhere, any time, to preserve the monopoly of a small elite minority over all that is advantageous and "desirable"—prestigious positions in the society, economy and polity; educational and cultural avenues and in today's context journalistic and media (both print and electronic) avenues; and life opportunities—and of typing down the vast majority almost irretrievably and irremediably to all that is disadvantageous and "undersirable"—productive agricultural labour and other forms of labour and service, on exploitative terms highly beneficial to the elite minority and grossly unfair to the rest. The Caste System is the Prison of the People.

The severe damage the all-embracing Caste System has inflicted and continues to inflict on the Scheduled Castes, Scheduled Tribes and Backward Classes has been well-documented elsewhere. Denial of space of minimisation of space for these three categories, though together they comprise about three-fourths of the population of India and the near-totality of its labouring population, is one of the features of Indian statistics including the Indian Census. Statistical darkness is more visible in the case of Backward Classes than in the case of Scheduled Castes and Scheduled Tribes. Even the minimal recording made in the decennial Census in respect of SC and ST was evaded for the BC, in spite of objective, well informed and full justified advice in the run-up to the last two Censuses, depriving the developmental agencies of valuable data relevant to development of BCs. Yet some rays of light have stole their way through the enveloping darkness. Thus, the Fifty-Fifth Round of the National Sample Survey has brought out the position of Backward Classes between SC and ST on the one side and the socially advanced category on the other in respect of poverty. The Second National Family Health Survey of 1998-99, the All-India Report of which was released in October 2000 contains valuable demographic and health data, *inter alia* bringing our differentials between SC, ST, BC and the Socially Advanced Categories. For example, the standard of living index based on different facilities and ownership of amenities in the household shows a low level in the case of almost one-third of the total sample. But, on disaggregation among the above four categories, it is revealed that this all India, all category total figure is actually true only of the BC whose value of the SLI is virtually the same (32.3% for BC as against 32.8% collectively for all). In the case of the SC and ST, the percentage of women with low SLI is more than half of their population (50.2% for SC and 53.9% for ST), while the percentage for the women of the Socially Advanced Category is much lower at about one-fifth of their population (20.3%). It is extremely revealing that all the shockingly and disturbingly low values for India on the various health, nutritional and other Social indicators/parameters are in fact virtually equal to the values for the BC. The values for the Socially Advanced Category are significantly better, while the values for the ST and SC are dismally worse, as though they belonged to another Continent. To give another example the percentage of women with low Body Mass Index (BMI i.e., the weight in kilograms divided by height in meters squared, is 36.1% for all and 36.2% for BC. The percentage of women with no media exposure is 40.1 for all and 40.6 for BC. Thus, BCs are the truest representatives of Indian backwardness, while the SC and ST seem to belong to another and infinitely darker Continent (some of the countries even of Africa fair better in some of the indices than our SC and ST). Obviously, India's backwardness can be removed only by removing the backwardness of BC along with SC and ST. Comprehensive road-maps for this have been prepared since about a quarter century age in the case of SC and ST, since 1996 in the case of BC and made available to successive Governments of India and States, successive Planning Commission regimes and different political parties, through processes with which I have been directly involved and am fully familiar. These road-maps can be made available on tap to any Government of Political Party whenever it takes serious and abiding interest, beyond mere electoral contexts and calculations, in the economic, educational, social and cultural progress of these three categories to a level of normalcy and equality, and thereby of India as a whole and consequently laying the foundation for an integrated and ultimately casteless India.

Unless the potential of the SC, ST and BC are full developed and harnessed, India will not be able to capture its due share of the opportunities of national growth potentially available. Nor will it be able to develop its manufacturing sector, for want of domestic demand for manufactured goods, unless the SC, ST and BC masses are developed and their purchasing power is raised to a level at which they can afford to buy essential manufactured goods, which they need but which they have to forgo now. According to the Nasscom and McKinsey forecast, the IT industry in India is expected to directly employ about 20 lakh people by 2008 as against the present estimated level of 7.70 lakhs and create indirect employment of 20 lakh more. But this is less than half of the number of the re-additions to the labour force force which is about 19 lakh per year over and above the existing 47 crores and the estimated number of more than 4 crores registered unemployed apart from the unregistered unemployed, seasonally unemployed and under-employed.

It is in this larger picture in which the Muslim Backward Classes have to be located. While there is tremendous ignorance of and bias against the SC and ST and BC, the ignorance is almost total in respect of Backward Classes who follow religions other than Hindu, among the educated Indian elite who occupy the commanding heights of the polity, the economy (in both public and private sectors), the society, the administration (governmental as well as private sector), the institutions of finance, (both governmental and non-governmental), the institutions of education (in the public as well as private sectors) print and electronic media, and other institutions, instruments and sectors of power. Ignorance at the source of power by itself is debilitating for the weak, but it is crushing when it is accompanied by bias. In this situation, the effort by Ashfaq Husain Ansari, whom I know as a distinguished member of a numerically large Backward Class among Muslims and an esteemed colleague who devotedly serves the legitimate cause of the Backward Class Muslims and BC in general and the causes of the education of the disadvantaged, in the shape of this slim volume with contributions from himself and other scholars is a valuable addition of the meagre knowledge of this sub-category of BC. This volume brings out the existence of the Caste System among those who follow Islam as their religion, some aspect of the nature of that Caste System, some of its implication and some of the problems arising the refrom.

Ashfaq Husain Ansari's Introduction marshals powerful and irrefutable evidence to show that the Caste System and the multifaceted dichotomy of Backward Classes and Upper Classes of Muslims do in fact exist. This evidence is drawn from eminent

Muslim Ulema, the Census of India 1901, Encyclopaedia Americana, Encyclopaedia Britannica and Justice Sawant's Judgement, in its entirety, is highly educative and valuable, it has to be pointed out with respect that the portions cited in the introduction contain a factual inaccuracy (for which Ansari is not responsible as it is in the Original). Labbais, Rawthars Marakayars in Tamil Nadu are included, not in the list of Scheduled Castes as stated therein, but in the list of Backward Classes. Similarly converts to Christianity from Scheduled Castes as also Latin Catholics, Christian Shanars, Christain Nadars and Christian Gramani—all four of whom are converts not from scheduled Castes but from Castes which have been categorised as Backward Classes from the time such categorisation started—are all in the list, not of Scheduled Castes, but of Backward Classes and there are similar instances of inclusion in the lists of the Backward Classes in some other States. However, the central point made in the Judgement that there are castes and caste-based inequalities among Muslims, Christians and followers of other non-Hindu religions (except Zoroastrians and in a sense Jains) is indisputable as social reality and Justice Sawant's observation in the subsequent two paragraphs have been followed in practice by the National Commission for Backward Classes from 1993 onwards in identifying Backward Classes among Hindus as well as Muslims and other non-Hindus.

The Caste System of India in particular and of South Asia in general does nor recognise or respect boundaries of religion. It is a religious in its aetiology and habitat, while of course being irreligious and even anti-religious in its nature and characteristics. What is the origin of Muslim Backward Classes? Apart from some sociological evidence, light is thrown on this by no less an authority-than Swami Vivekananda himself.

In one of his "Lectures from Colombo to Almora", titled "The future of India" (1897) he observed as follows, "The Mohammedan conquest of India came as a salvation to the down-trodden, to the poor. That is why one-fifth of our people have become Mohammedans. It was not the sword that did it all. It would be the height of madness to think it was all the work of sword and fire. And one fifth—one-half—of your Madras people will become Christians if you do not take care. Was there ever a sillier thing before in the world than what I saw in Malabar country ? The poor pariah is not allowed to pass through the same street as the high-caste man, but if he changes his name to a hodge-podge English name, it is all right; or to a Mohammedan name, it is all right ........ Shame upon them that such wicked and diabolical customs are allowed;........" Every region of the country has its special brand of such silliness including Bengal, but the silly as well as vile practices of Kerala came to this focused knowledge, thanks to the effort of a distinguished representative of the then 'untouchable' Ezhava Community, one of the two earliest Ezhava matriculates of Travancore, who were denied admission to college in Travancore on account of their caste status, vis Dr. Palpu, then working in Mysore, who is said to have gained confidential access of the Swami by posing as rickshaw-puller and taking him around in 'his' rickshaw. The social identity of "the down-trodden", "the poor" referred to by Swamin Vivekananda is clear from his words such as "the Poor Pariah" in the above quote and elsewhere, "the peasant, the shoemaker, the sweeper, and such other lower classes of India" who "have been silently working through long ages and producing the entire wealth of the land", 'the peasants' cottage ...... the huts of the fisherman, the cobbler and the sweeper" from which he envisages the rise of a "New India" in the place of the "Past India" of the moribund "upper classes of India", occurring in this various lectures. It is these sections of people who have been categorised as SC, ST and BC in modern Constitutional India. I shall lower down cite sample anthropological (Ananthakrishna Iyer) and scholarly (Logan) sources for Kerala. Another important source of help in indentifying the social origins and affiliations of Backward Classes among adherents of minority religions especially Islam is Nripendra Kumar Dutt, Former Principal, Sanskrit College, Calcutta, who in his "Origin and Growth of Caste in India", first published in 1931, has brought out the oppressive treatment meted out to Namasudras and the fact that the bulk of the Muslims in East Bengal are of

Namasudra and Rajbansi origin (both now classified as major SCs of West Bengal). Jagadish Narayan Sarkar, Professor of History in Jadavpur University, in his "Islam in Bengal (Thirteenth to Nineteenth Century)" has also pointed out the historical fact that those who embraced Islam in Bengal were mainly from the Lower Classes, such as "the poor aborigines of eastern and deltaic Bengal, – fishermen, hunters, pirates and peasants,—the impure or unclean out-castes, popularly called the untouchables, spurned and neglected by the caste-proud Brahmanical Hindu Society", who "Adopted Islam to escape from social injustice or secure social status."

Thus, the predominant social profile of the Muslims in India reflects the fact that the overwhelming bulk of their population is from Hindu castes which come under the present categories of SC and BC. There is also a small number of Muslim communities of very limited numerical strength, classified as STs, as in the State of Jammu & Kashmir and the Union Territory of Lakshadweep. There is also a proportion of Muslims of upper castes, such as those referred to as Ashraf in North India. But the predominant population of Muslims consists of castes/communities which are the counterparts of Hindu BCs and SCs, such Muslim castes/communities being referred to in North India as Ajlaf and Arzal. They share the characteristics of social, educational and economic backwardness of their counterpart Hindu BCs and SCs. The backwardness of the Muslim population as a whole compared to the Hindu population as a whole along a number of economic, educational and standard of living indices are really reflective of the situation of Muslim Backward Classes. Thus, just as it is the Backward Classes who correctly reflect the low social, economic, educational and standard of living indices of India, the indices for the SC and ST being much lower and that for socially advanced castes being much higher, it is the Muslim Backward Classes who correctly reflect Muslim Backwardness, the levels for the socially advanced castes like the North Indian Ashraf being higher and closer to their Hindu counterparts of socially advanced castes. This correspondence is accentuated by the demographic predominance of the Muslim BCs among Muslims which is significantly more than the proportion of Hindu SC + Hindu BC among Hindus. The landmark Mandal Commission first worked out the proportion of Hindu BCs (43.70%) among Hindus (83.84%), which works out to 52 out of 100 and mechanically applied the same proportion to all non-Hindu religious groups (Muslim, Christian, Sikh, Buddhist and Jain) namely 52% of 16.16% arriving at 8.4% as the proportion of backward non-Hindu communities as a whole, without distinguishing between Jains among whom there are no BC, Sikhs among whom there are BCs but in limited numbers and Muslims among whom BCs are preponderant. This methodology applied to Muslims results in a substantial underestimate. For example, in the major state of Uttar Pradesh, about 70% of the Muslim population belongs to castes which are the counterparts of Hindu BCs and an other 20% approximately belongs to castes which are counterparts of Hindu SCs. Therefore, just as the all-round socio-economic advancement of BCs (including BCs of all religious groups), along with the advancement of SCs and STs is a necessary condition for the removal of the backwardness of India, similarly the all-round socio-economic advancement of Muslim BCs is a necessary condition for the removal of the backwardness of Muslims. Unless there is focus on BCs along with SCs and STs, they will be left behind, deliberately and with an automaticity which does not require the strain of thought, keeping India as a whole down to backwardness compared to other countries. Similarly unless there is focus on Muslim BCs, they will be left behind in the same way, keeping Muslims down to backwardness compared to Hindus and even other religious communities.

I congratulate Ashfaq Husain Ansari in bringing into this compilation the paper of Asghar Ali Engineer which brings out clearly the relevance of social and economic parameters of the backwardness found among those who follow Islam as their religion and points to some of the important socio-economic factors and historical background of the backwardness of Muslims—which is really the backwardness of Muslim Backward Classes. The distinction between the arena of society, economy and polity on the one side and the arena of religion on the other, and the distinction, between rights pertaining to religious identity and rights arising from the principle of social justice have been conceptually brought out clearly and succinctly by Asghar Ali Engineer. Dr. Hasan Nishat Ansari's Paper breaks new ground in tracing the roots of the Caste System among Muslims in India not only to the system of discriminatory classification native to India and to the vice of High Lineage and low lineage which immigrated from Central Asia and throwing light on the discrimination, even under the Indian Sultanates and Mughals against Muslim weavers and other artisan classes, who are among those now classified as Muslim BCs.

In his Paper on "Truth of Muslim Reservation in Karnataka and Kerala", Ansari has dealt with facts about which there is little knowledge in other parts of the country especially in North India. In fact, while sitting on the NCBC's Benches for different states and earlier in my other capacities, I could see that the Muslims of South India too are unaware of the features of the social structure of their co-religionists of North India and other parts of the country.......such inter-regional ignorance is common among Hindus and people of other religions also. This brings in the larger issue of the diversity of the social profile of Muslims in different regions of India, while there are also some commonalities. One important difference in the social profile of Muslim BCs in North India and South India must be noted. In North India, their largest number consists of specific artisan/artisanal castes like those traditionally associated with weaving, blacksmithy, carpentry, cotton carding, meat processing etc. In South India, converts to Islam were not typically from such artisan/artisanal castes, though there are limited instances of such communities among them like the Dudekula of Andhra Pradesh (interestingly, this community combines Muslims as well as Hindu practices in their life, and are, therefore, looked upon as half-Muslims by the Hindus and as half-Hindus by Muslims). The bulk of the converts to Islam in the South were from Castes of agricultural labour and other general unorganized labour—Castes of the lowest stratum. This aspect of the profile of converts to Islam in the South is brought out be logan in his landmark Manual of the Malabar District (1906). What he says also chimes in with Swami Vivekananda's observations. According to him, "Conversion to Muhammadanism has had a marked effect in freeing the slave caste in Malabar from their former brethrens. By conversion a Cheruman obtains a distinct rise in the social scale, and, if he is in consequence bullied or beaten, the influence of the whole Muhammadan community comes to his aid". In his Tribes and Castes of Cochin (1912), Ananthakrishna Iyer writes that the Muslim population of the area are a community "composed of the descendants of mixed unions with very little of Arab blood and converts from the very lowest classes of Hindus, Large numbers of recruits came from the Thiyyas, of Malabar, Ezhuvans of (Cochin) State and also from the Pulayas, to whom the 'honour of Islam brings enfranchisement from the disabilities of their own caste". The Pulaya and Cheruman referred to by Logan and Ananthkrishna Iyer are synonyms of the same caste, which is included in the list of Scheduled Castes and is the largest scheduled caste of Kerala. Thiyya and Ezhuvan are regional variants of the same caste, which also suffered from Untouchability in the past and were consequently included among Depressed Classes in the Census of Travancore of 1921, but was able to struggle out of Untouchability by their own efforts by the Thirties of the 20th century and were, therefore, not included in the list of Scheduled Castes. The resultant post-conversion internal indistinquishability in terms of pre-conversion castes, along with perceptibility of general "low-caste" origin made it possible for certain parts of South India, like the princely States of Travancore and Mysore to perceive Muslims as a single backward castes. It is against this background that when, for example, as early as in 1915 the Maharaja of Travancore issued confidential circulars to the Heads of departments to give special consideration for "inadequately represented communities" in making appointments to certain categories of posts in the Government service, they contained the phrase "members of such communities as Ezhava, Muslim, etc., which are backward in education". In the first formal order of reservation issued in Travancore on June 25, 1935, the "Muslim community" was specifically included. Even in the early 19th century, when the Regent Maharani issued orders permitting women of depressed communities to wear gold and silver ornaments, which were prohibited for them till then, the order referred illustratively to some such communities, and Muslim was one of them. But, as the majority judgement in the Mandal case observed, the situation varies from State to State. In the State of Karnataka of which the princely State of Mysore forms a major part, certain specific identifiable and identified Muslim castes like Darvesu and Chapperband were mentioned in the list of Backward Classes apart from mentioning Muslim as a single BC. But in both these States subsequent immigrations and changes took place. Since Mandal, according to its consistent practice did not include in its lists of BCs any religion or followers of any religion as a totality, the Request for inclusion of the Muslims of Kerala, which essentially meant the Muslims other than those of the Malabar region (where they were known as Mappilla a name in the Mandal list as well as the State list and, therefore, in the initial Central list), came up before the NCBC. From an in-depth study by a premier research institute of Kerala, which the NCBC commissioned, the NCBC identified five distinct non-Mappila Muslim communities/social groups in Kerala which are not socially backward of which three namely Bohra, Cutchi Memon and Navayat (Bhatkali) are trading communities and two namely Turukkan (segmented into Sheikh and Syed are descendents of cavalrymen of Tippu Sultan's army and Dakhni Muslim (segmented into Syed, Sheikh, Pathan and Mughal) are descendants of migrants from Deccan who came as cavalrymen of the Travancore army. These five were excluded and the rest of the Muslims were included in the Central list of Backward Classes for Kerala.

In Karnataka under similar circumstances, the National Commission for Backward Classes excluded nine distinct Muslim communities/social groups which are not socially backward namely Cutchi Memon, Navayat, Bohra, Sayyed, Sheikh, Pathan, Mughal, Mahdivia/Mahdavi, Konkani or

Jamyathi Muslims and included the rest of the Muslims in the Central list of Backward Classes for Karnataka. The Commission also included specific communities of socially Backward Classes of Muslims like Baghban and Pandara/Pindari who applied for inclusion and were found to be distinct, inter-generationally continuous socially and educationally communities of Muslims, and Siddi a socially backward caste/community of African Black descent among whom there are Sunni Muslims, Hindus and a few Catholic Christians. This background will be of help not only to understand the different situations and social profiles of Muslims in North Indian States and South Indian States; this will also help to throw further light on the intellectual discussion mooted by Ashfaq Husain Ansari in his learned paper on "Truth of Muslim Reservation in Karnataka and Kerala". The North Indian pattern permitted, justified and required the identification of each specific Muslim backward caste/community and its inclusion in the list of BCs, leaving out specific Muslim castes/communities which did not fulfil the criteria of social backwardness. The South Indian pattern, especially in Karnataka, Tamil Nadu and Kerala permitted, justified and required the identification of each specific Muslim caste/community which did not fulfil the criteria of social backwardness and its exclusion from the list of BCs and the inclusion of the rest of the Muslims in the list of BCs. Thus, we have the bottoms-up approach in the North and the top-down approach in the South, arising from social reality and its inter-regional diversities and specificities.

This reality of the existence of BCs among Muslims and their demographic dimensions and the significance of comprehensive efforts for their all-round advancement to levels of normalcy and equality must be recognised, along with the reality of the existence of BCs among Hindus (and also among adherents of other religions) and the significance, for the advancement of India, of comprehensive efforts to their all-round advancement to the level of normalcy and equality. Failure to recognise these inescapable social realities emanates from elite ignorance as well as elite self-interest (not surprisingly, cutting across boundaries of religious affiliations).

All State-Level and Central-Level Commissions as well as Committees have uniformly recognised these realities. The Kaka Kalelkar Commission of 1953-55 (unconstitutionally aborted in 1955-61), in its chapter on Problems of Special Groups, noted with reference to Muslims that "there are a number of communities amongst them that are suffering from social inferiority and consequent educational backwardness. We have recognised..........and added the names of such backward communities found among them in the list of other Backward Classes". Accordingly they included in the BC lists prepared by them a large number of Muslim Castes/Communities in each State. In addition, in the Kalelkar lists there are many other entries of Castes in which there are Hindus as well as Muslims in a number of States.

This old tradition, rooted in social reality, of listing identified castes of Muslims, has been continued also by the Mandal Commission of 1978-80. Dealing with OBCs among non-Hindu Communities in its chapter on Identification of OBCs, the Mandal report noted that "there is no doubt that social and educational backwardness among non-Hindu communities is more or less of the same order as among Hindu communities" and that the Caste System "also pervades the non-Hindu communities in India in varying degrees". It relies on sociological sources for the existence of hierarchy and castes among Muslims with Sayyads, Sheikhs, Mughals and Pathans being comparable to Brahmins and Kshatriyas, and "occupational castes who are considered lower castes in the hierarchy". On the basis of this social reality, the Mandal Commission included in the list of Backward Classes "all untouchables converted to any non-Hindu religion" and "Occupational communities which are known by the name of their traditional hereditary occupation and whose Hindu counterparts have been included in the list of Hindu OBCs" like Dhobi, Teli, Dheemar, Nai, Gujar, Kumhar, Lohar, Darji, Badhai etc. Accordingly the Mandal lists for most States include many castes of Muslims and castes in which there are both Hindus as well as Muslims. This thread continued in the preparation of the first set of "Comman Lists" or "Central Lists" for 14 States in 1993 by the Expert Committee on Backward Classes set up in the aftermath of the Supreme Court's Judgment on 16.11.1992 in what is popularly known as the Mandal Case.

The same approach was also evident in the work of the National Commission for Backward Classes set up under a special statute in 1993 in its examination of applications of/on behalf of castes/communities/sub-castes/sub-communities/synonyms omitted in the first set of State-wise Common Central Lists because they were not in the State List or in the Mandal List for the State or in both.

The NCBC process resulted in the fresh inclusion, subsequent to the initial Central Common Lists, of a number of Muslim Castes which were found to be socially and educationally backward in the Central Lists for different States, which were not included earlier.

Awareness of the existence and problems of Muslim BC was also in the mental background of the Working Group on Empowerment of Backward Classes in the Tenth Plan (2002-07) set up in December 2000. The Working group, in its Report dated 12-04-2001, after grouping the Backward Classes into five different categories, has observed "these communities include people who follow different religions sharing the same traditional occupations. But difference of religion does not make any significant difference in their objective socio-economic conditions". In another context this report points out how the Muslim Caste of Halakhor traditionally engaged in safai work has been lost sight of in the context of *Safai Karamcharis* and all Backward Classes belonging to religious minorties (among whom Muslim Backward Classes are predominant) have been lost sight of in the context of minorties and pithily observes that the Backward Classes belonging to the religious minorties mostly belong to the More and Most Backward sub-categories of BCs – this is important in the background of the recommendation of the working group that in all schemes and programmes of the Centre as well as States, while all categories of BCs should be provided for, priority should be accorded to Most BC (MrBC) communities and to More BC (MrBC) communities.

The Report of the National Commission to review the Working of the Constitution has also taken into account the social reality of the existence of the Caste System among Muslims and its Nature and Impact, and the existence of Muslim Backward Classes and this is the basis of many of its general osbervations and detailed specific recommendations.

The understanding of the Commission, and the way in which it has deftly interwoven the themes of the religious and clutureal rights of the minorties in terms of the Constitutional safeguards; the developmental and empowerment rights of the Minority Backward Classes, among whom Muslim Backward Classes are numerically many times larger than the total of all other Minority BCs; national integration and national cohesion, can be seen in its observations and recommendations under the head Minorities, which have been cited in extenso by Ashfaq Husain Ansari in his illuminating Introduction in this book, which therefore I do not repeat here.

This can also be seen in the Commission's observations on the Report of the Working Group on the Empowerment of the Backward Classes in the Tenth Plan, which runs as follows–

"The Working Group on the Empowerment of Backward Classes in the Tenth Plan has given a clear and comprehensive approach to the development of backward classes. The best that can be said is that the Government should immediately implement everyone of the recommendations of the Working Group–the backward classes include identified castes/ communities of religious minorties who together constitute the bulk of the population of religious minorties of the country. The Commission's consequent recommendation for the immediate implementation of everyone of the recommendations of that Working Group is also significant from the same point of view, but does not need repetition here because Ashfaq Husain Ansari's Introduction cites it in full.

As a general approach to protection of the educational interests of the Weaker Sections, the Commission has observed that "social policy should aim at enabling the SC, ST and BCs (including BC minorties and especially the More and Most

Backward Classes among BCs) and with particular attention to the girls in each of these categories to compete on equal terms with the general category". For this purpose, while relying on Reservation at present, from the long term point of view, it has recommended the establishment of high quality residential schools for boys and girls of these three categories in every district, and share for them at State cost in private institutions of excellence and in foreign educational institutions. In its recommendation for the establishment of Residential Talent Schools of high quality in every district, one each for SC boys and SC girls, ST boys and ST girls and BC boys and BC girls, this is what it says about BCs – "the Commission recommends that residential schools should be set up for the BCs in every district, one each for BC boys and BC girls, including minorties who belong to BCs and with special attention to More and Most Backward Classes among BCs". It has also recommended that "Some of these schools for backward classes should be located in districts where BCs belonging to religious minorties are relatively more concentrated so as to facilitate BCs of such minorities getting adequate number of seats". The same recommendation had been made from 1996 onwards by a Committee (1996-97) set up for working out the modalities for the establishment of residential schools for SC, ST and BC girls in low literacy districts and in documents like the Dalit Manifesto (1996).

The phrase "including BC minorties" occurs also after BC in the Commission's observation, "in the context of the tectonic shift towards globalisation and liberalisation", about "the severe bias" "shared by the captains of the private sector with the rest of the advanced sections of the society" against SC, ST, More and Most Backward Classes including BC minorties and women.

While recommending remedial measures in every economical activity sector where the representation of SC, ST and BC is inadequate, the Commission has taken care to add the phrase "Including BC minorties"

Similarly while recommending reservation for SCs, STs and BCs in allotment of shops under the public distribution system, and other allotments like petrol stations, gas agencies etc., and provision of support mechanism to help entrepreneurs among these deprived sections, it has specified that BCs should include BC Minorites and especially More and Most Backward Classes.

The Commission has been repeatedly making specific mention of BC Minorities so that the existence of this sub-category of BC is deeply etched into the memory and consciousness of the policy-making, policy-implementing and resource-providing elite of India and of the people in general. The elite should not fail to take its cue from this even at the present rather late stage.

All in all, this pioneering work, which owes its origin to Ashfaq Husain Ansari's labour of love in the cause of Social Justice and on behalf of Muslim BCs, who are on the one hand an important part of India's Socially and Educationally Backward Classes and on the other the overwhelming majority (but short of the totality) of India's Muslims, is of great significance. I earnestly hope that this work will shake India's elite, both among Muslims as well and Hindus, out of their ignorance and prejudices against Backward Classes, both Muslims as well as Hindus. Elite nihilism—negation of inconvenient Reality—must end. The Elite, while enjoying the fruits of non-elite productive labour and services, has always denied the existence of the non-elite. In the social sphere, the beneficiaries of the Caste System,—both Savarna and Ashraf—even while continuing to reap its benefits, vociferously deny the very existence of the victims of the System—Avarna/Ajlaf-Arzal—and ingenuously deny the very existence of Castes. I would appeal to them to benefit by the present work and open their heart and mind to the BC and specifically the Muslim BCs along with other BC, SC and ST.

Recognition of the reality of the existence of Muslim Backward Classes and their all-round development and empowerment in unison with their Hindu and other non-Muslim BC brethren and neighbours is a categorical imperative in the moral, national as well as Constitutional perspectives. The lines and direction of such development and empowerment have been pointed out by the Report of National Commission for Review of the Working of the Constitution (2002), the Reports of the Ninth Plan and Tenth Plan Working Groups on the Development and Empowerment of Backward Classes (1997 and 2001), the Annual Reports of the National Commission for Backward Classes, the Proceedings of the First National Conference on Backward Classes (1997) organised by the NCBC, and the BC section of the Dalit Manifesto (1996). Their development and empowerment along these lines will have multiple benefits. The first benefit is that this will restore to the Muslims BCs their due, denied to them over the centuries and post-independence decades, which is a value in itself. This in turn will add strength to the efforts for the progress of India by harnessing their fully developed potential to this stupendous task. Thirdly, it will ensure that the combined and united energies of Religious Minorities as a whole and their well-wishers will be available, without distraction, for the important effort for the protection and promotion of the religious, cultural and security rights of the Muslims and other Minorties. Simultaneously, the experience of conjoint development and empowerment of Muslim Backward Classes and their Hindu and other non-Muslim brethren and neighbours will have an exhilarating effect on the ethos and mutual orientation of Hindu, Muslim, Christian, Sikh and Buddhist Backward Classes, will orient them towards development and legitimate self-improvement, eliminate mutual suspicions and hostile stereotyping and thus will help lay the social, economic and cultural foundation for the establishment of a cohesive, integrated Indian society and nation—the Elite willing. Amen—Tathastu.

From my five decades of work among and in the cause of the Scheduled Castes, Backward Classes and Scheduled Tribes, I am painfully aware of the sense of deep hurt, experienced by this Trinity of India's overwhelming majority and near-totality of India's physical labour force, and in the present context by the Muslim Backward Classes, on account of the daily humiliations, discriminations and deprivations and continuous neglect that has been and that continues to be their lot. India will come into its own when this deep hurt is banished by extirpating it at its root. This is the first step toward India's stable, sustained and steady progress.

**P.S. KRISHNAN,** I.A.S. (Retired)
Chairman, National Action Forum for Social Justice
Former Secretary to Govt. of India, Ministry of Welfare
Former Member-Secretary, National Commission for Backward Classes
Former Member, National Commission for Scheduled Castes & Scheduled Tribes
Former Member, Expert Committee on Backward Classes
Chairman, Working Group for Empowerment of Backward Classes in X Plan
Member, Steering Committee for Empowerment of SC, BC and Minorities in X Plan
Member, Jury for Dr. Ambedker National Awards

# 27

# INTRODUCTION

*Ashfaq Husain Ansari*

As part of a well-conceived strategy of the Muslim Ashraf leadership; an issue is being rasied that there is nothing like division of Muslims as backward and forward—Asharaf and Ajlaf. On the other hand, eminent Muslim ulema of almost all the schools including Mufti Mohammad Shafi Deobandi, who was counted as Amir-ul-Hind and Mufti-e-Hind-o-Pak, Maulana Ashraf Ali Thanvi and Maulana Ahmad Raza Khan Bareilavi, have in one way or the other clearly endorsed the presence of high and low, backward and forward, Ashraf and Ajlaf among the Indian Muslims. The statistics generated by the Census of India, the analysis of the Encyclopaedia Americana, Encyclopaedia Britainica, the recommendations of the Mandal Commission and the historical 1992 verdict of the 9 member special Constitution Bench of the Honourable Supreme Court of India, all confirm that like its Hindu counterpart the Muslim religious community is also displaying caste-based divisions. Backward Muslims have been getting OBC recognition in quite a few states. Since the Nineteenth Century, Muslim Ashraf leadership did not raise any hue and cry at that point of time, nor was the question of bringing all the Muslims under the purview of reservation ever raised. The importance of OBC reservation increased when on 16th Nov. 1992 the Supreme Court handed down its historical verdict and following its direction along with other OBC communities

Muslim OBCs also began to receive the benefits of reservation. As a consequence of the 73rd and 74th amendments to the Constitution, the OBCs Muslims also started getting reservation in the election of the different Panchayati Raj and urban local bodies.

The report of census of India 1901 refers to the backward and forward division among the Muslims in the province of Bengal as under:

> *"The conventional division of the Mohammedans into four tribes– Sheikh, Sayyed Moghal and Pathan–has very little application to this province (Bengal). The Mohammedans themselves recognise two main social divisions – (1) Ashraf or Sharaf and (2) Ajlaf Ashraf means 'noble' and includes all unboubted descendants of foreigners and converts from high caste Hindus. All other Mohammedans including the occupational groups and all converts of lower ranks are known by the contemptuous terms 'Ajlaf', 'worthless' or 'mean people they are also called kamina or itar, 'base' or Rajil, a corruption of Rizal, 'worthless', in some places a third class called arzal or 'Lowest of all' is added. With them no other Mohammedan would associate and they are forbidden to enter the mosque or to use the public burial ground."*

Within these groups there (sic) are castes with social precedence of exactly the same nature as one finds among the Hindus:

1. Ashraf or better class Mohammedans: (i) Sayyeds (ii) Sheikhs (iii) Pathans (iv) Moghals (v) Malik (vi) Mirza.
2. Ajlaf or lower class Mohammedans: (i) Cultivating sheikhs and other who were originally Hindus but who do not belong to any functional group and have not gained admittance to the Ashraf Community e.g. Pirali and Thankrai (ii) Darzi, Jolaha, Fakir and Rangrez (iii) Barhi, Bhatiara, Chik, Churihar, Dai, Dhawa, Dhunia, Gaddi, Kala, Kasai, Kula, Kunjara, Laheri, Mahifarosh, Mallah, Naliaya, Nikari (iv) Adbad Bako, Bediya, Bhat, Chamba, Dafal, Dhobi, Hajjam, Mucha, Nagarchi, Nat, Panwaris, Madaris, Tuntia.

(3) Arzal or degrades class: Bhanar, Halalkhor, Hirja, Kashi, Lalbegi, Mungta, Mehtar.

The Encyclopaedia Americana (International Edition) describes this division among the Muslims as under:

> *"All important communities including the Muslims, Chirstians and Sikhs have some sort of caste scheme. These schemes are patterned after the Hindu System since most of these people originally came from the Hindu stock. The large-scale conversions that have been going on for centuries have modified Indian Caste Society. Thus, traditional Hindu commensal and connubial rituals had emphasis on inherited social status or rank though generally rejected in the Islamic or Christain religious ethic nevertheless operate on social plain in these societies in India. In India, social rites and customs vary from region to region rather than from religion to religion."*

Similarly, Encyclopaedia Britanica describes the phenomenon as under:

> *"Among Muslims, it is pointed out, a distinction is made between 'Ashraf' (supposed to be descendants of Arab immigrants) and non Ashraf (Native converts). Both are divided into sub-groups, particularly, the non-Ashrafs, who are converts from Hinduism, it is pointed out, practice caste system (including endogamy) in a manner close to that of their Hindu counterparts."*

These documents are evidence of the presence of caste-based distinctions among the Indian Muslims as they have been prevalent among the Hindus. If someone is denying their existence, he is not recognizing the presence of an acknowledged empirical ground reality. The situation here is altogether baffling. The very existence of caste-based division among the Muslims is not only denied: the backward Muslims are in fact being blamed for having invented such a division. Some one might ask these worthies as to where did the words Ashraf, Ajlaf and Arzal come from ? Did the backward Muslims themselves prefer to be called as "Kamtar", "Kameen" or "Razeel"? On the one hand, these Ashraf Muslims look down upon the non-Ashraf Muslims but when the non-Ashraf Muslims began receiving benefits due to their low status and social and educational backwardness, these Ashraf Muslims began trying devoted moves to avail these very benefits themselves. Demanding inclusion of all the Muslims under the

OBC category and organising seminars and meetings to generate sustained pressure en the issue, are parts of the same clever strategy. Another method of depriving the backward Muslims of their legitamate due is to obtain take OBC certificates.

Several cases of obtaining fake OBC certificates have come to the public attention in Northern India. However, wherever backward Muslims are conscious and careful, such cases are being nailed.

A lot of hue and cry was made in the 12th Lok Sabha on the Women's Reservation Bill in a very shameful manner. Among other reasons it was so argued that there is total backwardness in an entire community specially the Muslim community as if the backward Muslims are not covered under the reservation of the OBCs. The male dominated society is unable to stomach one-third reservation being envisaged for the women. Keeping the Ashraf Muslim leadership in front, such people who claim to be the messiah of the Muslim, have supported the attractive proposition of granting reservation to the entire Muslim community. Although claiming to be well wishers of the Muslims and self-appointed messiahs of the backward, these elements are hard core opponents of the very principle of reservation for the women. These forces talk in a very low key fashion about 10% compulsory, reservation for women as against one-third reservation for women but are very noisy about reservation for the entire Muslim community and the Muslim backwards. These so-called well-wishers of the Muslims consciously hide this ground reality that if there is common agreement of reservation for the backward, around 85% Muslims, who figure in the list of the OBCs, are bound to get such benefits. They are already a wailing these benefits in rural and urban local bodies election, in most of the states.

Why there is so much opposition to follow the precedent of reservation given to the women under the 73rd and 74th amendments in the Panchayati Raj and Urban local body elections in U.P. and other states, to the Lok Sabha and Assembly Elections? The procedure for giving reservation to the SC, ST and OBCs in this mechanism is very simple and straight. One-third of the Quota reserved for the SC and ST is earmarked for the women. Similarly, out of 27% reservation quota for the OBCs in which the OBC Muslims are also included one third seats reserved for the women. There is provision for reserving one third seats out of the remaining 50% to general category seats. Under this arrangement, women of all the classes in which women from the OBCs Muslim women are included are getting reservation. Some how the Women's Reservation Bill has been introduced in the 13th Lok Sabha. But it is yet to be seen what fate awaits it. It is essential to know not only the policies very clearly but also the intentions behind them.

In the 1995 rural and urban local bodies election in U.P., a record number of OBCs Muslim males and Muslim women got elected. It appears as though this startling development of visibly large representation of the OBC Muslim males and females has un-nerved the Ashraf leadership of some parties and, therefore, they are as a part of their well-rehearsed strategy, creates an impression as if the Muslims are not included in the list of the OBCs.

Political parties claiming to be secular and well wishers of the OBCs and Muslims such as the Congress, Socialist Party, Bahujan Samaj Party, Left parties and Rashtriya Janata Dal of Bihar should clearly realise this fact that 85% of the total population of the Muslims is backward and most such communities are included in the OBC list. These parities have deliberately sidelined the OBCs till now. They should realise that the Muslim OBCs if given an appropriate opportunity might leave them in the lurch. Now they are going to support only that political outfit which is prepared to fight at every available forum for getting all the legitimate rights of the OBC Muslims.

The OBC Muslims are one with the non-Muslim OBCs in securing reservation in proportion to their percentage in the total population. However, this fact should not be lost sight of that the backward constitute 85% among the total Muslim population. Whereas all the OBCs are demanding reservation on the basis of population parity principle, they should also demand that the census enumeration in the year 2001 should follow the pattern of 1931 census in which caste affiliation was one of the columns in the census schedule. This would enable precise enumeration of caste-wise population break up instead of estimates/guesstimates. Mandal Commission figures are nothing but estimates, the figures generated by the rural and urban OBC surveys conducted in U.P. for the rural and urban local bodies are not accurate and correct ones and the majority of those who conducted the surveys, were belonging to the upper castes or anti-mandal ideology. When the society is clearly divided in two distinct ideological entity's and the Constitution, clearly recognising its existence has given reservation to the backwards on this basis, there should not be any objection to have empirical figures instead of estimates. The real clear picture of the Indian social structure would become available in 2001 if it follows the enumeration pattern of the 1931 census containing caste column.

Here I want to draw attention to an important issue. The Mandal Commission had emphasized and recommended reservation in educational institutions along with the reservations in the services under the state. Most of the states have provided for reservations in the educational institutions but no one is even talking about reservation in central educational institutions, ICSC, CBSE etc. On the other hand in the name of super specialty definite steps are being taken to roll back reservation in medical and engineering educa-tion. Merit and competence are mentioned only when upper caste elites talk about reservation for the backwards. However, these very elements have specifically provided for reservation for their wards. Under Staff quota NRI and donation in all educational institutions without any reference to merit and competence. There is discretionary quota available in institutions like Kendriya Vidhyalayas where Ealmsot the whole of it is cornered by the upper castes. Similarly almost 95% of the donations seats in medical engineering and other professional technical private colleges are being filled by the wards of the upper caste elites without merit and competence.

In the name of minority institutions even backward Muslims are deprived of their share. Most of the minority institution are dominated by upper caste elite Muslims. Some way out must be found for proper representation of backward Muslims in the governance, appointments and admission of minority institution.

The Dalit non-Hindus which includes among others Mulsim and Christian converts from Dalit Hindus (Scheduled Caste) demands restoration of their reservation that was formally withdrawn by the Presidential order of 1950 in gross violation of Indian Constitution and denial of fundamental and human rights. Article 15 of the Constitution of India prohibits any discrimination on ground of religion, race, caste, sex or place of birth.

**It states as under:**

15 Prohibition of discrimination on ground of religion, race, caste, sex or place of birth.

(i) The states shall not discriminate against any citizen on ground only of religion, race, caste, sex, place of birth or any of them.

Under Article 341 and 342 of the Constitution—The discriminatory Constitution (Scheduled Castes) Order of 1950 issued very clearly states in its clause 3, 'but in Order to become a scheduled caste under this Order a person profess to be either a Hindu or a Sikh.'

The Constitution has given direction in Article 15, 341 and 342 which contradicts clause 3 of the Presidential Order. No where in the above mentioned Articles or in any other Article there are any reference to the religion of the person or the group of persons for inclusion in the list of scheduled caste.

The Constitution (Scheduled Castes) Order 1950 violates the constitution by discriminating in mentioning the name of Religion in its clause 3. Dalit Muslims and Dalit Christians who are mainly converts from Scheduled Caste Hindu to Islam or Christianity remained Dalit socially, educationally and economically.

No other person but Mahatma Gandhi indirectly justified the demand for inclusion of Dalit Muslims and Dalit Christians in the list of Scheduled Caste. He states:

*"Whether the Harijan is nominally a Christian, Muslim or Hindu and now Sikh, he is still a Harijan. He cannot change his spots inherited from Hinduism so-called. He may change his garb and call himself a Catholic Harijan or a Muslim Harijan or Neo-Muslim or Neo-Sikh, his untouchability will haunt him during his lifetime." (Harijan Dated 26.12.36)*

It is a fact that his untouchability is haunting him not only during his lifetime but generation after generation.

Inspite of the above-referred discriminatory Presidential Order Justice Sawant clearly expressed his point of view in the famous nine Judges Constitution Bench Indira Sahani versus Union of India landmark judgement, 474. As far as Islam is concerned, Islam also does not recognise caste or caste system. However, among the Muslims in fact there are Ashraf and Ajlafs i.e. High born or low born. The census report of 1901 of the province of Bengal records the following fact regarding the Muslims of the Province of Bengal:

*"The conventional division of the Mohammedans into four tribes – Sheikh, Sayyed, Moghal and Pathan has very little application to this province (Bengal). The Mohammadens themselves recognise two main social Strata – Ashraf and Ajlaf. Ashraf means Noble and includes all undoubted descendants of foreigners and converts from high group and all converts of lower ranks are known by the contemptuous term Ajlaf, wretches or mean people. They are also called 'Itar, base as 'Rasil', a corruption of Rizal, 'Worthless.' In some places a third class, called Arzal or 'lowest of all' is added. With them no other Mohammedan would associate and they are forbidden to enter the mosque or to use the public burial ground."*

Within these groups there are castes with social precedence of exactly the same nature as one finds among Hindus.

Justice Sawant further states in para 475 of the Judgement:

*475-"Similar facts regarding the then other Provinces could be gathered from their respective census reports. At present, there are many social groups among Muslim which are included in the list of scheduled castes in some states For example in Tamil Nadu, labbias including Rawthars and Marakayars are in the list of scheduled castes. This shows that the Muslims in India have not remained immune from the same social evils as are prevalent among the Hindus."*

As regards Christianity Justice Sawant also states in para 476:

> *476-"Though Christianity does not recognise caste system here are upper and lower castes among Christians. In Goa for example, there are upper caste Catholic Brahmins who do not marry Christians belonging to the lower castes. In many Churches, the low caste Christians have to sit apart from the high caste Christians. There are constant bickering between Goankars and Gawdes who form a clear-cut division in Goan Christian society. In Andhra Pradesh, there are Christian Harijan, Christian Madras, Christian Reddys, Christian Kamma etc. In Tamil Nadu converts to Christianity from Scheduled Castes – Latin Catholics. Christian Shamars, Christian Nadars and Chirstian Gramani are in the list of scheduled castes. Such instances are many and vary from region to region."*

Hence, in the light of the above referred Articles of the Constitution of India and relevant paragraphs of the historic nine judges constitution bench Mandal Judgement the demand for inclusion of Dalit Muslim and Dalit Christian in the list of scheduled castes is fully justified in all respects. It is also constitutionally valid. Clause 3 of the Constitution (scheduled castes) order 1950 must be deleted without any further delay.

Muslims and Christians should fight untidily for their common cause.

It will not be out of place to conclude with the relevant paragraphs from the recommendations of Constitution Review Commission under the Chairmanship of Justice Venkata Challaiah:

Under chapter 10.11.1 it says:

> *10.11.1 "The general argument for creating a better cultural, economic and educational environment for protection of rights and of development of disadvantaged sections applies mutatis mutandis to the religious and linguistic minorities. Constitutional safeguards already exist. What is needed is a major breakthrough in educational and economic spheres. In this context, it is also to be noted that the bulk of the religious minorities consist of castes/communities, which are included in the list of socially and educationally backward classes. They are mainly counterparts of Hindu Backward Classes and to some extent of Hindu Scheduled Castes."*

> *10.11.2 The Commission recommends that:*

*(a) Steps should be taken for improvement of educational standards amongst the minority communities. Special programmes should be drawn up after the widest consultation with the leaders of minority communities including leaders of BCs, SCs and STs among Minorities from academic, professional, business and socio-political spheres and from low occupational spheres. Such programmes should be generously funded. Only educational and cultural advancement will help the cause of national integration as well as raise the capabilities of the communities. This is the high road to national cohesion.*

*(b) At present, the political representation of minority communities in legislatures, especially Muslims, has fallen well below their proportion of population. The proportion of BCs among them is next to nil. This can lead to a sense of alienation. It is incumbent for political parties to build up leadership potential in the minority communities, including BCs, SCs and STs among them, for participation in political life. The role of the state for strengthening the pluralism of Indian polity has to be emphasised.*

*(c) Backward classes belonging to religious minorities who have been identified and included in the list of backward classes and who, in fact constitute the bulk of the population of religious minorities should be taken up with special care along with their Hindu counterparts in the developmental efforts for the backward classes. This should be on the pattern of the approach to the development of Backward Classes formulated by the Working Group for the Development and Empowerment of Backward Classes in the Tenth Plan referred to separately under Backward Classes. This will on the one hand, help the development of the masses of religious minorities and on the other hand help bring about national cohesion.*

*(d) An effort needs to be made to carry out special recruitment of persons belonging to the under represented minority communities in the police forces of States, paramilitary forces and armed forces. This will instill confidence among minority populations as well as help them to develop responsible attitudes towards security issues confronting the nation.*

The Commission recommends that the Government should immediately implement everyone of the recommendations of the Working Group on Employment of Backward Classes in the Tenth Plan which covers all aspects and fields of their development—Economic, Educational, Social, Employment, Reservation etc.—taking in with particular care those backward classes who belong to religious minorities along with their Hindu counterparts in a cohesive manner. For example, some of the residential talent schools ear marked for Backward Classes should be located in areas of concentration of Muslims BCs. Further there should be residential talent schools for backward 'classes as separately recommended for SCs and STs at the rate of one each for boys and girls in each district, 75% being taken from backward classes and 25% from other categories. The Government should without any delay introduce reservation for backward classes in seats in educational institutions since absence of promotion of their education through reservation and other means when there is reservation of employment is anomalous.

Publication for larger circulation of the papers of these distinguished sociologists is needed in order to familiarise the backward Muslims with the central issues facing them at this juncture. They are blissfully unaware of the sinister conspiracy to wipe off their very identity. It is very easy to understand the logic of demand, for reservation for the entire Muslim community on the basis of their characteristics. However, it is very essential to understand the stark reality. This stark reality is mirrored by the contributions of these eminent sociologists. Dr. Ashghar Ali Engineer, Dr. D.L. Sheth, Dr. Hasan Nishat Ansari, Dr. K.Z. Amani, Dr. Anwer Pasha and also Prof. Shahabuddin Ansari, Besides introduction three of my own Articles on the subject are also included. To facilitate this larger objective these contributions are being published in English. The valuable addition to this volume is the foreword by Mr. P.S. Krishnan, IAS. (Retired). In fact, his foreword has become the main Article of this thin volume. He forcefully placed the facts and figures with relevant documents in his own style. His life long association and commitment to the welfare of S.C., S.T. and OBC's is fully reflected in the foreword.

I am grateful to the learned authors and the respective newspapers with whose acknowledgements these pieces are being published. I am also thankful to Principal Samiul Haq and Comrade Azizur Rahman for their co-operation in bringing out this publication.

**Ashfaq Husain Ansari**
Member of Parliament (Seventh Lok Sabha)
Member, State Commission
for Backward Classes U.P. (First)
Working President
Centre of Backward Muslims of India

# 28

# BASIC PROBLEMS OF INDIAN MUSLIMS

*Asghar Ali Engineer*

There is great debate in the country about the backwardness of the Muslims in India. Mostly it is theorised that it is their religion which is primarily responsible for this state of affairs. Such theorisation, to say the least, is utterly faulty and reflects either the anti-Islamic bias of the theorist or his/her lack of understanding of social roots of a problem. No religion can be held responsible for backwardness of its followers. This amounts to mixing up religious category with that of social one. Also such a theorisation seeks simplistic explanation. Any social phenomenon is a pretty complex one and a social theorist has to look into various factors—social, economic, cultural as well as religious. Also, no religious community can be treated by a sophisticated social theorist as a homogenous one. All religious communities are invariably divided in various groups, sects and classes and these groups, sects and classes have specificities of their own. No community can be either entirely backward or forward. If a section is backward another section will be forward. It hardly makes any sense to say that all Muslims in India are backward. A section howsoever small, will be construed as forward. Thus when we say Indian Muslims are backward, we mean a larger section of them compared to the Hindus, the majority community, is backward. And when we say Muslims are backward it should not imply that all Hindus are better off and have made it economically. There are millions of Hindus even from upper castes who are illiterate and poor in addition to those belonging to the scheduled castes i.e. Dalits. It is necessary to point these thing out in order to fight the stereotypes widely prevalent both among the Muslims and the Hindus.

First of all, it must be stressed that all Indian Muslims are not backwards. In contemporary India also, there are quite a number of Muslims who are quite wealthy, educated and well placed in society. They are quite influential in regional or central political power structure. Secondly, it must be understood that the main cause of Muslim backwardness is in their social origin. All Muslims in the medieval period did not belong to the ruling classes which were feudal in origin. Comparatively very few Muslims in India belonged to the upper classes. The vast majority of Indian Muslims were convert from amongst the Shudras of the Hindu society. Here we do not want to go into the controversy about coercive conversion. Suffice it may to say that such a stereotype is totally inadequate explanation of the complex process of conversion. It is more appropriate to say that conversion were by and large specially from amongst the Dalits of a voluntary and not of coercive nature.

As pointed out before, bulk conversion to Islam from amongst the Shudras, by and large account for general Muslim backwardness. These conversions took place because to these oppressed people Islam appeared to be much more democratic and egalitarian than the caste-ridden Hinduism. Among these Shudras, there were numerous jatis based on profession. Thus, there were Julahas (weavers), Khatiks (those slaughtering animals), Dhobis (washermen), Rangrez (dyers), Pinjaras (carders), Malis (gardners or those who grew and sold fruit and vegetables), Gorkans (grave diggers), Tambolis (those selling betel leaves and nuts), Hajjams (barbers), Lohars (iron smiths), Suthar (carpenter) and so on. When converted to Islam these professions were not given up by them. Thus what changed for them was the religion but not their social status. No wonder that these converted Muslims were generally looked down upon by the Muslims belonging to the ruling classes. As is well known, the upper class Muslims were known as Ashraf (i.e.

those of noble origins) and those belonging to the lower castes as Ajlaf (or of low origin). The latter were also known as Kamins a contemptuous term for these Muslims. Zia-ud-din Barani, a chronicler of the Sultanate period, refers to these converted Muslims in the most contemptuous terms and opines that they do not deserve higher education. It is enough if they are taught how to recite the Quran and say prayers which are obligatory for them as Muslims. Thus, it will be seen that a large majority of Muslims are utterly backward on account of the very nature of their social origin and it is these Muslims who constituted the vast majority of India.

It will be seen that in regions like Bengal where vast numbers converted to Islam from earliest days, poverty and illiteracy ruled the roast. It is well-known through various anthroplogical studies that in Bengal it is low caste Hindus who had by and large embraced Islam. Most of them were artisans in urban areas and small or landless peasants in rural areas. During early British period, a British civil servant W.W. Hunter also pointed out in his book that the Muslims of Bengal were quite backward and that their representation in government services was totally inadequate. Hunter's book was widely quoted by Muslims to get more concessions from the British. However, the position of Muslims in U.P. was not dismal. As there was Muslim rule in Owadh the Muslim Feudal class was quite well to do and was more than adequately represented in government services. The Muslim population in U.P. at that time was also around 15-16% and their representation, as a study by Paul Brass convincingly shows, in educational and police services was more than 20%. So wherever there was a large Muslim ruling class their representation in government services was far from being inadequate.

Thus, it will be seen that while in Bengal the Muslim representation in primary level education in English was nil, it was around 30% in Owadh in 1881-82. And in Punjab where Muslims were in majority there representation at primary level English education was just 31.1%. At college level in the same year the percentage of Muslim students in Bengal was 3.8% and in Owadh 4.5%, and in Punjab it was about 12.6% (see sharp

H. (1920), selection from Educational records, Pt. 1 1781-1893, Calcutta, Ch 27 in). Thus R.K. Kochhar observes in his article, 'English Education In India-Hindu Anamnesis versus Muslim Torpor' (Economic and political weekly, November, 28, 1992 pp. 2614). It is only in North-West provinces and Oudh corresponding to U.P. of today that the percentage of Muslim in schools and colleges was higher than it was in the total populations. Elsewhere Muslims, were under represented in education. In 1891-92 in NWFP and Oudh Muslim percentage in total population was 13.14 in secondary schools, 21.9 in arts colleges; and in professional colleges 17.7. In Bengal, Muslim percentage in total population was 32.3, in secondary schools 9.3, arts colleges 5.6 and in professional colleges 3.5. In Madras, percentage at school 5.3 was consistent with the percentage in total population 6.3, but the percentage of Muslim at college was a dismal 1.7 per cent.

Thus if Muslims, were backward because of their Muslimness or because of prejudices against them as some would like to argue it will be difficult to understand why they were adequately represented in education in Oudh, and NWFP and quite inadequately represented in Bengal despite much greater proportion of population there. The explanation lies in their social origin in these respective states. In Oudh there were more Muslims belonging to the upper classes than in Bengal as in Bengal large number were converted from amongst low caste Hindus. If one looks into corresponding figures for dalits and backward caste Hindus. It will be seen that their representation also was quite dismal in schools and in government services. Only in those states like Vadodara (in Gujarat) and Kolhapur (In Maharashtra) where the princely rulers made conscious efforts to disseminate education among dalits and backward caste Hindus that we find somewhat better representation of these sections of population in educational and government service.

There is another important factor one must focus upon in order to understand Muslim backwardness in the economic field. The Muslim ruling classes throughout medieval India were feudal and their prosperity depended on landed estates and agricultural surpluses extracted from the peasantry. They did not produce entrepreneur from the beginning. Even during the Sultanate or Mughal period the finances of the empire were handled by the Hindus. Mostly the finance ministry was in their (Hindu) hands.

Noted historian Toynbee has also drawn our attention to this fact. Since the upper class Muslim prosperity at least in North and East India almost entirely depended on feudal estates they came to grief when feudalism was weakened and modern economy replaced the feudal economy. It was, therefore, hardly surprising that for lack of experience and interest the Muslim jagirdari and zamindari did not take to modern commerce and industry. They ultimately lost all their economic clout with the abolition of the zamindari system. Many of them became deeply indebted to their financiers and had to mortgage their jagirs. There was no enterpruneur class among the Muslims in North India at all. No Muslim from North or East India ever owned big industrial or commercial enterprise.

Among Hindus on the other hand there always was an enterprising class. They were mostly in trade during medieval ages. When the British established their rule and modern industrial production system was gradually established in India, the Hindus took to it without hesitation. They soon established cloth mills and other industries. The tiny Parsi community from western India also gave the lead in this field. TATA's became one of the greatest industrial houses in India and they played a pioneering role in steel industry. Though Muslims were a much larger community we do not find such enterprising spirit among them for historical reasons as explained above. Among Hindus too the entrepreneur class was not found in every region it came mainly from Rajasthan, Gujarat and Punjab. In these regions, there was a strong commercial tradition among the Banias and Marwaris. The Brahmins too like the Muslim upper classes in general and of Punjab, Rajasthan and Gujarat, in particular, could not develop enterprising spirit. But unlike the Muslim zamindars, they did not have to carry the burden of feudal tradition and quickly took to modern education (after little initial hesitation) and became pioneers in this field. Thus, they at least made up for their non-prominence in economic field, with there prominence in cultural and educational field.

It should also be noted that feudal economy is fundamentally different from capitalist economy including its ethos. In feudal economy, there is no concept of saving and capital formation at all. As far as the feudal lords are concerned the whole emphasis is on consumption and showing off ones wealth. If there is not saving there will be no capital formation and no financial wherewithal for investment. Thus in feudal culture it is grand living which is important while in (developing economy at least) it is saving for investment which matters most. Since the Muslim ruling classes in the North India were feudal they believed in living a grand life and had no concept of saving and capital formation at all. Thus, they could not adjust to a capitalist and industrial economy and their affluence died down with feudalism. The trading classes among the Hindus, on the other hand adjusted themselves with industrial economy and made substantial investments in various industries in 19th century itself.

In Western India, specially along the coastal towns there were few Muslim sects like Bohras, Khojas and Memons who have been traders for many centuries. Their numbers, as compared to other Muslims in India is not very high. In all they are not more than 2.5 to 3 million, all told. They also did not take to modern industries. They were confined mainly to traditional merchantile sphere. One possible reason for this was lack of big capital for investment in big industries and second explanation could be their own traditional outlook. Thirdly, part of the explanation also lay in their avoidance of banking interest as the same is thought to be strictly banned by Islam. But it is certainly not the main reason, as some people think, some among the Bohras, Khojas and Memons did take to shipping and insurance on a large scale and it is these families who on migration to Pakistan after partition became big industrialist there, thus it will be seen that those who could have developed into industrialist of some significance in India migrated to Pakistan possibly to avoid competition. No doubt, they became big industrialist and are among the 22 top industrial families of Pakistan. But that is another story altogether, it is also interesting to note that all the top industrialists in Pakistan until recently were originally from western India and belonging to one of these three trading communities of Gujarat. It thus clearly shows that one needs to have certain economic outlook and upbringing in order to become an industrialist. There is no wonder if one does not find industrialists and big businessmen among the Muslims, specially in North India. One still finds some businessmen and small scale industrialists among Muslims in Western and Southern India. There has been a business community (specially in leather business) among Tamil Muslims, the rest of businessmen in South in Bangalore, Kochi, Coimbatore, Chennai etc. are all from those migrated from Western India.

## INDIAN MUSLIMS AND THEIR BACKWARDNESS IN CONTEMPORARY INDIA

As pointed out before the businessmen of some note from Western India migrated to Pakistan leaving behind only small businessmen who saw hardly any benefit in migrating to Pakistan. However, subsequently they prospered through sheer hard work and taking benefit of developing economy of India grew to some extent. Today these business communities are the most properous communities among the Muslims. In North India too the erstwhile ruling classes mostly belonging to the feudal families of Nawabs, Jagirdars and Talukdars migrated to Pakistan (with few exceptions of course). Also professionals (like lawyers, university teachers, doctors, engineers, civil servants those in police and military service etc.) and others belonging to highly educated and skilled middle classes form north and western India also migrated to Pakistan for greener pastures. It is important to note that except from Hyderabad very few Muslims from south migrated to Pakistan. It is north and North-Western India which account for largest migration to Pakistan-followed by the west. Thus, those Muslims who were left behind were those who saw no benefit whatsoever in going over to Pākistan. Thus, migration to Pakistan was restricted to richer and upper classes Muslims.

The Muslims belonging to lower castes and lower classes were left behind in India. Most of them were artisans from small and middle towns like Azamgarh, Maunath Bhanjan, Banaras, Aligarh, Moradabad, Ferozabad, Agra, Meerut, Deoband, Saharanpur etc. in western U.P. and small and marginal peasants from rural areas. Needless to say more migrations took place from urban than rural areas. One reason for this is economic (as they saw not much economic benefit in migrating to Pakistan and another reason of course is cultural rootedness, the people from rural areas are much more culturally rooted than those from urban areas. More culturally rooted a person is less inclined he/she will be to migrate to another area. Also those belonging to happen categories like Coolies, Tangawalas, Rickshawdrivers, Motor mechanic, Malis, Grave Diggers, Beggars, Weavers, Qassabs, Telis, Tambolies and several others also had no incentive in migrating to Pakistan and these were all economically and culturally backward Muslims. Thus, there are historical reasons for backwardness of Muslims in India today. Partition of India is nothing short of watershed in this respect. Not that before partition there was no backwardness among Indian Muslims. There was, in fact we have already argued that most of the conversions to Islam were from backward castes and they embraced Islam with their legacy of economic and cultural backwardness. There was great deal of poverty in Bengal, Punjab and Sind etc. But before partition there also was a section of Muslims which was highly affluent and influential. This section of Muslims either remained on the other side of the fence or migrated from India leaving very poor and backward Muslims.

This is dismal picture indeed. The overwhelming masses of Muslims are still living in poverty and ignorance. The economic and educational indices are very disappointing indeed. Usually when we complain about Muslims and their poor representation in services we refers to IAS, IPS and other prestigious services. It is true that their representation in these services is below two per cent. This is because the formation of educated middle class among Muslims is painfully slow. But concentrating on this will amount to betraying an elitist approach. The picture of poverty among Muslims at lower levels (relatively speaking) is very dismal indeed. We would like to quote some figures in order to give some idea. From available figures it can be said that more than 50% Muslims live below poverty line as compared to Hindus 40% of whom live below poverty line.

Thus, Muslims have to go a long way to imbibe education. Is it not surprising that Muslims whose prophet is reported to have said that it is obligatory for every Muslim man and Muslim woman to seek knowledge? But empirical reality is always very different from ideological desires or obligations. As pointed out before Muslims in India were converted to Islam from low castes with their cultural baggage and it is this cultural heritage which weigh down upon them even today. Unfortunately most of their Maulavis and Mullahs also come from these strata of society and thus having extremely backward outlook. It is they who sermonise Muslims in mosques on Fridays and thus keep on reinforcing the backward outlook the Muslims in general have on account of their backward social origin. This has become a vicious circle and it is very difficult to get out of it. No wonder then that Madarsa education is much mare popular among them than modern secular education. The huge Zakat amounts collected every year which certainly runs into several crores of rupees is mostly spent an Madarsa education. The Mullahs of course have a vested interest in running Madarsa as it gives them livelihood, recognition and power.

There is yet another reason why Madarsa education is more popular among Muslims. Religious Pathashalas among Hindus hardly exist today. One reason of course is as explained above backward cultural heritage of most of Muslims. Second and equally important reason is that most of the Muslims in urban areas are artisans and they prefer that their children work with their parents to learn the craft and supplement their income. However, they send their children to Madarsa firstly because they think it is obligatory for them to do so. Secondly, the Madarsa are more conveniently located as compared to municipal or government schools and their timings are also more suited as most of the Madarsa teach either in early morning or late evening when children are free from their economic activities and lastly education in these Madarsas is free and books also need not be purchased. Also, the syllabus in government schools is thought to be Hindu oriented which alienates Muslims.

These are some of the reasons for greater attraction for Madarsa rather than secular education among the Muslims. However, it is certainly impeding the economic progress of the Muslims as overwhelming number belongs to lower classes. With the so-called liberalisation and market friendly policies adopted by the Government of India, those who do not pay attention to modern secular education will be at much greater disadvantage. Muslims must go in for technical education in ever larger numbers to improve their artisanal skills and to face tough competition in the high tech orientation of market. How could it, be done? It is certainly not impossible. The Indian Christians are also converts from low and backward castes and tribals. But both among protestants as well as Catholics there is a great deal of emphasis in education. The Christian churches make it a point to open as many schools as possible and schools run by them are considered as among the best in the country. Even in Pakistan the best schools are those run by the Christians and there too, there is rush for admission in these schools. It is true that they receive aid from foreign countries but so do various Muslim organisations from different Arab countries. But Muslims utilize all these funds for running Madarsas only and rarely ever open schools or colleges for modern education. The Muslims can overcome their backwardness only if they pay attention to modern secular education.

Some Muslim leaders and intelligent have started making demands for reservation for Muslims in jobs and consider this as a viable solution. In my opinion it is not. There can be reservation for backward class Muslims on the basis of backward categories but not on the basis of religion. To demand reservation on the basis of religion is to play with communal fire. It will stoke Hindutva passions and benefit only the Sangh Parivar. In fact, there are very few qualified Muslims available for jobs. What is needed is to make concerted efforts to provide them facilities for acquiring these qualifications. The Ashraf Muslims produced a Sir Syed to motivate them to acquire modern education. Now in a democratic and egalitarian setup the backward and poor Muslims need an Ambedkar to motivate them for modern education. Today, the Dalits are ahead of Muslims in many respects because they produced their Ambedkar. The backward Muslim have yet to produce their own. And even after they do, they will have to struggle hard and for long to forge ahead.

*(The author is the Director of Institute of Islamic Studies, Mumbai and is also a prominent leader of the reform movement among the Bohras.)*

## 29

# MUSLIM RESERVATION: NO PROVISION FOR COMMUNAL QUOTAS

*D.L. Sheth*

For sometime now a section of the Muslim leadership has been demanding a separate ten per cent quota in reservation for Muslims. This is despite the fact that the majority of Muslims is already covered under the existing provision of reservation for the other Backward classes.

The new demand is not only for allocating a separate quota for OBC Muslim, but to extend the provision to all Indian Muslims. After Independence the argument goes, the Muslim community as a whole in Indian has become backward and should be declared as such. The demand concedes that the sub communities/biradaris of Muslims notified as backwards should get the first priority within the proposed separate category of 'Muslims'. The rest of the Muslim should get the benefits of reservation "only if and to the extend that Muslims quotas remain unfulfilled". A caveat is, however, added that the quotas unused by the 'backward' Muslim communities should go to the other Muslims.

This demand is part of the leadership's efforts to recover lost ground in the post-Babri Muslim politics. It is, however, not succeeding in Mustering popular Muslim support for the demand and making it an issue in mobilisational politics. This is because the poor and traditionally backward Muslim communities fear that if all Muslims become entitled to reservation their opportunities for upward social mobility will be severely curtailed, as the benefits will then go increasingly to the upper strata of Muslims. This situation may not continue for long. What can probably convert the demand into a symbolic issue of injustice done to Muslims is the frustration among poor and backward Muslim communities who deserve to be included in backward class lists but have been kept waiting.

**LONG TERM RESULTS**

The demand for separate reservation quota for all Muslims, however, raises an altogether different set of issue. Is the demand consistent with the rationale of the established policy of OBC reservation? What implications does it have for India's existence as a plural, secular democracy? It has become necessary to study the implications of this demand and prevent it from snowballing into the dangerous symbolic politics of mobilisation and counter mobilisation around ethnic-religious nationalism. First, it will reactivate the pernicious pre-partition discourse that essentialities religious communities as social-political monoliths, disregarding vital internal social economic and cultural differences within them a discourse now adopted by the Hindutva movement.

**SOCIAL JUSTICE**

It is a sociologically established fact that within every religious community there existed a vertical hierarchy of social groups marked by economic, social and educational differences. These differences do not undermine the religious identity of a community as such but that by itself, does not place different group following one religion within one single, horizontal, social, economic and cultural space. Cultural plurality in India is not just about the existence of different communities of faith. Plurality is more substantively manifested though the various micro-communities and cultures that have grown historically within and across religious boundaries. The Claim that a community of faith constitutes a unitary socio-economic and cultural entity, whether made by a majority or minority, in fact, represent a political strategy of a small elite to elicit majority support from its co-religionists. In effect, such elite politics towards aspirations for upward social mobility of a majority within a religious community and denies it the economic and social rights which state policy extends to the poor and the backward populations cutting across religions.

Second, by demanding reservation for all Muslims, the Muslim social elite has adopted a strategy of deliberate obfuscation of the terms of discourse on the issue of social justice. Again their strategy mirrors that of the Hindu upper caste elite which also refuses to recognize the social disadvantages and discrimination suffered by communities at the lower rungs of the Hindu social hierarchy. Just as the latter seeks to project the unity of all Hindus by including the lower caste. Hindus to get on the Hindutva bandwagon, the former wants to project the communal solidarity of the Muslims by taking over the reins of the backward Bandwagon.

Third, such a demand seeks to subvert the very rations of the reservation policy. The policy of OBC reservation is premised on the secular principle of social and educational backwardness of any class. It recognizes specific communities, cutting across religion as backward or non-backward on the basis of what the Supreme Court has described as a time-tested criteria of backwardness evolved by different states. Thus, any religious community almost invariably comprises backward and non-backward classes. Just as there are castes and classes among the Hindu majority, here are classes and caste like formations among the Muslims, Christians and Sikhs.

Backwardness is thus a congealed social reality of an occupational or a low traditional status group within a large macro-community of faith. This condition of backwardness among sub-communities of faith may or may not be theologically sanctioned but in reality it operates at the level of relatively closed hereditary cross-generational status groups which prevents the occupational and social mobility of its members. This is true, for example, of the Julahas or Halalkhors among the U.P. Muslims the Majhabis or Ramgharias among the Sikhs, the fishing communities among the Christians and so on. Similarly some groups within each community of faith are traditionally 'forward' for example, the Sayyeds, Sheikhs and other Ashraf communities of the U.P. Muslims, the Thangals, Arbis, Arakkals, Koyas and keys among the Kerala Muslims, the Khatris and Jats among the Sikhs, the Syrians among the Kerala Christian and so on. The claim that an entire community of faith is socially and educationally backward is a travesty of sociological truth and makes nonsense of the principle of social justice.

**NEW DEMAND**

We must, therefore, distinguish between the political principle of minority relevant for protecting cultural identities and rights and the social principle of backwardness meant to settle issues of equity and justice. Today these two separate logics are being deliberately tangled by the demand that the whole Muslim Community be allotted a separate quota of reservation as backward class. The proponents of reservation of all Muslims should in the interest of intellectual honesty and political candor, make their demand as a 'religious minority' but not as a 'backward class'.

Even this would mean a major amendment to the Constitution, one which would violate the secular spirit of the Constitution. India's Constitution recognises the cultural rights of minorities as fundamental rights and forbids discrimination on grounds of religious affiliation, but it is foundationally opposed to any idea of communal quotas. The new demand of Muslim reservation is simply a stratagem to introduce through the back-door the principle of communal quotas into the constitution.

*(The author a well known social scientist, is a former member of the National Commission of Backward Classes.)*

"The Large majority of the Muslims in India were originally recruited to Islam from the intermediate and lower rungs of Hindu society wherein status was rigidly defined in terms of birth and maintained by strong social sanctions. When these groups became incorporated into Muslim society through conversions either by peaceful persuasion, threat of force, offers of material and political advantages or aspirations of social mobility, they must have imported their social system with them. Since much of early conversion in Islam was a group process, this must have been easy. Some acculturative influence of Hinduism was thus inevitable. But if caste among the Muslim owed itself entirely to Hindu influence, then the Islamization of Muslim groups over the centuries should have resulted in the slow and gradual elimination of caste principles and ideology. However, such evidence as is available suggests that Islamization serves to reinforce rather than weaken or eliminate caste distinctions. Consequently, the question whether there are some elements in Islam which support caste distinctions becomes relevant."

# 30

# SOCIAL CLASSIFICATION OF INDIAN MUSLIMS: GENESIS AND CONSEQUENCES

*Hasan Nishat Ansari*

Various historical facts and circumstances ultimately led the members of the Indian Muslim Community to be divided into different castes and classes.

In fact the cult of 'high born' and 'low born' or 'forwards' and 'backwards' was propounded by the medieval ruling Muslim classes of Persia, central Asia and Afghanistan which was the main subject of Ziauddin Barani, the famous 'fourteenth century historian and political theoretician in his work 'Fatawa-e-Jahandari', completed in circa 1358-59 A.D. When the Central Asiatic Muslims entered and settled in India they also brought the vice of High Lineage and Low lineage and this to a great extent, together with Indian caste system had a direct impact on the Muslim society in complete derogation of the Islamic tenets of equality and fraternity among the human beings as a whole.

In modern times, the so-called upper caste Muslims spearheaded by Sir Syed Ahmed Khan (1817-98) were solely responsible for branding patriotic Muslim community as 'Badzat' or people of bad caste in order to obtain patronage of the British rulers for the Muslim gentry or the so-called high born Muslims. Sir Syed in his book 'Asbab-e-Baghawat-e-Hind' (The causes of the Indian Revolt) has categorically condemned the anti-British activities of the community of Muslim weavers and other backward Muslim Communities during the Indian Mutiny by stating that the members of the 'Badzat' or bad caste of weavers were most active in the Indian revolt of 1857. This sinister design to place the so-called upper castes in higher hierarchy of the Muslim society continued unabated and thus in the contextual facts and circumstances the actual champion of divide of Muslims into forwards and backward are the member of the so-called upper castes.

Ziauddin Barani in his book 'Fatawa-e-Jahandari', had advocated abrogation of higher secular and ecclesiastical education to the down-trodden Muslims and strongly recommended elementary religious education alone for the so called low born members of the Muslim society thereby depriving them altogether of any opportunity to claim higher temporal and ecclesiastical status in the society and maintaining the supremacy of the so-called upper strata of Muslim society. This philosophy of divide of Muslims into so-called high and low classes was ultimately adopted by Sir Syed who projected himself through his overt and covert activities in his political life as the greatest protagonist of society. In the nineteenth century, he was the chief exponent of the theory that the backward Muslim classes could not be tolerated to come up in the society as equals and it is an inherent right of the so-called higher Muslim Classes to be supreme and to relegate the backward classes in a state of serfdom.

The 'Tarikh-e-Firoz Shahi' of Barani and the earlier historical chronicle 'Tabagat-e-Nasiri' of Minhaj Siraj disclose that Muslim weavers and similar other vocational classes of Muslims were excluded from higher offices of the Sultan even under great Sultans namely Illtutmish and Balban. From Barani's 'Tarikh-e-Firoz Shahi' it is apparent that no sooner was it discovered that the imperial Wazir Nizamul-Mulk Junaidi was of weaver descent than he was removed from his office and along with him soma other officials of similar descent were also removed from their offices by Sultan Illtutmish. It also appears from the Tarikh that Muhammad-bin-Tughlaq inducted in various high offices backward Indian Muslims being attracted by their caliber and talent to encounter disaffection among the foreign Turkish, Arab and Afghan Amirs. The social discrimination among the Muslims infact emanated from the beginning to Turko-Muslim Sultanate which in effect was directly in conflict with the Islamic ideology of equality of mankind. In the circumstances, the first great Muslim social reformer Shaikh Kabir (A.D. 1440-1518), son of father Nur Ali alias Niru and mother Naima styled Nima of weaver descent, preached to Muslim and Hindu communities the gospel of social equality and universal brotherhood to create a casteless society and raze down the barrier of error and unenlightenment between the two communities. The movement initiated by Kabir was strongly resisted by caste extremists who coincidently dominated the Indian society but nevertheless the movement had desirable impact, on the social spectrum of India irrespective of caste and creed. And notwithstanding Kabir's movement against the evils of caste ism the malady of social discrimination based on caste and birth unfortunately continued till the end of Mughal rule and was ultimately inherited by a class of Muslims who had been regularly patronised by the Muslim rulers as higher ups of the Muslim society. This social vice was gradually adopted by the so-called superior Muslims as a spring board for using religion as a political instrument in the nineteenth and twentieth centuries.

The aforesaid historical facts which cannot be denied lead to only one conclusion that the sinister move was initiated and maintained by the so-called upper caste Muslim aristocracy. Such pernicious activities finally culminated in organised reaction among the oppressed Backward Classes and as a result the Momin and other backward Muslim classes had to organise themselves socially and politically to shake of the shakles of domination and such forces were led by the "All India Momin Conference" which played a dynamic role in freedom movement against British rule and took positive steps for the progress and development of the backward classes in social, intellectual, political and cultural spheres of the society. As a result of the social and political awakening created by the activities of the Momin Conference the backward Muslim communities now have various separate organisations that look after their needs and the long and arduous struggle waged by the Momin conference has further enabled these organisations to unite into the apex formation of the All India Muslims Backward Classes Federation.

There is absolutely no gain-saying about the fact that the perceptions of low born and high born is alien to the tenets of Al-Quran but the reality remains that the upper classes in the Muslim society flagrantly violated such Islamic tenets of equality, fraternity and universal brotherhood. These democratic principles were discarded by the so-called noble born Muslims who have now emerged as the so-called upper castes or forward classes Barani in the 'Fatwa-e-Jahandari' has grossly misinterpreted the verse of Al-Quran and sayings of the prophet underscoring equality of mankind by contending that only well born Muslims are capable of piety and virtues for they have adopted the nobler professions while from inferior born Muslims wickedness and destruction originate because they practice the baser arts and the meaner professions. The unambiguous ratio of the verse of the Al-Quran and the sayings of the Prophet is that persons irrespective of caste, race and colour are nearest to Allah by sole virtue of their piety and the abominable theory of High born and Low born is absolutely repugnant to the principles of Islam. There is no scope for social and political distinctions among Muslims as ordained by the Islamic scriptures and its very unislamic existence in the Muslim society is the direct outcome of the class attitude of the so-called superior born Muslims.

As Raghupati Sahai Firaq Gorakhpuri, an eminent intellectual of India says, "Living in India is not enough unless India lives in you". And this had actually happened in the attitude of the so-called Muslim higher ups who led by Sir Syed initiated a campaign to alienate the Muslims from the national freedom movement of Indian National Congress against the British rule and carrying out a separate platform in the name of religion in collusion with the British which ultimately led to partition of India. Sir Syed visualized that by joining hands with the Congress the interests of the higher ups in the Muslims community were likely to be in jeopardy because the Congress philosophy envisaged social equality of Indians and therefore, he preferred loyalty to the British rules and paved the way of Muslim separatism indirect opposition to the national mainstream. Subsequently, this fissiparous movement of Syedism, misquoted as Aligarh movement, was vehemently supported by the All India Muslim League.

During the Sultanate and Mughal periods of medieval history of India, the Momins or Muslim weaver class and similarly situated Muslim working classes were economically prosperous but socially suppressed. But with the advent of the British Raj the professional Muslim classes including weavers were subjected to economic disasters due to decline and ruination of handloom textile and other native industries. Their social status was already at a low ebb but with economic depression the professional Muslim groups were rendered as a class of destitute.

In pre-independence days, the only politically organized party of the Muslims with massive support was the All India Momin Conference which representing within its fold forty five million Muslim or fifty per cent of the total Muslim population of India openly and aggressively confronted the Muslim League and its two-nation theory and came to the rescue of congress and Maulana Abul Kalam Azad who was its President from February 1940 to July 1946. Then the following among Muslims of Maulana Azad was negligent. The Momin Conference under the stewardship of Abdul Qaiyum Ansari by supporting the Congress and its nationalist movement enabled the Congress to retain its national status and secular image or character and reinforced the personality of Maulana Azad as a Congress President with massive support of the Muslims comprising Momins and other backward Muslims. In the absence of the active support of the Momins the image of the congress would have been reduced to that of a 'Hindu body' and Maulana Azad would have been a 'Muslim show boy Congress President' and 'Puppet President of the Congress' as branded by M.A. Jinnah and the Muslim League. In such a view of the pre-Independence political scenario Maulana Azad and the Congress Party were in fact, representative of the Indians irrespective of Hindus and

Muslims and Jinnah was patently wrong in claiming the Muslim League as the sole representative body of the Indian Muslims.

Sir Syed in his 'Asbab-e-Baghawat-e-Hind' presented the role of the Momin and other backward Muslim classes implicitly as freedom fighters in the Indian Revolt of 1857, and simultaneously as a loyal subject of the British regime condemned them abusively as anti-British in disorderly upheaval. Although Maulana Azad like Sir Syed was well versed in Islamic theology, and author of commentary on the Al-Quran and infatuated with inherent bias against the backward Muslims but contrarily a nationalist has completely obliterated the glorious role of the Momins during India's movement for national Independence in his book 'India wins Freedom' including its thirty pages which were published later on.

The present attitude of the so-called forward Muslims is a legacy of pre-Independence Muslim League politics and they have focused the same bias against certain Muslim classes who are in fact completely free from the voice of casteism and religious fanaticism and have been struggling to come up in the hierarchy of the Muslim society and eliminate the virus of casteism which has been regularly pampered by the so-called forward with the sole design to maintain their socio-political and economic supremacy. The main object of providing reservation to backward Muslims and other in education and employment to improve their socio-economic and educational status is consistent with the Islamic concept of equality in as much as such governmental policy if pursued effectively shall fully bring the backward classes at par with the advanced classes in Indian society. It is absurd and at the same time maliciously motivated to suggest that such policy of the government contradict the tenets of Islamic equality.

It is well-evident that all the communal organisation particularly under nomenclatures synonymous to Muslim League have been sponsored by heir apparent of the leader of the pre Independence Muslim League. On the contrary, Momins and other backward segments of the Muslims of India took pride in addressing themselves as Indians and kept aloof from the secessionist movement of the Muslim League for Pakistan based on the two-nation theory which finally led to tragic and unfortunate division of the country.

The organisation of backward Muslim Classes has been wrongly accused of impeding social and national integration. The so-called Muslim upper classes will be well advised to shake off the outdated and un-Islamic attitude of superiority and abjure unhealthy communal politics and join other Indians in the main stream of Indian National Life which will solve all the problems of national integration and unity.

*(The author is Head of the Department of History, SMD College, Magadh University, Punpun (Patna) Bihar.)*

# 31

# MUSLIM DALITS AND CONSTITUTIONAL AND SOCIAL JUSTICE

*Anwer Pasha*

The word 'dalit' is a modern synonym of the word 'harijan' and today it is used for very backward social class. Since the word 'harijan' carried a connotation of humiliation the word 'dalit' has been adopted abandoning the use of harijan due to severe protests of dalit classes. The word 'dalit' in itself has certainly more vastness and meaningfulness and is the best expression for the depressed of backward classes. Not only this, whereas the word 'harijan' was used to mean the Hindu backward classes the word 'dalit' has the possibility to encircle the backward classes of other religions as well. But the irony is that inspite of vastness in meaning from constitutional and legal point of view the word 'dalit' is even today used for only Hindu backward classes, that is, the classes which were previously called harijans. Dalit is still used only and only to mean the same Hindu backward classes even though the word has amassed vastness and relevance in its meaning yet constitutionally and legally its idea is limited and discriminatory. This is because whereas the word 'dalit' carries the idea of universality in its meaning and urges separate recognition for certain classes in the society on the basis of social and economic backwardness alone beyond religious and regional barriers. The idea behind this word is being consciously suppressed to keep it limited constitutionally and legally and behind this attitude a certain kind of prejudice is at work and that prejudice is based on communalism. Otherwise there is no reason as to why a non-Hindu backward class with equal condition should not be included within the word 'dalits' and why should it not be entitled to the same constitutional and legal safeguards and concessions as the Hindu dalits enjoy.

Keeping in view the described background the constitutional and legal safeguards and concessions bestowed on Hindu dalits were compulsory and based on justice because the constitution-makers had the feeling that despite attainment of freedom and establishment of democracy it would be self deceit to rely on Brahmanical mentality. They had the estimate that Brahmanical and Manuwite thinking and attitude were rooted so deep in the Hindu social system that it was not easy to rid the society of them. So with the coming up of democracy, expansion of education, and extension in broad mindedness, injustice and discriminatory mentality and attitude towards dalits cannot be rooted out completely. So they made legal and constitutional safeguard, and concessions sure for the dalits.

But while our legislative leaders kept in view the interests of Hindu dalits and adopted just attitude in offering them constitutional safeguards they completely neglected the Dalits belonging to Islam and Christian religion who had the same social and economic condition and adopted an unjust and discriminatory attitude towards them. This was because while the legislative leaders kept the dalits of Muslim and Christian community deprived of any kind of constitutional and legal safeguards and concessions they saw to it that if Hindu Dalits converted to Islam or Christianity they would lose the safeguards and concessions which they had as Hindu dalits but if they entered Buddhism or any other Indian religious sect other than Islam or Christianity they would be entitled to the safeguards and concessions as usual. This prejudicial attitude of the legislative leaders and our Government can never be considered to be based on justice, none the less it has a tinge of communal prejudice.

So far as the use of the word 'dalit' for Muslim backward class is concerned, what to say of Hindus, the majority of Muslim intellectual leaders do not accept it because this word and its connotation are opposed to the Islamic social idea in theory and they take the Muslim dalits aspect as a conspiracy to divide Muslim society. But the solution of the problem is not in looking askance from reality. The Islamic ideal of equality in the society notwithstanding, in India and the Sub-continent, the reality under the influences of caste system of the Hindu social setup on Muslim society has to be seriously analysed and in the light of this analysis the attitude and mentality taken by the upper caste Muslims towards lower caste Muslims will have to be taken into consideration. An honest study in this respect will certainly lead us to the fact that though under Muslim social setup the Muslim Backward castes did not suffer the same inhuman, unjust and depressive attitude to that extent which exists in Hindu social system yet on some level the elements are active in our mind and subconscious which encourage unequal, un-Islamic and discriminatory behaviour towards Muslim backward castes. This very mind set and attitude has generated the reaction among Muslim Backward classes to the extent that today they are bent upon to identify themselves with Hindu dalits for political recognisation. Thinking of this class on such lines is quite natural because in democratic rule establishment of political alliance on the basis of equal economic and social status and reaching out for power after the alliance and making efforts for sharing power is quite normal.

But it is sad that on this front too Muslim dalits do not seem to get justice. The Hindu dalits are very much interested to include Muslim dalits in their political front in order to beef up their strength but in matters of political power and constitutional safeguards and concession to them their attitude too does not seem to be fair. So, the Dalit Muslim are prey to the situation *'Na Khuda Hi Mila Na Visale Sanam Na Idhar Ke rahe Na udhar ke Hum.*

The other but very important side of the problem concerns the so-called upper caste Muslim. It is true that in the Islamic social system there is no possibility for up or low on the basis of caste, race or colour for any human what to say of the followers of Islam. But have the Indian Muslims really adopted the Islamic ideal social system in their actual life? Have we not established caste differences on lines of Hindu social system? True, there is no religious justification for the caste system among Muslims, but are we not untrue to our religious belief by adopting this social system based an discrimination? Why not our religious contractors ever raised a serious campaign against this differentiation and discrimination? Why no fatwa ever came up against this dishonesty and perjury? Apart from that, this question is also important as to why in the Muslim community only the socially backwards are also backward economically and educationally? And is their level of backwardness is different from Hindu dalits? If not, then why should they not be called Muslim dalits and also why we never put in collective effort to get them rights of constitutional and legal safeguards and concessions?

In Muslim social system, there may not be distinctions on caste basis in most matters of life but I know of at least two spheres where the discriminatory mentality of upper caste Muslims is distinctly seen working.

First, a considerable section of the Muslim Community does believe in caste distinction and looks down upon backward Muslim castes, and like Hindu upper castes the Muslim upper caste persons in their oral expression use derogatory words and remarks for the Muslim backward castes. Does this not reflect the Manuvadi mentality of the upper caste Muslims? True that generations before coming into the fold of Islam, in the mind and unconscious of upper caste Hindus the former racial prejudice and discrimination is rooted in one form or the other and it is not possible to get totally rid of these elements in a country and society where superiority of Hindu social system reins. But this argument is totally opposed to the system of equality in Islam. It cannot be accepted as justified. Total extradication of this malignant is the only remedy. So, serious consideration in this respect is essential.

The other important matter is the attitude pertaining to marriage. It is a confirmed fact that in the Muslim society the most intensity of caste feeling is found in matters of marriage, that is, expression of caste distinction in its worst form is shown by Muslims in connection with marriage. Otherwise in practical life no particular distinction is visible in various matters because, be it religious matters or social, distinction of upper caste and the lower is generally not observed among the Muslims. But when it comes to matters of marriage very rigidly a Saiyed parfers a Saiyed a Sheikh to a Sheikh, a Pathan to a Pathan is preferable. With the show of big heartedness a Saiyed is married to a Pathan or Sheikh, a Khan to a Sheikh or Saiyed and a Shaikh to a Pathan or Saiyed but this too is considered to be unpleasant conjugation. But limited as it is, this big heartedness never steps out towards Ansari, Dhunias, Darji, Teli, Dhobi, Nai, Churihar, Sabzifarosh, Hajjam, Qussab, Halalkhor, Khanabodosh, Nat, Sapera and other backward Muslim classes, Although exception in this respect is at times seen yet this is very insignificant in proportion.

It is not a mere chance that seventy per cent of the population belonging to Muslim Backward class comes in alignment economically with Hindu dalits. The same causes have remained active behind this as were active for the backwardness of Hindu dalits. Conversion to another religion brought no economic betterment to these Muslim dalits whereas during the last fifty and odd years constitutional safeguards and concessions have generated proportional improvement in the wretched conditions of Hindu dalits. But deprived of those constitutional and legal safeguards the Muslim dalits are being day by day pushed to more backwardness and if solid steps to eradicate the backwardness of Muslim dalits are not taken the matter world get uglier. So, sooner than later steps must be taken to provide constitutional safe guards to the Muslim dalits as well, at par with Hindu dalits. And like the Muslim OBCs having been included along with other OBCs, on that pattern Muslim dalits, after identification, should be placed in the list with Hindu dalits and they should also get the constitutional safeguard and concession as the Hindu dalits are provided with.

There can be two methods for providing constitutional safeguards and concessions to Muslim dalits. One, the Muslim dalits should have a share in the safeguard and concession provided to Hindu dalits following an amendment in the Constitution in so much) as proportionate shares are allotted so that Hindu and Muslim dalits get their due share and they can get it according to their share in population. The other method could be to allot constitutional safeguards to Muslims as a whole and out of those safeguards proportionate share may be fixed for the dalits Muslims in proportion to their population. This way in every walk of life and power system on a countrywide scale the backwardness and dwindling representation of Muslims can be prevented and justice would be done to the Backward classes of the country's largest minority.

# 32

# TRUTH OF MUSLIM RESERVATION IN KARNATAKA AND KERALA

*Ashfaq Husain Ansari*

According to some Muslim intellectuals and politicians in Karnataka and Kerala, all Muslims are included in Backward Class list and all Muslims are enjoying the benefits of reservation. This matter is being raised off and on by Saiyed Shahabuddin and political leaders and intellectuals sharing his opinion. Salman Khursheed has also raised this issue and has put out the demand that all Muslims in Uttar Pradesh should be included in the list of Backward Classes on the pattern of Karnataka and Kerala and must be provided with all the concessions of Backward class.

Be it Salman Khursheed or Saiyed Shahabuddin everyone agrees that both are intellectual politicians and, whatever they say or write they will say it after thorough study and verification. Politician as they are, Mulayam Singh Yadav, Ram Bilas Paswan or Laloo Prasad Yadav could make statements keeping in view, political gain and loss as they perceive which may or may not be related to reality. But intellectual politicians like Saiyed Shahabuddin and Salam Khursheed must look into the facts before issuing such statements.

The most dependable way to find out whether all Muslims in Kerala and Karnataka have been included in the Backward class list is to go through all the available lists concerning

Backward classes issued by National Backward classes Commission and then conclusion can be drawn and brought cut in writing. People expect intellectual politicians like Saiyed Shahabuddin and Salman Khursheed would not say anything but based on study.

Now a look at the Central list of Backward classes of Karnataka and Kerala will show the truth. First, the Karnataka list is taken. The Karnataka list is contained on pages 18 to 21 and serial Nos. 51 to 184 and there it is very clearly stated on page 20, serial 125 "Other Muslims excluding" and those excluded are "Kacchi, Memon, Navayat, Bohra, Bhuraya, Borha, Saiyed, Sheikh, Pathan, Mughal, Mahad Yoma, Mohdadi, Konkani or Gomati Muslim".

Some Muslim professional castes are also included in the Karnataka lists. Similarly, the Kerala list which is noted on pages 22, 23 and 24 contains Backward classes of the state from serial No. 1 to 82. In it on serial No. 46 is written Other Muslims excluding and those excluded are "Bohra, Kachchi, Memon, Navayets, Turkan, Dakhini Muslim".

Saiyed Shahabuddin, Salman Khursheed and intellectual politicians like them must understand where they stand now as they have been off and on demanding inclusion of all Muslims on India level in the Backward class list on the pattern of Karnataka and Kerala.

Intellectual politician and along with them leaders of political parties must clearly understand that neither Muslims nor Sikhs and Christians can achieve reservation of Backward class on the basis of religion. Similarly all the followers of Buddhism cannot be included in the list of Backward classes. Those Buddhists Christians or Sikhs who are converted to Buddhism, Christianity or Sikhism from Dalits have already been included or may be included in the Backward class or S.C. list but not all the Christian Buddhists or Sikhs.

Our political leaders and even those who are regarded as intellectuals make tall claims of sympathy with Muslims but instead of making demands for their advancement they are knowingly or unknowingly trying to snatch away those very rights from Muslims who are included in the Backward class list owing to their social and educational backwardness and are getting a little concessions in education and jobs. No intellectual or politician of the Millat nor a Muslim political leader comes forward for the cause that Muslims who are already part of OBC list should get concessions proportion-ate to their population. No doubt, Backward Muslims have the vote power. Their population is 70 to 80 per cent to the whole population of Muslims. But so far as political leadership is concerned they are almost no where. Only leaders of social status are running around top leaders of almost every political outfits. No party gives weightage to socially backward Muslims. Sometimes, under misguidance they raise slogans for reservations for all Muslims from their own platforms. Some of their own opportunist and self-interested political leaders of the community do not hesitate even cutting the branch by their own hands on which they are themselves sitting. Broadly speaking they are oblivious to the fact as to why their representation is dwindling day by day so much so that in the 13th Lok Sabha out of 31 Muslims elected to it not a single backward Muslim could get elected. How long shall we shout slogans in favour of others and detrimental to our own selves without giving deep consideration to it?

# 33

# IMPORTANCE OF RESERVATION FOR MUSLIM BACKWARD CLASSES

*Ashfaq Husain Ansari*

The question of Muslim reservation has again begun to crop up in Urdu newspapers and journals. A group of Muslim intellectuals along with some persons belonging to different political parties and some Journalists who earlier established an organisation by the name of "Movement for Empowerment of Muslim Indians" met at Lucknow as its Lucknow chapter. It goes by the short name of Moemin which is pronounced as Momin in Urdu. Its first conference was held in Mumbai in 1999 and probably the second conference took place at Bangalore in 2001. An English fortnightly has rightly called it an organisation of "Five per cent Muslim elite which has nothing to do with 95% Indian Muslims".

Some Urdu newspapers have been strongly pleading as to why no organised movement is being started for Reservation to all Muslims. It has been stated that whatever movement came up it proved only short lived. In an article reference has been made about Mayawati's order granting 8.44% reservation to Muslims. Firstly, it is far from truth that Mayawati during her first tenure as C.M. issued any such distractive order through which, if not all Muslims, at least Backward Muslims had been separately given their rightful share out of 27% reservation for Backward class. At that time, I was a member of Uttar Pradesh

Backward Class Commission. So I am fully aware of the government notification which is referred to time and again and I keep a copy of it safe with me. Those who often raise the issue of 8.44% reservation must seriously think over it, consider each and every aspect, study the relevant sections of the Constitution and thoroughly go through the Judgements of Supreme Court and then take the decision. This must also be taken into account that there is scope for reservation in the Indian Constitution on the basis of caste, community and group, but so far reservation to followers of one religion all over India on the basis of religion is neither allowed by the Constitution nor by the Supreme Court.

So far as empowerment of Muslims is concerned no one can deny its importance. But when the issue of empowerment will be raised the question as to which class of Muslims is deprived of empowerment most will naturally arise. Who can deny the fact that at the national level in both the Houses of Parliament and at the State Level in State Legislatures representation of Muslims is quite low in proportion to their population, but when considered in detail the fact that out of 31 Muslim members elected to the 13th Lok Sabha not a single member representing the Muslim Backward classes could get elected. Same is the case with Rajya Sabha and the Houses of the State Legislatures. Same is the story of representation of backward Muslims in the Central and State Government and also other services including civil police, defence, paramilitary and public enterprises. So much so that in all secular political parties to including the Congress representation of Muslim backward class is miserable from National to State, District and block level, whereas general estimate of the Backward Muslim population is more than two-third of the whole Muslims population. According to the figure of Mandal Commission based on the census of 1931, out of 12% of the Muslim population as a whole in the country 8% of the population belong to Backward Muslims.

Muslim community leaders of the "Movement for Empowerment of Muslim Indians" and leading Journalists and intellectuals all should think why representation of backward

Muslims in the 13th Lok Sabha has come to nil, why representation of this class is dwindling day by day in the State Legislatures? Why their representation in decision making bodies is in such a bad shape? Believing even the Mandal Commission Statistics, the strength of Backward Muslims in the Lok Sabha should be 45 while those of non-backward 20 but the story is totally the other way round. Non-backward Muslims have cornered far more representations in proportion to their population where as representation of Backward Muslims has fatten to zero. Now let us see which side should the Movement for Empowerment of Muslim Indian (Moemin) people or slogan raisers for reservation to all Muslims are going to take. The real aspect of the picture is that non-backward Muslims have pocketed representation much more in proportion to their population. If there is any class in Muslims which has been deprived of its rights and which is not getting representation in proportion to their population it is the Backward Muslim classes. The need of the hour is to fight for their empowerment. They must get due representation at all levels in proportion to their population.

The absence of reservation has made no difference to the representation of non-backward Muslims. In case of reservation to all Muslims where will they reach? And the poor Backward Muslims will be further pushed far behind in competition. This must be given thought to. In the last Panchayat elections in Uttar Pradesh and in the rural and urban local bodies polls there was 27% reservation for Backwards, out of it Muslim, Backwards got representation though not to the proportion of their population yet better representation was available. One can see Backward Muslim men and women, as chairpersons and members of local bodies at various rural and urban local bodies.

Out of 27% reservation for Backward classes, the Backward Muslims have got their right and under it they will be getting the concessions and representation at various levels though lesser than their population proportion. Imagine what will be the position of Backward Muslims in case reservation is granted to all Muslims? It requires serious thinking. In the present Scenario it looks that only the share of non-backward Muslims will go up if reservation for all Muslims becomes a fact. In case reservation to all Muslims is granted will it be certain that Backward Muslims would get representation proportionate to their population in the 14th Lok Sabha or corresponding State Legislatures or in other seats of power or office bearing positions of political parties.

The slogan of reservation to all Muslims has also complicated the issue of reservation of seats for women in the Lok Sabha and State Legislatures. As far as the issue of reservation for women belonging to Backward class and Scheduled castes is concerned, a common opinion has been formed and is already in practice in local rural and urban organisations and everyone has accepted it willingly or otherwise and it has been practiced more than once in most states. They consciously or unconsciously do not understand that in case the backward class women get a share in reservation the backward class Muslim women too will get if not full, at least some share in it. They also try to hide that the population of backward in the whole Muslim Society is two-third to three-fourth and legally no one can stop them from taking due share from the reservation to backward class women. There is absolutely no provision in the Constitution of India to grant reservation on the basis of religion. So please do not stalk reservation for women in the name of Muslim reservation. Reservation for entire Muslim women, or entire Sikh or Christian women is simply not possible under the Constitution. So do not stop Backward Class Muslim women to get their reservation share in Lok Sabha and State Legislatures. Backward Muslim women are getting their share of representation in local, urban and rural organisations. Let them have their share in Lok Sabha and State Legislature too. Let the movement for Empowerment of Muslim Indians spell their position clearly in this regard.

# 34

# TRUTH OF MUSLIM REPRESENTATION IN LOK SABHA

*Ashfaq Husain Ansari*

In Democracy only those are heard who have their own voice. At each level representation of Muslims and particularly Backward Muslims is getting lesser and lesser day by day. Justice Venkat Challiaiah, Chairman of the Constitution Review Commission formed by the Central Government has said in his report:

> *"At present, the political representation of minority communities in legislatures, especially Muslims, has fallen well below their proportion of population. The proportion of BCs among them is next to nil."*

Further he states:

> *"Backward classes belonging to religious minorities who have been identified and included in the list of backward classes and who, in fact, constitute the bulk of the population of religious minorities should be taken up with special care along with their Hindu counterparts in the developmental efforts for the backward classes."*

Against this background is stock of Muslim representation in the first to thirteenth Lok Sabha is taken the picture which comes up shows that Muslim representation in the 1st to 13th Lok Sabha has been very low in proportion to their population and in that too worse is the case of Backward Muslims representation. For the 13th Lok Sabha which has been recently dissolved only 31 Muslims could get elected and among those 31 'none was a representative of Muslim Backward classes'. Similarly, the number of Muslim members elected to the 12th Lok Sabha was 28 and there was none belonging to Muslim Backward classes. In 11th Lok Sabha, the number of Muslim members was 29, whereas in the 10th Lok Sabha this figure was only 25. In the 9th Lok Sabha Muslim representation was 27. In 1984 when election was held against the background of Indira Gandhi's martyrdome and whereby Congress registered more than two-thirds majority while the Bharatiya Janata Party sank to only 2, even then the number of Muslim members in the Lok Sabha could not go beyond 42. The tradedy of the 1984 Lok Sabha election was that this time Congress gave lesser number of tickets to Muslims as compared to the 7th Lok Sabha, resulting in a cut in the number of tickets to backward class Muslims. Congress came back to power in the 17th Lok Sabha. In this Lok Sabha, the number of Muslim members was as high as 48 and Muslim Backward class members totalled six. The Janata wave in 1977 could fetch only upto 31 seats for Muslims in the Lok Sabha and out of it not more than two were from the Muslim Backward classes. Both in the 4th and 5th Lok Sabha Muslim representation remained 28 whereas in the 3rd Lok Sabha of 1962 Muslim representation was only 20. Under the Constitution of the Republic after the first election for the Lok Sabha, only 11 Muslims could succeed and this number increased to 19 for the second Lok Sabha in 1957.

This is the picture of Muslim representation in the Lok Sabha. Generally, Muslim population is 12% of the total population of India. That means Muslim representation remained between 2.5 to 8%. This percentage shrank to 6% from 9th to 13th Lok Sabha, Now, it is clear that in the Lok Sabha Muslim representation has been not even half in proportion to it population and more startling point is that after the Seventh Lok Sabha, representation of Backward Muslim started dwindling and by the 9th Lok Sabha it almost came to nought. If studied deeply the facts are even more startling. Muslim population is estimated as about 12% of the entire population of India and of this according to the facts and figures of Mandal Commission 8% are Backward Muslims. In proportion to Muslim population at least 64 of them must get seats in the Lok Sabha and if one-third are supposed to be estimated as non-Backward their share of seats comes to 21. The conclusion is obvious that non-Backward Muslims are generally getting more representation in comparison to their population, while even the meager representation of Backward Muslims which used to be limited to only a few in number came to nil after the 9th Lok Sabha.

Demand for representation of Muslims according to the proportion of population has been raised off and on and with the election round the corner every organisation has been putting up this demand by holding seminars, meetings and rallies in Delhi. But Muslim leaders never wish to disclose the fact that non-Backward Muslims have been enjoying much more representation than their proportion in Muslim population whereas leaving side the representation according to ratio of population of B.C. Muslims which has come to zero. For this neither the Backward Muslim leader unitedly raise a voice nor do the leaders of secular parties claiming sympath for Muslims seriously give a thought to it. Almost the same picture of Backward Muslim representation obtains in State Legislative Assemblies. The upper Houses also do not present a different look. There is no practice or convention that in case Muslim representation in the Centre is low the repair is done in the Rajya Sabha. At State level, too no such convention exists for the Vidhan Parishads. Be it Rajya Sabha or Vidhan Parishads at both places representation of Muslims particularly that of Backward class Muslims is receding day by day.

## 35

# DALIT MUSLIMS DEMAND RESERVATION

*K.Z. Amani*

The caste system is so pervasive in India that it has become a feature of life of all the religious groups in the country. While the Hindus are divided into four classes (Brahmin, Kshatriya, Vaishya and Shudra) which had divine sanction, the Indian Muslims were placed in two well-defined social divisions (1) Ashraf (noble) and (2) Ajlaf. The first included all undoubted descendents of foreigners and converts from upper castes (Hindus). All other Muslims, including the occupational groups and all low/caste converts were known by the contemptuous term Ajlaf (mean people).

Within these groups, there are divisions with social precedence of exactly the same nature as one finds among the Hindus. It must, however, be mentioned that this division is unique and has been practiced and perpetuated only in the Indian sub-continent. Elsewhere in the Muslim world, no such gradation of Muslim society is found because it is not permitted in Islam.

### CASTE AMONG MUSLIMS

The census reports, district and state gazetteers of the British Raj provide invaluable information about various population characteristics including the caste divisions and sub-divisions of Indian society. The 1921 census had a special report on caste among Muslims. The detailed discussion about the Muslim castes, their place in the social hierarchy and educational status was not to the liking of the intelligentsia, mostly Ashrafs, who argued that an analysis of caste stratification among the Muslims was uncalled for since it was against the Islamic principles of equality and social justice. However, caste has been a social reality and sociologists and the basis of empirical research have come to accept, that caste divisions exist in Muslim society. The basic difference between the Muslim and the Hindu castes is that while the Muslims have caste division and have practiced it, among the Hindus one finds not only the practice but also the theory of caste.

## U.P. EXAMPLE

But the practice of collecting caste-wise data among Muslims was discontinued after the 'Independence'. However, research on social stratification among the Muslims continued and social scientists have made seminal contribution in this field.

A study of Muslim castes in U.P. made by Ghaus Ansari discusses the origin and existence of caste, caste structure and organisation and inter-caste relation among the Muslims. Writing about the Awadh region (central U.P.), he says:

> *The region is well known for majority of Muslim zamindars (landlords) while the cultivators and serving caste are derived from the lower ranks of both Hindus and Muslims. The Ashraf (Sayyed, Sheikh and Pathoo) have been associating themselves with the high status of the feudal system – the zamindars, while serving castes of the villages have been regarded as people of inferior or low birth. Birth alone decided an individual's social status. Even if a person of low caste, such as Nai (barber) or Gaddi (grazier) acquired some property and thereby raised his economic status, he would never rank equal with those born as Ashraf, no matter how poor these Ashraf might be. Inspite of his wealth, he has to remain within his class and caste limits, in the rural areas the caste impact is still great and the Ashraf (Sayyed, Sheikh, Mughal or Pathan) are clearly distinguishable from the rest of the serving castes (Julaha, Kabaria, Dhunia, Manihar, Nai, Qassab, Teli, Gaddi and others).*

Ansari further added that in the urban areas the picture is not much different. In towns most of the professions such as office clerk, school teacher, lawyer, doctor and businessman are predominantly monopolised by those who claim Ashraf descent. However, in the urban centres, in contrast to the rural life in the villages, education and economic condition played a significant role in reducing the importance of birth.

Here one can find examples of educated individuals of lower rank who hide their caste distinctiveness and identity themselves with Ashraf by adding to their names titles like Sayyed, Khan, Siddiqi and Kidwai.

## LITERACY LEVEL

Studies made by Imtiaz Ahmad, Zarina Bhatt, M.K.A. Siddiqui and published in Caste and Social Stratification among the Muslims, have further supported the findings of Ghaus Ansari. It is obvious from the studies that the Muslims of low social ranking had no opportunity of education and upward mobility. The following table shows the level of literacy of selected Muslim castes of U.P. and is self-explanatory.

| *Caste* | *Total population literate* | *(% of the total)* |
|---|---|---|
| Sayyed | 2,79,470 | 12% |
| Mughal | 58,864 | 9.0% |
| Nau Muslim | 55,972 | 2.3% |
| Julaha | 8,06,397 | 1.9% |
| Darzi | 2,28,536 | 1.9% |
| Manihar | 90,224 | 1 9% |
| Qassab | 1,52,019 | 1.4% |
| Dhunia | 3,53,000 | 1 2% |
| | | 0.7% |

*Source:* Census of India 1921 United Provinces of Agra and Awadh, Vol. XVI, Part- II, Table IX pp. 136-137.

## VIEWS OF DR. AMBEDKAR ON MUSLIMS

Hindus had political leaders and social reformers like Gandhi, Phule, Perrier and Dr. Ambedkar who were not only concerned about the plight of Dalits but also actively fought against the evils of the caste system. However, it would be hard to find a solitary example where Muslims social reformers, religious preachers or politicians have written, spoken or made any concerted effort to get rid of social evil which is opposed to the teachings of Islam.

Dr. B.R. Ambedkar admirably sums up the realities of Muslim society in India where a privileged minority had believed in practiced and perpetuated a hierarchy, which is based on the concept of high and low social gradation :

The existence of the evils (caste system) among the Muslims is disturbing enough. But far more distressing is the fact that there is no organised movements of social reforms among the Musalmans of India on a scale sufficient to bring about their eradication. The Hindus have their social evils. But there is this relieving feature about them namely, that some of them are conscious of their existence and a few of them are actively agitation for their removal. The Muslims, on the other hand, do not realize that they (castes) are evils and consequently do not agitate for their removal.

(B.R. Ambedkar: Pakistan or the Partition of India, Thacker & Co. p. 223).

One interesting area of research on caste among Muslims has remained unexplored so far. Vertical stratification based on high and low social ranking had been studied but horizontal segmentation of Muslims castes in most urban and rural settlements of North India remains to be investigated closely. In the towns and cities having a sizeable Muslims settlement, it is common to find localities having names, which indicate the caste configuration of the population. For example, localities such as Mohalla Sayyadwara, Qazitola, Qazipara, Pathanan, Sheikhpura, Minyan Pura, Sarai Minyan, Mir Ka Mohalla, Jolahtola, Basti Jolahan, Basti Atishbazan and Kanjar Wali Sarai etc. make it obvious that members of a particular class inhabit these localities. Moreover, like the Hindus, among the Muslims also the top-ranking castes have their settlements near the city centre but those placed at the bottom are to be found close to the periphery of the urban settlement.

**WANTED RESERVATION**

The Constitution of India provides a blue print for an egalitarian society. It promises equality of opportunity to all the citizens of the country. However, it is not possible to eradicate age-old inequalities simply by adopting new principles in a Constitution. It, therefore, becomes imperative to adopt special measures in order to at least minimize, if not, bring to an end inequalities of the past. Reservation is aimed at reducing the levels of inequalities where people are segregated and denied opportunities of education and upward mobility on grounds of birth. It should be noted that equality of status is not possible unless all sections of the people are impartially in a position to benefit from the existing social order.

## MANDAL COMMISSION REPORT

The Constitution says that the state may take such steps as are needed to safeguard the interest of the socially deprived groups of communities. Such communities fall into three broad divisions: (i) Scheduled Castes, (ii) Scheduled Tribes, and (iii) Other Backward Classes. The basic argument in favour of reservation of socially deprived has been that special opportunities should be created for this section over and above the general provision for equality of opportunity for all.

Dr. Ambedkar, while placing before the Constituent Assembly such a proposal argued that the aim of providing equal opportunities to all irrespective of caste, creed and community is very important. However, he was of the view that special opportunities must be created for those sections of society, which have been severely deprived and disadvantaged.

In the Constitution of 1950, special provisions were made for SC/ST. However, one of the directive principles of state, policy said that some measures might also be adopted for the benefit of OBC's without specifying what these measures should be and who the OBC's are. Therefore, Commissions (Katekar 1953. Mandal 1980) were set up which identified caste and communities and placed them in the category of OBC. Mandal Commission Report makes interesting revelations about the representation of different social groups in government jobs.

But reservation has provided some scope for SC/ST/BC's, nearly half of India's population, were hopelessly behind.

So, the casteless Indian Muslim is a complete myth. No non-tribal Indian community is free of the evils of caste system. Imtiaz Ahmad's pioneering work on social stratification, caste and kinship among the Muslims has shown that conversion to Islam could not break the caste structure, especially those based on occupation and hierarchal division of labour. It perpetuated discrimination. Inequalities and its removal required affirmative action and positive discrimination. The Kalekar and Mandal Reports took into consideration this fact and included 'low caste Muslims' in the list of OBC on the ground that they are socially and educationally backward as the Hindu backward classes and need the benefit of reservation.

The Muslim backward classes feel that their deprivation, because of low social ranking on grounds of birth, has been noted and they will get the benefit of reservation. However, it is strongly felt that two decisions need to be reviewed and changed if they we to get any worthwhile advantage from the policy of affirmative action. Under the Government of India Act of 1935, a list of extremely backward castes was drawn Lip and was known as SCs. Some of these castes such as Dhobi (washerman), Mochi (cobbler) and Halalkhors (sweepers) had both Hindu and Muslim members and special provisions were made for their social and economic uplift. However, in 1950 a Presidential Order was issued according to which these special benefits would be available to Hindu SCs only. In this way, non-Hindu SCs were denied the benefits that 1935 Government of India Act had provided to them. Through and amendment in 1956, the benefits were extended to Sikh SCs, and in 1990 this was extended to neo-Buddhists.

The Muslim backward classes feel that the denial of benefits of reservation to Muslim SCs is unjust and contrary to the spirit of the Constitution and its principles of secularism and equality.

Much is also being made out of the advantages, which have come to the backward classes because of the implementation of the Mandal recommendations. It should be noted that in giving assent or its implementation the Supreme Court in 1992 not only limited the overall reservation to 50% but also inserted an economic exclusion clauses under the name of 'creamy layer'

It meant that BCs having slightly improved economic condition were out of the purview of reservation. It is obvious that the decision not to provide benefits to Muslim SCs which is given to Hindus, Sikhs and neo-Buddhists and denial to the creamy layer among BCs, the advantage of affirmative action is bound to seriously jeopardize the cause of social justice.

# 36

## MOMIN CONFERENCE KI DASTAVEZI TAREEKH

***(Compiled by Ashfaq Husain Ansari from "Delhi Momin Media, 2000) Review by Shahabuddin Ansari***

Attainment of freedom by the country and the partition of the subcontinent in its wake was calumination of a long-dream battle fought at various fronts—political, social and economic. The struggle also proved eatalyst in infusing confidence among the so-called 'Dalits' both in Hindus and Muslims in asserting their role and in raising their voice against himself and injustice inflicted upon them by the high-caste, 'the Ashraf'. Any attempt at chromicalling definitive history of freedom movement, therefore, will have to wait till such time as accounts of assertion made by these down-trodden classes and documents of their efforts become available.

The volume under review is one such attempt in which Mr. Ashfaq Husain Ansari, an ex-M.P. and Chairman of the Centre of Backward Muslims of India, has retrieved and put together documents of the India Momin Conference. The Conference as representative body of the largest group among the backward class Muslims was formed in 1925 at a time when in the wake of Khilafat Movement and Non-Cooperation Movement political consciousness had spread among the Muslim masses. No less important factor in an urge to organize among the Momin Ansari was the reaction in the community against the tyranny and ill-treatment to which members of the community were subjected to by the so-called 'Ashraf' or upper caste Muslims. The various presidential addresses of conference echo the agony and pain for the insult inflicted upon this class in calling them 'Razeel' (of low birth) by the 'Upper Caste' Muslims who even went to the court to get them declared as 'low-born.'

Welcoming the delegates to the seventh Conference held in Gorakhpur in 1939 Mr. Riazuddin Ahmad, Advocate has narrated how when the representatives of the Conference met Sir Stafford Cripps and Pt. Nehru and gave them an account of the plight of the class at the lands of 'Caste' Muslims, the Muslim press, dominated as it was by the Caste Muslims termed the conference representatives as stoogies of the Indian National Congress. The documents in the book reveal that it was the Momin Conference, which raised to voice against the Lahore Resolution of the Muslim League soon after it was adopted in March 1940.

The documents included in the book comprises Presidential addresses of the conference from 1925 onward as also welcome addresses by Chairmen of various reception committees. In addition there are some records of the Provincial Momin Conferences. In the first fifty pages, Mr. Ansari has given a resume of the activities of the conference upto 1955.

The third part of the book entitled "Miscellaneous" contains a few articles tracing the history of the early efforts at organizing the Momins. A valuable article reprinted in the book on the history of attempts made in bringing out newspapers and magazines to further the movement will be of immense value to scholars of history of Urdu Journalism. The book is both a history of Momin Conference and a study in social anthropology in exposing the caste conflict among Muslims and in high lighting the cleave that continue to exist even to this day.

The book displays considerable effort on the part of Mr. Ansari in unearthing valuable documents and in safeguarding them from going into oblivion. One wishes equal efforts were made in editing the volume to make it more compact and readable. Inclusion of some biodata and photographs of persons who had no role in shaping the conference or in conducting its affair prior to 1947 gives the book a partisan look and to some extent has marred its documentary value. It is hoped that a new edition as and when it in brought and will clear it from such blemishes.

*Hon. Director, Dept. of Lib. & Tuf, Sc. Jamia Millia Islamia and
Hon. Advisor, Dr. Zakir Husain Library, Jamia Millia Islamia

The most mind boggling and shocking reality is that not a single OBC Muslim got elected to the Lok Sabha in 1999. It is this political stagnation, social neglect and economic deprivation which has generated a new political consciousness among the Dalit and OBC Muslims and given birth to a new layer of Muslim leadership desiring due share in the government, administration and Parliament. Surely, this is a cause of concern to the monopoly of political power of the upper caste Muslims.

This newly found awakening is more particularly visible among the OBCs of the Muslim community. The possibility of clash between this emerging new OBC Muslims leadership and the present Muslim leadership cannot be ruled out. This new Muslim leadership has sensitivity towards poverty, deprivation and educational backwardness of the Muslim and yet, it is devoid of unnecessary religious fundamentalism. This leadership among Muslims is developing along the lines of leadership of the OBCs among the Hindus.

Editorial of Hindi Daily 'Aj'
14th December, 1999